History of The Boston Synagogue 1888-2013

A 125th Anniversary Celebration

by Michael Weingarten

and The Boston Synagogue Archival/Historical Committee: Bette L. Siegel, Chair; Charles S. Fineman; Ruth Fein and Marlene Meyer

Copyright © 2013 by The Boston Synagogue,
55 Martha Road, Boston, Massachusetts 02114-1206 U.S.A.

All rights reserved. No part of this publication may be translated, reproduced, stored in a retrieval system or transmitted, in any form or by any means, electronic, mechanical, photocopying, recording or otherwise, without express written permission from the publisher.

ISBN 978-0615805139

First edition 2013

Table of Contents

		Page
	Preface	iii
	Summary of Findings	vii
1.	The Founding of Congregation Beth Jacob 1888	1
2.	Developments in the North and West Ends 1888-1905	9
3.	Early Rabbis and Lay Leadership	21
4.	The Early Shuls and their Communities	47
5.	Developments in the West End 1905-1925	59
6.	North Russell as Leading West End Shul	78
7.	Shul Buildings and Architecture	91
8.	Developments in the West End 1925-1945	99
9.	Developments in the West End 1945-1965	121
10.	Urban Renewal and Survival	131
11.	The Maurice Saval Era 1971-1989	157
12	The Post-Saval Era 1989-1999	184
13.	The Recent Era 1989-2013	191
14.	Looking Back: The Past 125 Years	204
15.	Looking to the Future	210
Appendix 1	A Geography Lesson	213
Appendix 2	Listing of Predecessor Shul Rabbis and Ritual Directors	220
Appendix 3	Bylaws: North Russell Street Mishnah Study Group	226
Appendix 4	Rabbi Moses Margolies Boston Shul Affiliations	230
Appendix 5	Rabbi Solomon Friederman Boston Shul Affiliations	231
Appendix 6	Rabbi Isaac Baritz Boston Shul Affiliations	233
Appendix 7	Charles River Park/Boston Synagogue Officers	234
Bibliography		236

Preface

On the occasion of the 125th anniversary of the founding of The Boston Synagogue's earliest predecessor shul (Congregation Beth Jacob) in 1888, the Board of the Synagogue decided to celebrate the event by commissioning a history of the shul and its predecessors.

To implement this project, the Board formed an Archival/Historical Committee consisting of Bette Siegel as Chair, with Charles S. Fineman, Ruth Fein, and Marlene Meyer as members. Michael Weingarten joined the Committee as editor/author. None of the members are professional historians, although Bette is a librarian at the Massachusetts State House; Charlie is a former Western European bibliographer at Harvard and is now a freelance translator; Ruth is a former Chair of Combined Jewish Philanthropies (and of The Boston Synagogue) with extensive knowledge of Boston Jewish history; Marlene is a retired anesthesiologist and President of the West End Civic Association; and Michael in an earlier lifetime received an M.A. in Eastern European History from Columbia before deciding to pursue a career in business. The Committee also engaged Sarah Gluck as an archival intern to sort though the shul's records.[1]

In the spirit of honoring our predecessors, we wish to remember our late Board member and Historian Muriel Kantor Z"L, who would have greatly enjoyed participating in this exercise.

In preparing this retrospective, we faced a major problem, which is that we (a) knew very little about our predecessors, and (b) were writing about immigrant shuls that did not archive records and were torn down years ago. The lack of published information became apparent when some of us reviewed our copies of the Sarna et al. landmark work *The Jews of Boston* and found that the only mention of our predecessor shuls in the main text is a picture of a 1931 Purim Party at North Russell Street.[2] For 'The Boston Synagogue' or

---

[1] Sarah is a graduate of the archives management program of the Simmons Graduate School of Library and Information Science.

[2] See photo in Chapter 8. There also is a buried footnote in a separate chapter of *Jews of Boston* that includes a cursory mention of the founding of Beth Jacob and Beth Hamedrash Hagadol, as well as their merger in 1940.

'Charles River Park Synagogue,' there is only a brief discussion of the current building's architecture. The same occurred when we approached the people at the Vilna Shul Jewish cultural center, thinking that they might have amassed some useful materials – only to learn that there was nothing available.

We therefore realized that we were on our own, and if we wanted to learn more we would have to do some digging.

Acknowledging Some Key Sources

Fortunately we were able to uncover an interesting and eclectic set of data. One important find was Carol Clingan's 575-row spreadsheet *Massachusetts Synagogues and Their Records, Past and Present*,[3] which compiles key data for each synagogue that ever existed in Massachusetts. This helped us assemble the chronology charts that are shown throughout this history.

Another critical source was Bette Siegel's examination of the annual *Boston City Directories*, which listed the nkames of the rabbis for the predecessor shuls from 1888 through 1930. Out of fifteen rabbis, we uncovered useful information for eight; their stories became a central element of our history.

We received valuable support from Judi Garner, head archivist at the American Jewish Historical Society's Boston facility, who provided access to important documents such as the board minutes of Anshei Libavitz and the beautifully illuminated 1909 North Russell Street Mishnah study group bylaws. The New York office provided us with a copy of one of the few extant copies of the 1892 *History of the Jews of Boston*.

We also want to thank those people who provided oral history recollections of our shuls in different eras, including Oscar Epstein (1930s); Leonard Nimoy of *Star Trek* fame (1940s); David Wizansky (1950s); and David Fishman (1980s). Live long and prosper!

---

[3] Prepared in 2010 for the Jewish Genealogical Society, and available at www.jgsgb.org/pdfs/MassSynagogues.pdf; a.k.a. "Clingan Spreadsheet."

Editorial Choices

In researching and writing this book, we made several important editorial choices:

- We decided early in the research process that the project's goal was to prepare a history, not a genealogy. As a result, compiling lists of officers and their descendants was of lower priority than finding materials that tell a coherent story of the establishment and development of a group of immigrant shuls over a 125-year period.

- We have erred on the side of excess with respect to exhibits and quotations, because we want this document to represent a repository for difficult-to-find materials.

- We decided that this book should comprise an objective history (warts and all) – just as the Torah points out negative aspects of the person that Congregation Beth Jacob was named after (Jacob). The history of our shul includes prolonged periods of decline as well as successes. Highlighting these emphasizes the achievements of some immigrants (and one rich benefactor) who created something that has endured despite the crises. Without them, we would not be here today.

- While any history necessarily deals with major events and important people, the shul's basic function has always been to serve the needs of ordinary Jews. Accordingly we have included stories such as: Minnie Kasser's wedding at North Russell Street at the turn of the last century; Oscar Epstein's bar mitzvah in the 1930s; and Holocaust survivor Ryfuel Abosh's poignant request in the 1970s that the synagogue officers install a memorial plaque for him (posthumously) next to those for his father, mother and sister -- since he was the only one left in his family.

- We recognize that we violate the goal of objectivity when we reach the modern era and write about things that some of us have been involved in personally. We shall leave it to our successors to correct our biases. However we thought that it was important to let readers know how things turned out over the last fifteen years.

Other Acknowledgements

We want to thank Charles Fineman for his work as bibliographer and proofreader. Gerald Kleinstein and David Fishman provided translations of Hebrew and Yiddish texts. Kelly Burnett helped with preproduction editing and formatting.

We also want to thank our fellow shul officers and members of the board (not already named) for their support throughout this process: Susan Schreiner Weingarten, Chair (who had the vision that we should write a history as a centerpiece of our celebration); Jeffrey Steinfeld, Secretary; and board members Ruth Aaron, Leslie Blachman, Chris Connelly, Florence Einhorn, Stephanie Goldberg, David Kreisler, Shlomo Pinkas, Marshall Schribman, Gail Semigran, Howard Speicher, Marc Siegel, Ruth Raphael, Heather Stein and Carol Trust.

In Closing

This work is intended to be a living document with periodic updates. We encourage anyone with additional information to email us at office@bostonsynagogue.org.

We hope that the reader finds this history to be interesting as well as informative.

* * *

The Archival/Historical Committee:
Bette L. Siegel, Chair
Charles S. Fineman
Ruth Fein
Marlene Meyer
Michael Weingarten

March 2013/Adar 5773
55 Martha Road, West End
Boston, Massachusetts

Summary of Findings

In total, The Boston Synagogue had six predecessor shuls, each formed between 1888 and 1900 in the West and North Ends. They then merged over the next sixty years to form what today is the only active synagogue in downtown Boston holding Shabbat and holiday services 52 weeks a year.

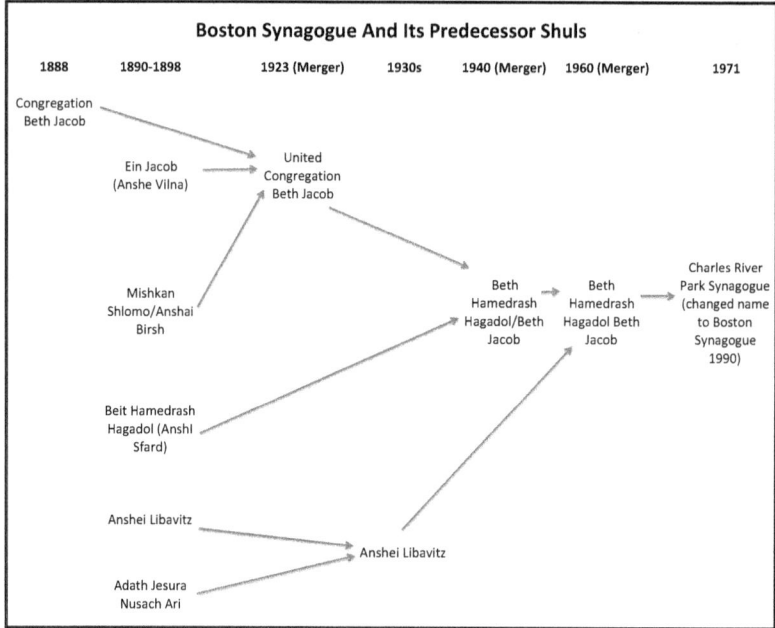

Clingan Spreadsheet and Boston Synagogue analysis

The first of these predecessors was Congregation Beth Jacob (CBJ), which incorporated in 1888, established a shul on Minot Street in the West End in 1889, and then moved to nearby Wall Street (thereby becoming known as the Wall Street Shul). Today's location is by the Propark Garage on Lomasney Way.[4]

The Boston Synagogue's other major predecessor shul, Beth Hamedrash Hagadol (or as it was spelled in its incorporation papers,

---

[4] Showing that nothing is forever, Propark's owner is proposing to replace it with high-rise housing.

"Beth Amedrish Agudal Anshi Sfard"),[5] was founded in 1896 on Poplar Street and relocated to 28 North Russell Street in the early 1900s (thereby becoming known as the North Russell Street Shul). Today the site is part of the parking lot and adjacent building at the Charles River Plaza shopping center near the Wyndham Hotel (formerly Holiday Inn).

The establishment of these shuls was the result of a wave of Jewish immigration from Eastern Europe starting in the 1880s. Initially most settled in the North End.[6] Once the North End became overcrowded, Jews began moving to the West End.

The extent of the West End's growth is startling. In the period from 1870 through 1910, the Jewish population exploded from 100 to 40,000. By 1919, there were 24 synagogues in the West End, an area of only a few blocks.

In response to this growth surge, Congregation Beth Jacob (CBJ) was the first synagogue established in the West End, followed within the next decade by the other predecessor shuls.

Although the North Russell Street Shul location only dates to the early 1900s, it soon become known as *the* place to go for concerts by famous cantors, and it had its own choir. As a result, it rapidly became the largest shul in the neighborhood. Fifty years later, the famous West-End born author Charles Angoff fondly said, "In [North Russell Street's] days of glory it was one of the great synagogues of America."[7]

Between 1888 and the 1920s, CBJ, North Russell Street and the other predecessor shuls benefitted from their affiliations with prominent rabbis such as Moses Zebulon Margolies. Margolies served as rabbi of Beth Jacob as well as five other shuls, and was the leading Orthodox rabbi in Boston in the 1890s. He apparently was

---

[5] Given that today's readers are more familiar with the 'Beth Hamedrash Hagadol' transliteration than 'Beth Amedrish Agudal,' the former is used in this book unless there is a specific reference to historical documents or plaques.

[6] The West End was not the original locus for Jewish immigration. The first wave (German Jews) settled in the South End, where they established Ohabei Shalom in 1843 as the first synagogue in Boston.

[7] Source: Angoff, "Memories of Boston" in *The Menorah Journal*, 1962

so strict on kosher meat certification that the butchers and a rejected suitor collaborated to poison all 2,000 guests at the rabbi's daughter's wedding (fortunately no one died). He became the Babe Ruth of rabbis, moving from Boston to New York to head Kehillat Jeshurun, where, among other things, he helped expand the RIETS rabbinical seminary into what is now Yeshiva University. The Ramaz day school in New York was named in his honor (**R**av **M**oshe **Z**ebulon).

By the 1920s, as Jews prospered they began to move out of the West and North Ends to the (then) more upscale neighborhoods of Dorchester and Mattapan. As a result, the Jewish population of the West End decreased by half by 1925, and by 1945 was down to 2,500. By 1957, the Jewish population in the West End was only 900.

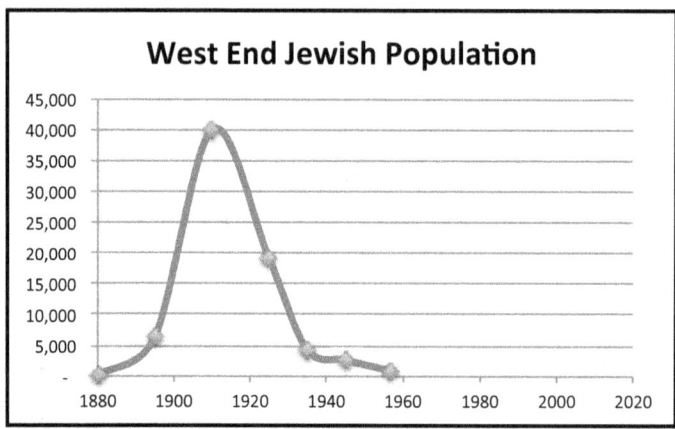

Boston Synagogue analysis based on multiple sources

The necessary result of the population surge and equally dramatic decline was a substantial drop in the number of West End shuls after 1920.

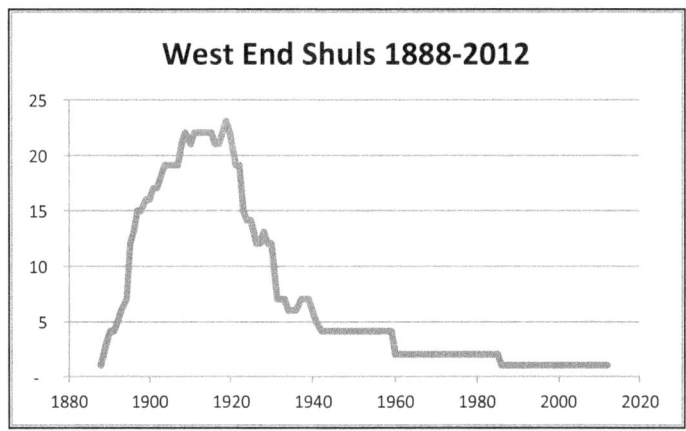

Clingan Spreadsheet and Boston Synagogue analysis

In response to this decline, three of The Boston Synagogue's predecessor shuls merged in 1923. In 1940, there was an additional merger in which Beth Amedrish Agudal Anshi Sfard and Beth Jacob formed Beth Amedrish Agudal Beth Jacob, with the joint congregation occupying the North Russell Street building. The cornerstone from this merger has been re-installed in the current 55 Martha Road building.

By the 1950s, the Boston Redevelopment Authority and its predecessors decided that the West End was a blighted neighborhood that needed to be bulldozed and replaced with what is now Charles River Park. The urban renewal zone included the location occupied by North Russell Street, with no provision for a replacement shul.

To the extent that there is a functioning synagogue in downtown Boston today, it is due to the determination of Maurice Saval of Back Bay, who: (a) decided that there needed to be a shul, (b) negotiated/litigated with the Boston Redevelopment Authority for the necessary money and land, (c) oversaw construction of the new building in a cutting-edge modern style, and then (d) ran it for twenty years until his death in 1989, paying the bills when money was short. Among other things, Saval and his friend Judge John Fox hired intelligent young people as rabbis and ritual leaders on a part-time basis (they typically were studying at Harvard or Brandeis at the same time, and/or were graduates of Maimonides or Yeshiva University). A number of these people have gone on to prominent positions in the Jewish community and elsewhere (Rabbi Allan Nadler, Rabbi

Marc Gopin, Professor David Fishman and Professor Noah Feldman).

If there were flaws in Saval's management during this period, it relates to two issues. The first was fiscal. The synagogue was not self-supporting, and relied on Saval's willingness to cover deficits. When Saval died without leaving a sufficient endowment, the shul faced serious financial problems. The second was Saval's failure to deal with the fact that there was an insufficient core of Orthodox Jews in downtown to sustain the synagogue's Orthodox practices.

After Saval's death, a succession of presidents worked hard to maintain the shul over the next decade. During that time, progress was made in a number of areas (for example, setting up a Hebrew school). However the board's disinclination to address the shul's Orthodox status made it difficult to deal with membership and financial losses.

In 1998, Susan Schreiner Weingarten became President, and was succeeded by Michael Rubin, Michael Weingarten (Susan's husband), and Bette Siegel. During this era, the shul made a number of changes whose goal was to attract the increasing number of Jews who were choosing to live in downtown Boston as the result of gentrification – also benefitting from the fact that for committed Jews, smallness and intimacy were becoming more important than largeness and formality. This played to the shul's strengths.

The Boston Synagogue made three fundamental changes during this period. First, Susan developed a relationship beginning in 1999 with Rabbi Daniel Lehmann at Gann Academy/Hebrew College, in which The Boston Synagogue benefitted from access to world-class rabbinical talent. In recent years, it supplemented this with talented (and mostly young) rabbinical students from the Hebrew College Rabbinical School. This profoundly improved the quality of the synagogue's services and attracted new members. Second, the shul decided to become egalitarian in 2002, making it a more acceptable place for non-Orthodox women and for families with daughters who wanted to hold bat mitzvahs (but could not under the shul's previous rules).[8] Third, the shul placed greater emphasis on Hebrew school,

---

[8] The first woman to conduct services as a *chazzanit* was Rabbi Sara Zacharia, at that time a teacher at Gann Academy.

Young Professionals activities and community events, such as Friday night dinners.

As a result, The Boston Synagogue is now financially self-sustaining and growing.

History, however, shows that nothing is forever and that the shul must adapt to changes as they occur.

It will be interesting to see what the Committee's successors say about the shul in 2038 and 2083 at the shul's 150th and 200th anniversaries.

The Boston Synagogue today

Chapter 1

The Founding of Congregation Beth Jacob 1888

The history of The Boston Synagogue begins on March 3, 1888, with the incorporation of Congregation Beth Jacob ('CBJ') in the state of Massachusetts "for the purpose of Hebrew worship."

Congregation Beth Jacob Articles of Incorporation

The incorporation papers did not list a specific location other than "City of Boston," which may reflect the fact that CBJ did not yet have a building with a mailing address. In 1889, CBJ moved into facilities at 11 Minot Street in the West End; and in 1894, it relocated nearby to 30 Wall Street, in the old Dean School. As was characteristic of the street-centric shul nomenclature of those days, CBJ became known as 'the Wall Street Shul.'

Determining the locations of these synagogues has been made difficult by the fact that the entire neighborhood, including the street layout, was destroyed by urban renewal in 1958-1960. However, using a map that superimposes the pre-urban renewal streets on a current street map (Appendix 1), Minot and Wall Street were located where Martha Road/Lomasney Way runs today. The Propark garage facing North Station occupies the 30 Wall Street site.

CBJ was the first synagogue established in the West End,[9] but it was the eleventh synagogue in Boston. Based on the Clingan spreadsheet, Boston's first synagogue was built in 1843 in the South End (Ohabei Shalom) and the North End's first synagogue was established in 1872 (Shomrei Shabbos). The West End was only the third Boston neighborhood with a shul.

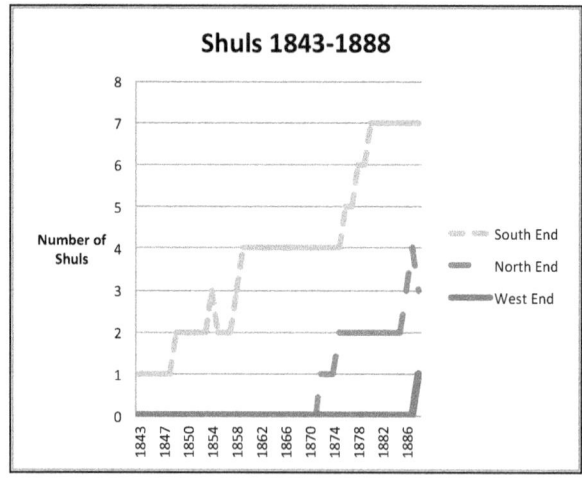

Clingan Spreadsheet and Boston Synagogue analysis

---

[9] For the term 'West End,' this book uses the definition adopted by the Clingan spreadsheet, which includes the flat of Beacon Hill – and with it, the Vilna Shul on Philips Street as well as Anshei Libavitz/Adath Jesura Nusach Ari at 8 Smith Court.

Of the preceding ten shuls, seven were in the South End and three in the North End. CBJ's founders get high marks for recognizing that being first in the West End was better competitively than being fourth in the overcrowded North End.

Underlying Demographic Trends

CBJ's formation was in response to an immigration surge by Eastern European Jews starting in the 1880s to Boston generally and the West End in particular – the result of pogroms triggered by the assassination of Czar Alexander II in 1881. This surge can be seen in the following table showing Jewish population as a percentage of total Boston population, growing from 1.2% in 1880 to 7.1% by 1900.

Jewish Share of Boston Population

	Jews	Total Boston	Jewish %
1845	40-100	114,000	0.1%
1850	350-500	137,000	0.3%
1860	1,000-2,300	178,000	0.9%
1875	3,000		
1880	4,000-5,000	363,000	**1.2%**
1895	20,000	504,500	**4.0%**
1900	40,000	561,000	**7.1%**

The Jews of Boston and Boston Synagogue analysis

These new immigrants moved initially into the relatively poor North End, supplanting what was once an Irish immigrant neighborhood. As Italians also moved into the North End it became overcrowded. As a result, Jews began to move into the adjacent West End, which offered better living space, although it still was a relatively poor neighborhood. As Mary Antin, (who upon immigrating to Boston in 1894 lived briefly on Union Place off Wall Street in the West End, near CBJ), noted in her 1912 autobiography *The Promised Land*:

Anybody who knows Boston knows that the West and North Ends are the wrong ends of that city. They form the tenement district, where poor immigrants foregather, to live as unkempt, half-washed toiling foreigners; pitiful in the eyes of social missionaries, the despair of boards of health, the hope of ward politicians, the touchstone of American democracy. The well-versed metropolitan knows the slums as a sort of house of detention for poor aliens, where they live on probation till they can show a certificate of good citizenship.

Mary Antin, *The Promised Land*, 1912; photo from: http://jwa.org/encyclopedia/article/antin-mary

Union Place off Wall Street (near Congregation Beth Jacob) – Antin, *The Promised Land* 1912

The Jewish inhabitants of the West and North Ends tended to come from different places in Eastern Europe. Arnold Wieder, in *The Early Jewish Community of Boston's North End (*1962), comments that "although the groups on both the North End and the West End were mixed, some interviewees observed that the North End had more of a *Litvak* character, while the West End had more *Russishe* Jews" (p.

18). Despite this statement, some West End shuls like Mishkan Shlomo/Anshei Birsh and Ein Jacob (Anshe Vilna) had *Litvak* origins (see Chapter 2).

The following pictures of Salem Street in the North End and the Boston Matzo Baking Factory illustrate what the street scene looked like (with the West End not being too dissimilar).

Salem Street, Jewish North End 1891

Boston Matzo Baking Company, North End Boston 1894.
Jews of Boston, from *American Jewish Historical Society* archives

These photographs suggest that shuls such as CBJ were not 'our crowd'[10] places – they were poor immigrant shuls. The richer Jews in Boston (who had arrived from Germany decades earlier) lived in the South End and went to Ohabei Shalom (founded in 1843) or Adath Israel (founded in 1854; later changing its name to Temple Israel). The contrast between the photos of the North and West End and the following 1908 photograph of Temple Israel (which looks like a set from *Masterpiece Theatre* on PBS) illustrates the lower socioeconomic status of CBJ and the other immigrant shuls.

Well-dressed congregants leaving Temple Israel's Commonwealth Avenue Synagogue, 1908. *Temple Israel Archives*

> **"By the 1880s, membership [of Temple Israel] ... included the most wealthy and influential Jews in Boston."**
> *Temple Israel website*, http://www.tisrael.org/TIHistory.asp

On the other hand, an essay titled "The Jews at the North End" in the contemporaneous book *History of the Jews of Boston* (1892), suggested that this disparity would be temporary:

---

[10] In 1967, Stephen Birmingham wrote a book, *"Our Crowd": The Great Jewish Families of New York*, in which he coined the term "our crowd' to refer to rich German Jews who looked down on the new wave of poor Jewish immigrants from Eastern Europe.

[Jews] have been buying up the real estate, on which they have in many cases raised the values very greatly. Their method of purchase is typical: they will generally pay more than others; but as a rule, they pay only one or two thousand dollars down, with an agreement to pay the balance on installments, the whole being secured by a mortgage. Most of the Jews of the North End are poor, though they rarely remain so long. This is the first stopping-place of the immigrant. Here if he has no money to start himself, he will find some one to fill his back pack on credit and send him out to the country to peddle.... The Jew is essentially a business man, and is generally progressive. It is therefore not uncommon to see the immigrant who starts out with a borrowed pack, blossom out in a few years as a merchant with a large capital, or, what is the same to the Jew, a large credit.

"The Jews at the North End," in *History of the Jews of Boston* (1892)

While upward mobility was good for the Jewish community, it meant that over time, an increasing share of Jews would choose to move to better neighborhoods. This would have profound long-term implications for the West End shuls.

CBJ's Heterogeneous Founders

In contrast to other shuls established in the 1880s and 1890s, CBJ was not formed by immigrants from a single town in Eastern Europe, the so-called '*landsmannschaften*' shuls (German/Yiddish for fraternal societies), often called '*Anshei*' (people of), e.g., Anshei Zvill, Anshei Libavitz, Anshei Poland of Warsaw, Anshe Zaslave, Anshe Slavuta, Anshi Volin, Anshe Wilkomeer and Anshi Lecovitz.

Instead, 'Congregation Beth Jacob' without an *anshei* tag suggests the intent to form an inclusive community synagogue rather than a sectarian '*shtibl*.' This is reinforced when one examines CBJ's incorporation papers, because the founders' names were surprisingly heterogeneous. Not only were they not all *Russishes* or *Litvaks*, for the most part they were not even Eastern Europeans:[11]

- CBJ's officers were: H. Robensohn, President; Luis Sondon, Treasurer; Charles Garb, Secretary; with A. Moshkowitz, R. Krensky and Marks Rudman as Trustees. Other board members included A. Godinski, S. Quint, M. Hoffenberg and S. Scion.
- Only three out of the ten names are clearly Eastern European (Moshkowitz, Krensky and Godinski).
- In contrast, five are German (Robensohn, Garb, Rudman, Hoffenberg and Scion); one is Sephardic (Luis Sondon);[12] and Quint is nondescript and presumably was changed from the original name.

---

[11] In contrast, most of the twelve signers of the May 16, 1899 Mishkan Shlomo/Anshai Birsh incorporation papers were Eastern European. The same is true of the April 5, 1902 Beth Amedrish Agudal Anshi Sfard incorporation papers -- suggesting that Beth Jacob was more heterogeneous than other West End shuls.

[12] In Boston City Council reports of proceedings for 1903-4, Lewis Sondon, owner of 55 and 57 North Russell Street, was cited for defective flagstone coverings over coalholes (holes in the sidewalk used to deliver coal into basements) and was given ten days to repair. This suggests that Luis/Lewis was relatively affluent.

Chapter 2

Developments in the North and West Ends 1888-1905

During this period, there were three major developments:

- The number of synagogues in the West End grew to twenty, (all Orthodox), while the North End lost half of its shuls.
- CBJ grew substantially and built a major new building on Wall Street
- The shuls in the North and West Ends began hiring rabbis, of whom at least two became prominent (Rabbis Margolis and Friederman) and helped define Jewish culture in the immigrant neighborhoods.

Chapter 2 deals with demographic trends and West End synagogue growth. Chapter 3 discusses the rabbis of this era; and Chapter 4 discusses how the shuls interacted with congregants for life cycle and other events.

Demographics

In the seventeen years after CJB's founding, there were substantial changes in the North and West End Jewish populations:

- The North End's Jewish population peaked in 1895 and then dropped 25% in the next decade, as the Italian population surged and Jews moved out -- largely to the West End.
- In contrast, the Jewish population of the West End increased by a factor of 6-7 times from 1895 to 1910, with Jews becoming a majority of the population (Gans in *The Urban Villagers* says 75% by 1926).

North End and West End Population Trends

Year	North End Jews	North End Italians	West End Jews	West End Italians
1880	500	1,000	100	125
1895	6,200	7,700	6,300	1,100
1905	4,700	18,000		
1910			40,000	
1920	Negligible			

Jews of Boston

The following charts from the *Boston Advocate's* June 15, 1906 issue (quoted by Lisa Kleinstein in her unpublished study *Echoes of the Old West End Boston, 1900-1914*) illustrate the changing demographics of two typical West End streets:

Real Estate Ownership: Hale Street

	1885	1895	1905
Hebrew	0%	55%	62%
Italian	0%	11%	11%
Irish	12%	8%	8%
American	88%	26%	19%

Real Estate Ownership: Poplar Street

	1885	1895	1905
Hebrew	0%	26%	56%
Irish	18%	18%	3%
American	82%	56%	41%

Kleinstein, *Echoes of the Old West End Boston, 1900-1914*

Synagogue Count

The impact of these population changes on synagogue count was substantial:

- In the North End, the number of shuls, after peaking at ten in 1899/1900, dropped to five by 1905.
- In the West End, the number of shuls grew from CBJ in 1888 to twenty shuls by 1905.

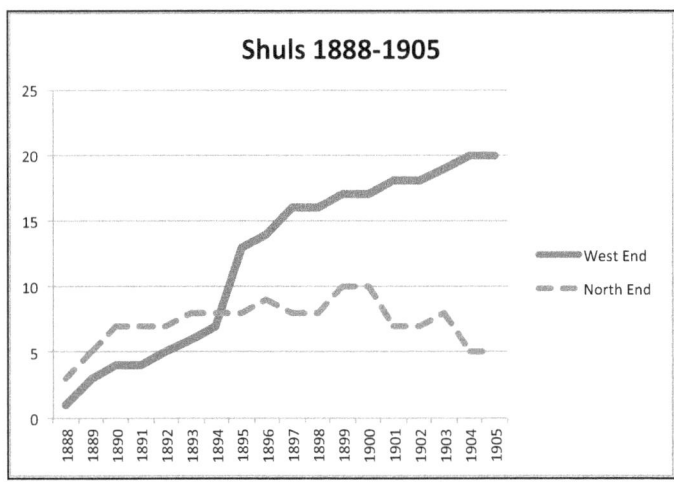

Clingan Spreadsheet and Boston Synagogue analysis

The 20-fold increase in West End shul count is particularly impressive, given that it occurred in a small geographic area (48 acres; now occupied by Charles River Park).

Unlike the South End shuls' shift to Reform and Conservative Judaism, the West End shuls remained Orthodox. Therefore there were limited differentiation opportunities:

- One way to survive (at least short-term) was to go the *landsmannschaft* route appealing to immigrants from a particular town. As shown in the chart below, ten of the twenty shuls were *landsmannschaften*.[13]
- Another differentiation vehicle used by five shuls was to be Chassidic or claim Chassidic influence (the shuls called Anshei Sfard,[14] Nusach Ari[15] or Anshei Libavitz (from the town that

---

[13] The *landsmannschaft* strategy had an inherent time limit, since with each successive generation there would be less attachment to the original hometown.

[14] The references to Sfard (as in Anshi Sfard) do not refer to Sephardic Jews or Spain, but rather to Chassidic Jews who, like the Baal Shem Tov (the founder of Chassidism), were attracted to the mysticism of Sephardic Jews. As a result, as stated in Chabad.org, "the prayer text used by Chassidim actually came to be known as *nusach sephard* ("Sephardic version"), while the prayer text of the "real" Sephardim is commonly referred to as *nusach sepharadi* (prayer version of the Sephardic Jews)."

spawned the Lubavitch movement).

- The remaining shuls (including CBJ) were more inclusive.

West End Synagogues 1900
Bold = Boston Synagogue Predecessor Shuls

	Landsmannschaft	Chassidic	General
Anshei Libavitz	x	x	
Beth Hamedrash Hagadol Anshi Sfard		x	x
Cong Beth Jacob			x
Ein Jacob (Anshe Vilna)	x		
Adath Jesura Nusach Ari		x	x
Mishkan Shlomo/Anshai Birch	x		
Adas Israel			x[16]
Agudath Achim (1)			x[17]
Agudath Achim (2)			x
An Tagi Jacob			x
Anshai Kieve	x		
Anshe Austria	x		
Anshe Slavuta	x		
Anshe Zytomir	x		
Anshei Sfard		x	
Linas Hazedek		x	
Russian Sphard	x		
Sharei Zion (Anshe Lechowitz)	x		
Tifereth Israel			x
Vilna Shul (Anshe Vilner)	x		
Total	**10**	**3-5**	**6-8**

Clingan Spreadsheet and Boston Synagogue analysis

---

[15] The *Nusach Ari* designation "means, in a general sense, any prayer rite following the usages of Rabbi Isaac Luria, the *AriZal*, in the 16th century, and, more particularly, the version used by Chabad Hasidim." (source: Wikipedia)

[16] Moved from the North End.

[17] Clingan lists this as a separate shul from the other Agudath Achim. It was located on Lowell Street and survived until the 1930s.

So CBJ, which began in 1888 as the only shul in the neighborhood, faced substantial competition by 1905, all from Orthodox shuls. In the short term, this was sustainable, due to the large and growing Jewish population. Longer term, however, if and when the Jewish population in the West End began to decline, the twenty shuls could not all survive, with the choices being to:

- Build a better shul building with better services,
- Differentiate,
- Move,
- Merge, or
- Die.

Ultimately CBJ and the other predecessor shuls would choose the merger route (although not for some time). Here is what is known about each synagogue:

The Other Predecessor Shuls

Anshei Libavitz[18]

Anshei Libavitz was founded in 1890 at 189 Hanover Street in the North End (two years after CJB). As the 'Anshei' tag suggests, it was founded by people from the Russian town of Lyubavichi, a small *shtetl* town near Smolensk in Russia (population approximately 1,516 inhabitants in 1880 including 978 Jews; source: Wikipedia). Given that Lyubavichi/Libavitz was where the Lubavitch/Chabad movement was formed and headquartered, the 'Anshei

Anshei Libavitz

Libavitz' name suggests that the shul had a Chassidic relationship -- although the first Chabad rabbi in Boston, who arrived in 1904, served as rabbi at North Russell, not Anshei Libavitz (more on this later).

---

[18] Libavitz is sometimes transliterated as 'Libovitz,' 'Lebowitz' and 'Libawitz.' Unless used in a quoted source, 'Libavitz' will be used, since this is how the congregation spelled its name.

In 1904, Anshei Libavitz moved to 8 Smith Court on Beacon Hill, when it bought the former African Meeting House from a third party.[19] The congregation then "made many repairs and upgrades, including: installing electric lighting, in 1908; repairing the roof, plumbing, sidewalk, sewage system, flooring, fence, and windows, from 1908-1912; and upholstering the old church pews in the summer and installing steam heat in the fall of 1923" (Source: work conducted by Alex Goldfield and quoted in the *Vilna Scribe* [Fall 2009 issue].

The Anshei Libavitz building had two floors, which allowed it to share facilities with Adath Jesura Nusach Ari from 1910 to 1915, and with North Russell Street from 1960 to 1971.

Adath Jesura Nusach Ari

Adath Jesura Nusach Ari was founded in 1897 at 80 Lowell Street and moved to 2 Smith Court in the 1910-1915 period. In 1918, it shared space with Anshei Libavitz at 8 Smith Court but with different rabbis (Appendix 2). It ceased operating around 1930, folding into Anshei Libavitz.

The 'Nusach Ari' part of the name suggests that Adath Jesura had a Chabad association, although like Anshei Libavitz it did not hire Chabad rabbis. Instead, Adath Jesura generally employed (on a part-time basis) the same rabbi as the Baldwin Street Shul in the North End, effectively making it a subsidiary branch.

Mishkan Shlomo/Anshai Birsh

Mishkan Shlomo/Anshai Birsh was founded in 1898 at 89 Lowell Street; then moved to Leverett Street and Minot Place. The Anshei tag suggests that it started as a *landsmannshaft* for *Litvaks* from Birsh.[20]

By 1917, Mishkan Shlomo had its own building at 71 Poplar Street. However, the map in Appendix 1 shows that 71 Poplar was a

---

[19] In the mid-to-late 19th century, the flat of Beacon Hill had a substantial African-American population, which (like the Jews in the 20th century), moved out as new immigrant populations moved into the area (it is ironic to think of African-Americans moving out because the Jewish immigrants were 'ruining the neighborhood,' given the reverse stereotype about what later happened in Dorchester/Mattapan/Roxbury). In 1971, the property was resold to the African American community, and is now part of the Museum of African American History.

[20] Birsh, or 'Birzh,' is a town in Northern Lithuania. In Lithuanian, it is called Birzai.

relatively modest row building, not a grand edifice.

Mishkan Shlomo had a short life, merging with CBJ in 1923.

Ein Jacob (Anshe Vilna)

Ein Jacob was founded in 1895 at 16 Poplar Street (a block north of Massachusetts General Hospital, near the Blossom Street cul de sac at Charles River Park). Given that the 1916 property rolls show that 16 Poplar was owned by "Harry Bachner et al," Ein Jacob may have been a *shtibl* rather than a free-standing shul.

Ein Jacob (Anshe Vilna) was not affiliated with the Vilna Shul (Anshe Vilner) on Philips Street – although both shuls presumably were formed by Lithuanian Jews from Vilna.

The name 'Ein Jacob' is an interesting choice, because it is unusual as an American synagogue name. Aside from Boston's Ein Jacob, an Internet search only surfaced a Congregation Ein Jacob established in the Bronx in 1894 and another in Newark, New Jersey, neither of which still exists. In contrast, there are numerous 'Beth Jacobs.'

To a Talmud scholar, 'Ein Jacob' (or *Ein Yaakov* in Hebrew) is a book written by Rabbi Yaakov ben Solomon ibn Habib (c. 1460–1516) which collected all of the agaddah (the non-legal) material of the Talmud. "Scattered among the more than 2,700 pages of the Talmud, aggadah focuses on the ethical and inspirational aspects of the Torah way of life. Through a wealth of homilies, anecdotes, allegories, pithy sayings, and interpretations of biblical verses, it has been said that the aggadah brings you closer to God and his Torah" (https://rowman.com/ISBN/9780765760821; accessed: January 2013).

In this context, naming one's shul 'Ein Jacob' honors this tradition and dedicates the shul to Talmudic learning.

From the perspective of this history, Ein Jacob was a short-lived shul that merged into CBJ in 1923. Its most important contribution to this history is that it was the only Boston Synagogue predecessor shul that hired one of the most prominent rabbis in Boston at the turn of the century – Solomon Friederman (more on him in the next chapter). It then jointly hired Rabbi Isaac Baritz (with Mishkan Shlomo and several other shuls) – thereby becoming part of a general West End shul transition away from traditionalist rabbis and asserting lay control.

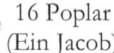

16 Poplar
(Ein Jacob)

Poplar Street Towards Chambers Street, 1910.
Boston Public Library, Print Department

Beth Hamedrash Hagadol (Anshi Sfard) – North Russell Street Shul

Beth Hamedrash Hagadol (Anshi Sfard) was one of the two most important predecessor shuls (along with CBJ).

According to Clingan, Beth Hamedrash Hagadol was founded in 1896 by Lithuanian Jews[21] and was incorporated in 1902. It was located initially at 30 Poplar Street, but moved to 28 North Russell Street when it bought the African Methodist Episcopal Zion Church[22] – in the process becoming known as the North Russell Street Shul. The site is currently occupied by the parking lot at the Charles Plaza Shopping Center.

The Anshi Sfard part of the shul's name (see footnote 14) suggests North Russell's use of Chassidic nusach, and its first listed rabbi (D.M. Rabinovitz) was Lubavitch. However, there is no indication that the shul itself was Chassidic. Instead, "Hagadol" ("The Great") suggests a desire to be a large broadly-based congregation rather than

---

[21] The shul's Lithuanian origin is questionable, since the 'Anshi Sfard' part of the name is Chassidic, and therefore Russian/Polish, not Lithuanian. Additionally a *Beacon Hill Times* article dated Aug 4, 1998 ("Boston Synagogue: A David-and-Goliath Story") suggests that the founders were from Zaslov in Russia/Ukraine.

[22] "Former Church Now a Synagogue," *Boston Globe* article June 7, 1903, mentioned in *Jews of Boston*. As with Anshei Libavitz, North Russell purchased a building formerly used by African-Americans, who vacated the West End and Beacon Hill as the Jews began populating the area. After selling its church to Beth Hamedrosh Hagadol, AME Zion then moved to Columbus Avenue.

limiting itself to what in 1896 was a small Chassidic sect.

The North Russell Street address would become the location of the merged synagogues in 1940, and it was the major shul in the West End. [More on North Russell Street in Chapter 6.]

CBJ History Through 1905

CBJ experienced substantial growth and prosperity during the period through 1905.

The first post-incorporation document that includes CBJ is the 1894 *Boston City Directory*, which indicates that its rabbi was "Rev. M.F. Margolis, pastor," with "Louis Kamper, Sexton." Apparently the directory editors either did not know or did not want to use the word 'rabbi,' (until the 1900 edition) and they provided the wrong middle initial for the rabbi. By 1895, he became "Rev. M.S. Margolis." [the S was for 'Sebulon'.]

In 1899, there is substantially more information on CBJ in the *American Jewish Yearbook,* volume 1, with the following reference to what by then was an eleven-year-old shul (there are no listings for the other predecessor shuls):

> **CONGREGATION] BETH JACOB,** 27 Wall Street. Founded 1888. Rabbi, M[oses] Z[ebulon] Margolies,[23] 3 Baldwin Place; Assistant, J. Rathchkovsky. Officers and Board of Trustees: President, Elias Kamberg, 98 Leverett Street; Vice President A. Shine, and 8 directors. Board Meeting monthly. Members, 125. Services, three times daily. Religious School daily, 4 to 7 p.m. Pupils, 100. Annual income $3000. *American Jewish Yearbook,* Volume 1

In addition, the *Yearbook* included information for six other Boston synagogues, which facilitates making inter-shul comparisons.

---

[23] An interesting side note regarding the *AJY* listing is the change in the spelling of the rabbi's name. By 1899, Margolis apparently decided that a better English transliteration of his Yiddish name was 'Margolies,' and 'Sebulon' should be 'Zebulon.' His name in the 1899 *Boston City Directory* was similarly changed to "Rev. M.Z. Margolies"

American Jewish Yearbook **1899 Directory Information**

Shul	Location	Members	Hebrew School Size	Annual Budget	Budget Per Member
Beth Jacob	West End	125	100	$3,000	$24.00
Beth Israel	North End	300	150	$8,000	$26.67
Shaarei Jerusalem	North End	100	NA	$2,500	$25.00
Chevra Tihilim	North End	125	NA	$2,000	$16.00
United Sephard	West End	60	60	$600	$10.00
Adath Israel (Temple Israel)	South End	125	NA	NA	
Mishkan Tefila	South End	125	NA	NA	
Ohabei Shalom	South End	275	150	NA	

American Jewish Yearbook and Boston Synagogue analysis

From the *AJY* information, one can observe several things:

- CBJ was an Orthodox shul with daily shaharit, minchah and maariv (morning, afternoon and evening) services.
- It had an intensive Hebrew school that met three hours a day 5-6 days a week, roughly equivalent to the amount of Jewish studies that students get at Jewish day schools today.
- The $3,000 annual budget is equivalent to $78,000 today. Given that average salaries in those days were substantially lower than today,[24] $3,000 could support a full staff plus operating costs.
- The budget per member is at the upper end of the five shuls with data, showing that CBJ was a full-fledged synagogue, not a *shtibl*.
- Compared to other shuls in the *AJY* 1899 Directory, CBJ was 2.5 times smaller than Beth Israel (the Baldwin Street Shul) in

---

[24] In Angoff's *Something About My Father*, around 1916 Rabbi Sharfman was paid $10.00 per week from Vilna Shul and earned $2-3 per week from lifecycle events. At $12.50 total per week, this came to $650 per year, worth around $15,000 today. In 1906, Rabbi Margolies was induced to leave Boston for Kehilath Jeshurun for a salary of $1,000. These are relatively close to the US average family income, which was $687.
(http://www.dailypaul.com/86536/historic-value-of-work-comparison-1915-2009)

the North End[25] and half the size of Ohabei Shalom in the South End. On the other hand, it was as large as Temple Israel and Mishkan Tefila in 1899, despite the fact that the latter were better established.

During this period, CBJ avoided damaging political infighting. This contrasts with the history of the first synagogues in the South End (Ohabei Shalom) and the North End (Shomrei Shabbos), both of which suffered from schisms that are well documented in *Jews of Boston*.

In part due to this tranquility, CBJ was sufficiently prosperous in 1903 to build a 5,400 square foot building on Wall Street – which warranted substantial *Boston Globe* coverage. Frederick A. Norcross, a prominent architect who was active in rebuilding the tenements of the North and West Ends, as well as the Boston University buildings on Bay State Road, designed the building:[26]

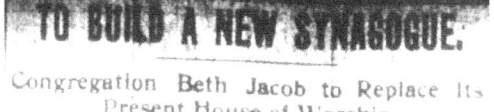

Congregation Beth Jacob to Replace Its Present House of Worship.

---

[25] Beth Israel's larger size helps explain why Rabbi Moses Margolies considered it his primary shul, as would Margolies' successor Rabbi Wolf Margolis.

[26] From Boston University Preservation Studies alumna Maura FitzPatrick's M.A. thesis: "Fred A. Norcross (1871-1929) conducted a prolific 34-year career as a designer and architect in Boston, beginning with the rebuilding of Boston's tenement neighborhoods in the North and West Ends and the North Slope of Beacon Hill." (www.bu.edu/history/about/history-of-the-department/the-history-building/) (accessed January 2013)

The Jewish congregation Beth Jacob will soon erect a fine new synagogue on the site of its present house of worship the old Dean school, 30 Wall St. It will be 85 feet wide and 63 feet deep and will be built of brick, with limestone and granite trimmings, from plans by F.A. Norcross of Boston. The building will be completed next summer.

The main entrance is under the tower, and from this fireproof stairs with marble treads lead through a staircase hall, fireproof from basement to garret, with a marble dado and terrassmo floor, to the small synagogue on the first floor. A rear door also communicates with this staircase, furnishing an additional means of exit and entrance.

Beside this small synagogue on the first floor there are a large lecture hall, two rooms for the study of the Talmud and a check room containing 300 boxes. The synagogue, lecture hall and one study room are divided by sliding partitions and can be [combined] into one large room to be used as a place of worship on special occasions.

On the second floor is the large synagogue with a seating capacity of 600 on the floor and 350 in the gallery, which extends around three sides. In the center of the auditorium is the cantor's desk and at the end opposite the entrance is the ark.

There are no columns to obstruct the view and the walls are to be handsomely decorated. The finish throughout the building is whitewood and the floors are of hardwood.

On the gallery floor are two committee rooms. The basement contains a large banquet hall with kitchen, which will be used for social gatherings, weddings, etc., the heating appliances, the men's and women's lavatories and two storerooms.

An excellent and effectual system of ventilation is provided for and ample arrangements for escapes in case of fire.

Electricity and gas will be used and the building will be heated by steam. Louis H. Levenson[27] is chairman of the building committee. -- *The Boston Globe* September 5, 1903

---

[27] Levenson shows up in the 1916 Boston property list as owning 52, 62, and 64 Nashua Street, and so was relatively prosperous.

Chapter 3

Early Rabbis and Lay Leadership

Substantial information exists about two rabbis, Moses Margolies and Solomon Friederman, who served at CBJ and other predecessor shuls during the 1888-1905 period; as well as information on early lay leadership. For a list of rabbis for each shul by year, see Appendix 2.

Both rabbis were traditionalist immigrants who helped form the structure of Orthodox Judaism in Boston at the turn of the last century. However Margolies would prove to be much more accommodating to the need for flexibility (in a manner that presaged Modern Orthodoxy), while Friederman opposed all change.

Rabbinical Biographies 1903

In the *American Jewish Yearbook* volume 1, there is a compilation of "Biographical Sketches Of Rabbis And Cantors Officiating In The United States" for the year 1903. The survey includes two rabbis who served at least one of The Boston Synagogue's predecessor shuls (in italics below):

> **Margolies, Moses Z.** Rabbi of Congregations Beth Israel, *Beth Jacob*, and *Anshei Libavitz*, Boston, Mass. Born April, 1851, at Kroz, Russia. Son of Solomon Margolies. Rabbinical diploma received from Rabbi Heilpern, Bielostok, Russia, and others. Held Rabbinical positions in Russia for thirteen years. Address: 3 Baldwin Pl, Boston, Mass.

> **Friederman, Solomon Jacob.** Rabbi of Congregation Shaarei Jerusalem, Zitomir, and *Ein Jacob,* Boston, Mass. Born May 10, 1866, at Vilna, Russia. Son of Boruch M. Friederman. Rabbinical diploma received from Rabbi Isaac E[l]chanan Spector, Kovno. Was Rabbi in Congregation Kol Israel, New York City. Publications: "Emeth Weemuno," "Minchos Jacob." Address: 116 Salem, Boston, Mass.

American Jewish Year Book 5664, 1903.

Looking at these biographies suggests the following:

- Neither rabbi listed CBJ, Anshei Libavitz or Ein Jacob first in his affiliations, suggesting that these shuls were of secondary importance to them. Margolies' primary affiliation was Beth Israel in the North End (the 'Baldwin Street Shul"); whose 1899 budget was 2.5 times larger than CBJ's. Friederman's primary affiliation was Shaari Jerusalem in the North End (slightly smaller than CBJ).
- Both rabbis were born and received rabbinical ordination in Eastern Europe. They served as rabbis in Europe or New York before coming to Boston.
- Rabbinical ordination was received from an individual rabbi in Europe. While this initially might appear less prestigious than receiving *semicha* from a rabbinical school, Rabbi Friederman's mentor Rabbi Yitzchak Elchanan Spektor was "considered the pre-eminent Halachic authority of his time" (source: Wikipedia). As illustration of Spektor's prominence, the Rabbi Isaac Elchanan Theological Seminary (RIETS) at Yeshiva University, which today is the center of Modern American Orthodox Judaism, was named in his honor (RIETS stands for "Rabbi Yitzchak Elchanan Theological Seminary").

Left: Rabbi Yitzchak Elchanan Spektor. Right: RIETS Seal (in Hebrew, Yeshivat Rav Yitzchak Elchanan)

- Each man served as the rabbi for at least three congregations (the Boston City Directory for the year 1900 shows Margolies as the rabbi for six shuls, with Friederman listed for three). Obviously the small and newly established immigrant shuls could not provide full-time employment, so rabbis needed to find part-time jobs (with shammases and others leading services when the rabbi was absent).

**Rabbi Moses Margolies:
Shuls Served in the Boston 1900** *City Directory*
* Boston Synagogue Predecessor Shul

1.	Beth Jacob*	2.	Anshei Libavitz*
3.	Adath Jesura Nusach Ari*	4.	Shaari Jerusalem
5.	Beth Israel	6.	Chevra Tehilim

- In 1900, Rabbi Margolies was 52 and Rabbi Friederman was 37. Based on their age difference as well as other sources discussed later in this chapter, Margolies was the dean of Orthodox Judaism in the North and West Ends.
- The younger man (Friederman) touted his academic capabilities, listing two publications (and writing two more in later years).
- Neither was a rabbi's son. This is in contrast to the stereotype of Eastern European *shtetls*, where sons of rabbis succeeded their fathers. Perhaps if one were the son of a rabbi with guaranteed dynastic employment, the natural inclination would be to stay in the old country.

Orthodox Versus Reform Rabbi Credentials

Margolies and Friederman's backgrounds were substantially different than those of rabbis at Reform temples such as Raphael Lasker and Samuel Hirschberg at Ohabei Shalom. From the *American Jewish Yearbook*, here are Lasker's and Hirshberg's biographies:

> **Lasker, Raphael.** Rabbi Emeritus of Congregation Ohabei Shalom, Boston, Mass. Born February 19, 1838, at Zirke, Prussia. Educated by his father [rabbi of Zirke] Rabbi Caro of Pinne; Rabbi Hirsch Schneidemihl, Obornick; and Rabbis Moses Feilchenfeld and Mendel Rogasen, all in Posen; and at the Gymnasium of Gleiwitz and the University of Giessen. Was Rabbi and founder of Congregation Bnai Abraham, Portsmouth, Ohio, 1858; Rabbi of Congregation Shaar

Hashomayim, New York City, for nine years; of Temple Israel, Brooklyn, N. Y., 1871-1876. Member of the Boston Public School Board for six years. Editor of the *New Era Jewish Magazine*. Address: 31 Doane, Boston, Mass.

Hirshberg, Samuel. Rabbi (since 1895) of Congregation Ohabei Shalom, Boston, Mass. Born December 14, 1869, at Cincinnati, Ohio. Son of Maurice A. Hirshberg and Sarah Samuels. Educated at Hebrew Union College (Rabbi, 1891); University of Cincinnati (B.L., 1891); and Harvard University (M.A., 1902). Was Rabbi of Congregation Achduth Vesholom, Fort Wayne, Ind., 1891-1895. Married, October 24, 1899, Jeannette Rosalie Hirshberg. Address: 30 Coolidge, Brookline, Mass.

American Jewish Year Book 5664, op. cit.

Looking first at Rabbi Lasker: in 1903 Ohabei Shalom was 60 years old, and therefore sufficiently well established to have a 65-year-old rabbi emeritus like Lasker. Unlike Margolies and Friederman, Lasker came from Germany (Prussia). He was university-educated and received rabbinical ordination from a *bet din* of four rabbis, including his father. He then served as rabbi of three congregations in 1858 through 1876 – at which point Ohabei Shalom employed him as rabbi for eighteen years from 1877 to 1895.

In short, Rabbi Lasker is stereotypical of the type of rabbi that a big city Reform synagogue would have hired: someone from Germany with university as well as rabbinical credentials; with demonstrated success in leading congregations. Lasker's ability to participate in broader Boston society is illustrated by his serving on the Boston Public School Board. He lived not in an immigrant neighborhood, but on Doane near Milk Street in what is now the Financial District.

In 1895, Rabbi Lasker was succeeded by Rabbi Hirschberg. Unlike his predecessor, Hirschberg was a native-born American and graduate of Hebrew Union College (the Reform seminary) as well as the University of Cincinnati. After serving at the age of 22 as rabbi in Fort Wayne, Indiana, he came to Ohabei Shalom at 26. He also held an M.A. from Harvard, which would have impressed his Boston congregants.

Rabbi Hirschberg's biography is typical for Reform rabbis. With the establishment of Hebrew Union College (HUC), there no longer was a need to go to Germany for replacement rabbis. Instead, Ohabei Shalom could hire an HUC graduate with strong secular academic credentials. Rabbi Hirschberg lived in Brookline, not Boston, and so was one of the earliest Jews who chose to live in the suburbs.

So there was a world of difference between the West and North End rabbis and the rabbis from Ohabei Shalom.

More on Rabbi Margolies

Despite his comparatively modest *American Jewish Yearbook* biography, Congregation Beth Jacob's and Anshei Libavitz's Rabbi Margolies ultimately had a more impressive career than the Ohabei Shalom rabbis. In the years when Margolies lived in Boston (1883 to 1906), many considered him to be the leading Orthodox rabbi in the city. Some commentators called him Chief Rabbi, although this appears to be an honorary rather than an official title. In this sketch from *History Of the Jews of Boston* (1892), Margolies was credited with being the leader of the united Orthodox congregations of the North and West Ends:

> The subject of this sketch, Rabbi M. Z. Margolies, of the United Hebrew Orthodox Congregations, of Boston, first saw light on the 17th of February, 1851, in the city of Kross, Russia. Under the guidance and influence of the celebrated Rabbis Volper, Huroitz and Alpert, the famous Rabbi of the city of Bialistock, he studied the Talmud. Endowed with a keenly intellectual faculty, added to assiduous study, he soon acquired a masterly knowledge of the Talmudical lore. After receiving his Rabbinical diploma he was chosen as assistant Rabbi with the sanction of the Russian Government, in the city of Meretz, in his

Rabbi Margolies

21st year. His second Rabbinical position was at the city of Roslow, where he served as Chief Rabbi for 12 years. His usefulness and influence soon felt itself beyond its spheres. While being Rabbi at Roslow he received a unanimous call from the Congregation "Shomre Beth Abraham"[28] of this city, the largest Hebrew Orthodox Congregation at the North End, which position he accepted. The Rabbi succeeded, by his able and impressive sermons, which bear the stamp of sincerity and earnestness, in uniting the various congregations of North and West Ends, of which he is now the spiritual guide and leader, which confidence and respect he enjoys and commands. The Rabbi fondly enjoys his family life with his wife and four children.

History of the Jews of Boston, 1892

There are two other descriptions of Margolies in his Boston years. The first comes from Ephraim Lisitzky, who immigrated to Boston in 1900 from Slutzk, Russia at the age of 15. As recounted in his autobiography *In the Grip of Cross Currents* (written years later in 1949), Lisitzky, who had been an observant *yeshiva bocher* (young man; student) in Slutzk, visited Margolies shortly after he arrived in Boston. He refers to Margolies by his acronym Ramaz (short for **R**av **M**oshe **Z**evulon),[29] and comments favorably on the rabbi's learning and presence:

---

[28] The Baldwin Street Shul.

[29] Prominent rabbis often were honored with acronyms. The most famous examples are Rabbi Solomon ben Isaac (Shlomo Itshaki), or Rashi; and Rabbi Moses ben Maimon (Maimonides), or Rambam.

The Chief Rabbi of Boston at that time [1900] was Rabbi Moshe Zebulon Margolies, known as The Ramaz... Ramaz' face glowed... with its chiseled lines, delicate skin, and brilliant expression. He had a grand air and dressed elegantly. His tall figure was accentuated by a top-hat, whose blackness contrasted with the white of his long full beard and of the hair falling down on the nape of his neck where it was trimmed in a straight line.

Ramaz was a modest man, but his very appearance commanded respect.

* * *

Shortly after I arrived in Boston my father presented me to Ramaz, who invited me to visit him at home. I eagerly responded to his invitation. Each time I visited him I basked in his learning – Ramaz cleared up obscure passages in the Talmud for me.

Rabbi Moses Margolies. www.ramaz.org.

Lisitzky, *In the Grip of Cross Currents*

Lisitzky portrays Margolies as a surprisingly 'progressive' rabbi along several dimensions. First, he was strongly pro-Zionist:

> Zionism encountered great difficulties in making its way at the beginning of the century in America. Some Orthodox rabbis were hesitant to help it; others opposed Zionism actively, seeing it as subversive of traditional Judaism. But Ramaz became one of the champions of Zionism. A portrait of bare-headed Herzl hung on the east wall of his home together with portraits of great Jewish scholars; he pronounced Herzl's name with reverence. He also propagated the idea of a Jewish renaissance in Palestine in both his synagogue sermons and in his private conversations.... The Ramaz' home in Boston became a meeting place for Zionists.

Second, Lisitzky notes that Margolies accepted the fact that his son Sam was "educated both at the yeshiva and at Harvard University" and gave speeches in English as well as Yiddish. Many traditionalist rabbis rejected secular learning and demanded that all sermons be in Yiddish.

Finally, Lisitzky emphasized Margolies's belief in the need to develop Jewish rabbinic leadership in America, rather than viewing America as a place where Jews were losing their faith and therefore looking to Eastern Europe for rabbis. When Lisitzky spoke to Margolies about returning to Slutszk for rabbinical training, Margolies instead recommended that he attend the new Rabbi Isaac Elchanan seminary in New York:

> Ramaz ... foresaw that American Jewry was destined to become the center of world Jewry, and he was concerned lest it deteriorate spiritually for lack of higher educational institutions. When the Rabbi Isaac Elchanan Yeshiva was founded in New York (today Yeshiva University), Ramaz became its patron. Even when he still lived in Boston he was a staunch supporter of the yeshiva: when he settled in New York, Ramaz became its chief leader and benefactor till his death.
>
> ...I had told Ramaz of my decision to return to Slutzk Yeshiva: and ... I came to ask his advice as to the best way to go about becoming a Rabbi.
>
> "My son," he replied, "wherever Israel has gone the Torah has followed. It has followed us into our American exile, too. A modest beginning has, with God's help, been made at the Rabbi Isaac Elchanan Yeshiva which has been founded in New York. The yeshiva provides for its students. Go there my son, study at the yeshiva, and He Who causes His Name to dwell wherever the Torah dwells will surely aid you."

So based on Lisitzky's portrait, Margolies, despite his traditionalist background, was surprisingly broad-minded, making him a precursor to what Joseph Soloveitchick would develop into Modern Orthodoxy.

* * *

In a second (and amusing) vignette about Margolies (published in the *New Yorker* in 1953), Samuel Behrman recounts what happened sixty years earlier in 1893 when Margolies' daughter Ida married into the author's family. Apparently Margolies was so important a rabbi and so strict on kosher meat certification standards in Boston that in retaliation, the local butchers paid $1,500 to poison the 2,000 guests at Ida's wedding (equivalent to $37,000 today). Fortunately no one died:

> About the time I was born, a radiant event took place in my family. ... the totally unexpected engagement, in 1893, of my Uncle Harry, who lived a couple of blocks away on Providence Street, to a Boston girl named Ida, the daughter of the Ramaz ....
>
> The Ramaz, who was then presiding over the Baldwin Place Synagogue, in Boston, to which he had been summoned from Lithuania seven years before, traced his descent from a celebrated rabbi known as the Rashi, one of the greatest of Talmudic commentators, who lived in France in the eleventh century...
>
> [Ida's] marriage to my Uncle Harry, which took place in Meinhard Hall, in Boston, received more than the conventional reporting in the social columns, because most of the two thousand guests, as well as the bride, were poisoned. In Worcester, the event was known for years as Ida's Poisoned Wedding. "BEAUTIFUL BLONDE IN A BLUE SATIN DRESS POISONED AT HER OWN WEDDING," went one headline, and another declared, "RABBI'S DAUGHTER AND TWO THOUSAND GUESTS POISONED BY DEJECTED LOVER." The dejected lover was Perrele Greenbaum. Perrele had everything; he was successful in business, lively, generous, and very much in love with Ida. But he was a materialist and couldn't resist the Saturday influx of business at his store. ....
>
> As [Ida] was standing under the wedding canopy, a visitation came to her: a voice like an angel's whispered, "Don't sit at the head table and don't eat!" This injunction

she did not obey. Presently, there was panic in the hall and Ida understood why the voice had whispered to her. The guests all became very ill, those at the head table experiencing the first paroxysms; she became very ill herself. The Ramaz spoke to the guests quietly. The guilty ones would be discovered, he said, and God would punish them.

The Ramaz's prediction came true soon enough. The very next day, while the two thousand guests were still writhing, the wife of a butcher who had wanted to supply the meat for the wedding but who had been refused came rushing to the Ramaz crying hysterically. Her small son had just fallen off a roof, and she took this as a punishment from God. The Ramaz had turned this particular butcher down because he did not consider that his product met the ritual requirements for kosher meat. The Ramaz had many enemies among the Boston butchers, who found he could not be bribed to give certificates, or Hashgohes, qualifying their meat. The turndown for this big wedding was more than they could take. Some of the illegal butchers got together and raised fifteen hundred dollars, with which they bribed a druggist to concoct a poison that would not be fatal but would make the guests violently ill. When the plot was revealed by the butcher's hysterical wife, the Ramaz, instead of demanding that the offenders be sent to jail, rushed off to see the injured child, and this convinced the mother that the boy would get well, which, indeed, he did. God, said the Ramaz, would punish the plotters; revenge was not his province. So it came to pass. The druggist, who had been prosperous, gradually lost his business as the news got around; the illegal butchers and their leader, since the Ramaz continued to refuse to give them Hashgohes, were forced eventually to seek other trades.

"Daughter of the Ramaz," S.N. Behrman, *The New Yorker*, November 21, 1953

In 1906, Margolies left Boston to become senior Rabbi of Kehilath Jeshurun, a nationally prominent Orthodox synagogue in Manhattan.[30] He then played a major role in the formation of Yeshiva University, and was one of the speakers at a major 1933 anti-Nazi rally held at Madison Square Garden in New York. The famous Ramaz School in Manhattan was named after him posthumously, using his Ramaz acronym. In a 1936 obituary in the *New York Times,* he is called the "dean of the orthodox rabbis in North America."

Margolies' story is reminiscent of Babe Ruth being traded from the Boston Red Sox to the New York Yankees in 1919. While Margolies was prominent in Boston, he became much more important in New York.

Rabbi Margolies addressing 1933 Mass Rally at Madison Square Garden in NYC against the Nazi persecution of Jews.
http://www.ramaz.org/public/legacy.cfm

---

[30] He was paid $1,000, equivalent to $25,000 today. (source: *Modern Heretic and a Traditional Community: Mordecai M. Kaplan;* Jeffrey S. Gurock, Jacob J. Schacter; p.51.

Rabbi Margolies *New York Times* Obituary, August 26, 1936

RABBI MARGOLIES DIES OF PNEUMONIA

Dean of Orthodox Synagogue Heads, 85, Zionist Leader and Jewish Educator.

FOUNDER OF RELIEF GROUP

Rose From Sickbed in 1933 to Address Meeting of Protest Against Anti-Semitism.

Special to THE NEW YORK TIMES.

BELMAR, N. J., Aug. 25.—The Rev. Moses S. Margolies, dean of the orthodox rabbis in North America and head of the Kehilath Jeshurun Synagogue of New York, died at the Carlton Hotel here shortly after 5 A. M. today. He became seriously ill of pneumonia a week ago. His age was 85.

His wife, a son, Hyman Margolies of New York, and a daughter, Mrs. Ida Newman of Newark, N. J., were at the bedside when he died.

Funeral services will be held tomorrow morning at the Kehilath Jeshurun Synagogue, Eighty-fifth Street near Park Avenue, New York.

Associated Press Photo.
RABBI M. S. MARGOLIES

Spoke at Protest Meeting

Failing health after he reached the age of 80 did not diminish the active participation of Rabbi Moses S. Margolies in Jewish affairs. Anti-Semitism in Germany moved him so deeply that he rose from a sickbed on March 27, 1933, to address a protest mass meeting at Madison Square Garden.

Dean of the Orthodox Jewish rabbinate in this country, he brought the audience of 20,000 to its feet as he pronounced a prayer in Hebrew asking that the persecutions cease and that the hearts of the enemies of Israel be softened.

No religious or cultural activity here or abroad was foreign to the scope of Rabbi Margolies's interest. His chief objective was the establishment and expansion of institutions of Jewish learning throughout the world, and he was one of the first to recognize the necessity of combining religious and secular knowledge in these institutions.

Rabbi Margolies was born in Kroza, Russia, in April, 1851. His rabbinical training was obtained in the yeshivas of Kroza and Bialystok. At the age of 26 he became a rabbi in Sloboda, where he served until he was called to Boston in 1889 as chief rabbi of the Orthodox community there.

Came to New York in 1906

In 1906 he came to New York to fill the pulpit of Congregation Kehilath Jeshurun, 117 East Eighty-fifth Street, one of the largest and most influential Orthodox congregations in the country. He continued to serve as rabbi there until his death, although in recent years most of the actual duties of the post devolved on his grandson, Rabbi Joseph H. Lookstein, who was associate rabbi of the congregation.

For many years president of the Union of Orthodox Rabbis of the United States and Canada, Rabbi Margolies took a leading part in most Jewish movements. At his death he was honorary president of the Union of Orthodox Rabbis and of Yeshiva College, which he did much to build.

He was founder and honorary chairman of the Central Relief Committee, which was merged later into the American Jewish Joint Distribution Committee. He was chairman of the Rabbinical Board of New York, head of the board of education of the Uptown Talmud Torah and a director of the Rabbi Jacob Joseph School and of the Hebrew Sheltering and Immigrant Aid Society.

A pioneer Zionist, he was active in the Mizrachi, the Orthodox Zionist Organization of America. He organized the supervisory system under which kosher meat was distributed in this city and, in cooperation with other Jewish leaders, he founded the Kehillah here.

Former Head of Yeshiva College

His concern with problems of Jewish education led him to seek the organization of the secular high school department of the Rabbi Isaac Elchanan Theological Seminary, out of which grew Yeshiva College. He was president of the college and seminary for several years.

Many institutions in Palestine held his interest. More than 1,000 trees were planted in his honor there. A special tract, known as the Ramaz Forest, was established and friends, acting through the Jewish National Fund, contributed to the tree planting. The name was taken from the word "rabbi" in conjunction with Mr. Margolies's initials.

Among the institutions in Jerusalem which he served as chairman were the United Charities, the Kneseth Israel, the Diskin Orphan Asylum, the United Home for the Aged and the Rabbinical College Torah Chayim. He was also treasurer for many yeshivas in Poland and Lithuania.

Rabbi Margolies had four children by his first wife, who died in 1912. A daughter, Mrs. Etta Schlang, died in 1932, and a son, Rabbi Samuel Margolies of Cleveland, died in 1918. The surviving children are Mrs. Ida Newman of Newark and Hyman Margolies of this city. There are twelve grandchildren and three great-grandchildren.

Rabbi Margolies was married four times. His fourth marriage was on March 24, 1927, to Mrs. Ida M. Braz.

TRIBUTES BY LEADING JEWS

Work and Personality of Rabbi Margolies Are Praised.

Jewish leaders in the city joined yesterday in praising the work of Rabbi Moses S. Margolies. Among the tributes were:

Dr. BERNARD REVEL, President of the Faculty of Yeshiva College—Dr. Margolies was a recognized and revered leader of the American Orthodox rabbinate. He was a unique spiritual personality. Master of the entire field of Jewish lore and law, he dedicated his life to the dissemination of Jewish learning and idealism and was a great force for God and good, for selflessness and spirituality in the life of the Jewish community in this land.

Rabbi HERBERT S. GOLDSTEIN, Honorary President of the Union of Orthodox Jewish Congregations of America—Rabbi Margolies was above all a great authority on Jewish law, which enabled him to be a liberal interpreter of it. He was not a cloistered scholar, but a friend to all who sought his aid.

Borough President SAMUEL LEVY—The sense of personal loss sustained through the passing of my revered rabbi and teacher is transcended by the loss to American Israel and world Jewry. Though his supreme contribution was to the cause of Jewish learning in this land and everywhere, he nevertheless gave of his spirit and leadership to every cause for the welfare of Israel. He was the uncrowned head of Orthodox Jewry.

Rabbi J. L. HOROWITZ, President of the Descendants of Rashi Association—He was the most noble man in American Jewish life and his kind cannot be duplicated.

SAMUEL D. LEIDESDORF, President of the Federation for the Support of Jewish Philanthropic Societies of New York—New York has lost a great religious and communal leader. He was influential in the philanthropic life of the community. His counsel and guidance will be greatly missed.

More on Rabbi Friederman

Separately from Friedman's *American Jewish Yearbook* capsule profile, there is an in-depth biography in *Orthodox Judaism in America*. From this, one learns that Friederman came to Boston in 1895 from New York City (and stayed, in reversal of Margolies' path). In addition to serving as a pulpit rabbi, he was interested in Jewish education (in which he was less than successful), working with Chassidic rabbi Pinchas Horowitz. He also was well known as a traditionalist preacher who published sermons. In these, he opposed Reform Judaism and urged American Jews to follow Old Country religious practices:

> **FRIEDERMAN, ZALMAN YAAKOV** (c. 1860-1934). Rabbi. Zelman Yaakov Friederman (son of Baruch Mordechai) was born in Meretz, near Vilna, Lithuania, in the 1860s. At the age of 12 he went to Siobodka to study the Talmud with Rabbi Moshe Danishevsky, head of the Slobodka rabbinical court. Later he studied at several small yeshivas in Vilna.
>
> At the age of 20, Friederman received rabbinical ordination from the rabbi of Bialystok. Additional letters of ordination were received from Rabbi Isaac Elchanan Spektor of Kovno, Rabbi Aaron Moshe Lapidus of Rassein, and Rabbi Yitzchak Lipa Shereshevsky of Neshvitz. Following his marriage in 1889 to the daughter of Rabbi Yaakov Lifshitz, personal secretary to Rabbi Isaac Elchanan Spektor of Kovno, Friederman continued his Talmud studies with the financial assistance of his father-in-law.
>
> Immigrating to America in 1893, Friederman settled in New York's Lower East Side, where he was appointed rabbi of Congregation Kol Israel Anshei Polin. While in New York, he played an important role in the development of the East Broadway Talmud Torah and the Kupat HaRamban charity. In 1895 Friederman accepted a position as rabbi of a consortium of Orthodox congregations in Boston known as the Agudar ha-Kehilol. A notable preacher in Yiddish, Friederman often bemoaned the condition of American

religious life to his congregants in Boston, chastising them for not adhering more scrupulously to Orthodox observance. In 1895 he also published his first book, *Emet v'Emunah;* a polemic against Reform Judaism. A supporter of the founding of the Agudath haRabbonim, Friederman was hopeful that a rabbinic union of European Talmud scholars might improve the religious condition of American Jewish life.

Together with Hasidic Rabbi Pinchas David Horowitz,[31] who had come to Boston from Palestine in 1914, Friederman established a Talmud Torah yeshiva where boys studied Talmud after public school hours. But the yeshiva did not receive the support of some community leaders and Orthodox rabbis who feared that a Talmud Torah yeshiva would undermine their afternoon school program. Without widespread support of the community, the yeshiva ... was eventually closed.

Friederman maintained an ongoing correspondence with the leading scholars of Europe and Palestine regarding matters of halakha. Rabbi Israel Meir HaCohen (known as the Chofetz Chaim), Rabbi Yehoshua Leib Diskin, Rabbi Chaim Ozer Grodzinski, and Rabbi Chaim Sonnenfeld were in contact with Friederman and familiar with some of the problems he faced as a rabbi in America.

A long-time activist on behalf of religious Zionism, Friederman was in close communication with Rabbi Abraham Isaac Kook and in 1934 left Boston for a visit to Palestine. While in Palestine Friederman became seriously ill and died on December 16, 1934...

Beside the polemical work *Emet v'Emunah,* Friederman authored several books of sermons, including *Minchat Yaakov, Nachalat Yaakov, and Shoshanat Yaakov.* He submitted several articles to Judah David Eisenstein's *Ozar Yisrael* and

---

[31] Friederman married Rabbi Pinchas Horowitz's daughter in 1920 in a wedding held in Roxbury with 6,000 guests. Later, in a controversy over kashrut (the Lebanon Kosher Sausage Factory division of Swift Premium Meats), Horowitz appointed Friederman to represent him in a beth din proceeding (source: *A Chassidic Journey*).

wrote dozens of essays in *Ha-Ivri* and *Ha-Peies*. Writings: *Emet v'Emunah* (New York, 1895); *Minchat Yaakov* (New York. 1901); *Nachalat Yaakov* (New York, 1914); *Shoshanat Yaakov* (New York, 1937) ...

Orthodox Judaism in America: A Biographical Dictionary and Sourcebook by Moshe D. Sherman

Based on the *Orthodox Judaism* citations, The Boston Synagogue purchased Friederman's works for review. The *Yakov* books are collections of sermons for Shabbat and holidays, and are written in Hebrew with English and Hebrew end papers (see *Shoshanath Yaakov* in Hebrew; *Shoshanath Jacob* in English). In these books, Friederman uses the title "Rabbi of the United Congregations" (in Hebrew, *Rav d'Agudath ha-Kehiloth*) rather than listing his congregations separately (he is never listed as the rabbi for more than three shuls in any one year; see Appendix 5). For European readers who did not know where Boston, Massachusetts was located, the Hebrew page notes in parentheses that Boston is in "Medinath America."

One suspects that the asserted title was meant as a challenge to Margolies' status as head Orthodox rabbi in Boston. As noted earlier, *History of the Jews of Boston* (1892) stated that Margolies "of the *United Hebrew Orthodox Congregations*, of Boston" ... had succeeded "in *uniting the various congregations* of North and West Ends, of which he is now the spiritual guide and leader." Thus, for Friederman to use the title *"Rabbi of the United Congregations"* in *Nachalat Yaakov* in 1901 (while Margolies was still in Boston) was provocative.

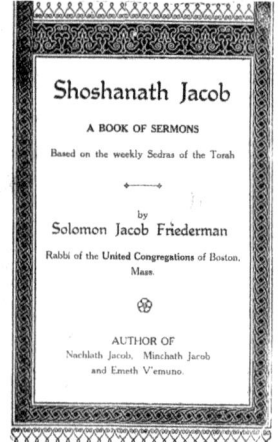

If Friederman's intent was to challenge Margolies' supremacy, it did not succeed, since there is no indication that others recognized him as "Rabbi of the United Congregations."

As suggested in the *Orthodox Judaism* biography, Friederman was a traditionalist who opposed what he saw as dangerous assimilation by American Jews. A good example of his beliefs is seen in this translation from *Emet v'Emunah* (Truth and Faith), which, as noted in the biography, is "a polemic against Reform Judaism:"

> ...and what can we say to deceitful acts that were done in the past and are still being done today by connivers and wise guys who are scheming to make our people forget their heritage and religion and let them be immersed in the pleasure of assimilation and absorption into the nations, from the time of the early Hellenists such as Simon the Traitor, Jason, and Menelaus, and all the various other heretics, to the new Sadducees in our own time, and all those who ignore the Mitzvoth that are explicitly stated in the written Torah, and all who seek amendments and reforms to the religion of Moses and Israel while deviating from the way of life of the Jewish community and live an unfettered life by themselves. The difference between their deceitful acts today to the deceitful acts at the generations of the Judges till the destruction of the Temple, is only the difference that exists between the laws of the nations in their generations to the way of life of the nations today. In the past they believed that they can benefit from being close to the gentiles so they assimilate and learn their ways, which were in accordance with the spirit of that time. While today they are seeking to imitate the gentiles and assimilate in them with a passion: they follow their laws and find delight in their mores, in accordance with the spirit of the present time. All that they do, in spite of the spirit of the Torah that speaks to them from experience in the same way as the Torah spoke in days past through the mouth of the prophets; namely, that the more they are going to copy like monkeys the deeds of the gentiles, the more will the gentiles hate them and vomit them out of their midst. And if, from their past acts of

duplicity, you could have concluded that they did not know the Torah, from all their deceitful acts of today we must conclude that they don't know and don't comprehend the shape of a single letter in Moses' Torah!

Friederman, *Emet v'Emunah*, p. 47-48; translated by Gerald Kleinstein

As illustration of his uncompromising attitude, Friederman demanded that Jews wear kippot (skullcaps) at all times, in an era when few Jews did this outside the synagogue.

Rabbi Zalman Yaakov Friederman ... quickly gained a reputation for hard-line opposition to any deviation from the strictest Orthodoxy. Predictably, his contribution echoed [the] position that bareheadedness is never sanctioned and the view ... that uncovering the head amounted to *hukat hagoyim,* and was therefore absolutely prohibited. Friederman even cited sources supporting male head covering during sleep and at the bath house. He found room for leniency only in a case where one must swear before a Gentile court of law, and the judges required bareheadedness.

Katz and Bayme, *Continuity and Change*

Educationally, Friederman pushed for traditional cheder Jewish education. Unlike Margolies, he opposed the new Zionist-inspired movement in Boston that taught modern Hebrew, feeling that this distracted students from learning Jewish religious practices and values.[32] When graduates of the Zionist Evrio School at 31 North Russell Street[33] (which included modern Hebrew in its curriculum) approached Friederman for Talmud instruction, Louis Hurwich of the Bureau of Jewish Education recounted the following story:

The school could not financially sustain hiring a special faculty member for these graduates. But they desired to study Torah and particularly Talmud. When they realized

---

[32] In this context, the statements made in the *Orthodox Judaism in America* biography about Friederman's pro-Zionist stance may have been a later position.

[33] Evrio was located directly opposite the North Russell Street shul (the latter was located at 24-30 North Russell Street).

that Evrio could not accommodate them, they split into groups and knocked on the doors of local rabbis pleading for someone to teach them. But they were graduates of a school whose reputation was that it taught heresy. Who knows what would happen to a rabbi who took these young heretics under his wing? One by one the rabbis rejected the young people with different excuses. One group... came to Rabbi Freiderman [sic]... and said: "We have finished Evrio. They cannot accommodate us any longer, but we wish to study Torah. We want to learn Talmud and we have come to ask you to teach us."

"Do you really want to learn?"

"Absolutely."

"How many of you are there?"

"Eighteen to twenty."

"Fine, I will teach you, but as you can tell, there is not enough room in my home for such a large group. You must find a place."

"We have a place: The Evrio School."

Rabbi Freiderman pounded his fist on the table: "I need a holy place! The Evrio school is not a holy place."

The Evrio School.
Jews of Boston

Louis Hurwitz, translated by Farber in *An American Orthodox Dreamer*, pp. 22-23

Finally Friederman was unhappy with American synagogue structure, in which rabbis had to accommodate the requirements of lay-led boards, in contrast to the monarchical control that heads of yeshivas or Chassidic rebbes enjoyed. As he complained in *Shoshanat Yaakov* in 1927:

> The rabbis must satisfy the wants of the audience, for that is the foundation for their survival, since their prodders – the officers of the synagogues – order them: "expand the membership of the congregation, increase the audience, attract the affluent to hear your sermons," so as to increase the income.
>
> Friederman, *Shoshanat Yaakov*, in Sollers, *Multilingual America*

In sum, for people who were less than 100% old country Orthodox, Friederman was not their ideal rabbi. As a result, Friederman's 'fit' with the members of Ein Jacob would prove tenuous. By 1910, the *Boston City Directory* shows that its rabbi was Isaac Baritz, who remained there until 1923, at which point Ein Jacob merged into Beth Jacob.

World-view: Margolies Versus Friederman

From the above descriptions, one might conclude that Margolies was 'progressive' while Friederman was 'traditionalist,' but the actual distinctions between the two are not so clear-cut. Both Margolies and Friederman came from traditional Eastern European backgrounds and were involved in the founding of the haredi organization Agudas Harabbonim, founded in 1902. As Sarna notes, this placed both rabbis at the right wing of American Judaism:

> In a bid to gain greater attention, sixty European-trained rabbis who most vocally represented Judaism's right wing convened on July 29, 1902… to formalize the creation of what they called, carefully avoiding the profane English tongue, the Agudath ha-Rabbanim (United Orthodox Rabbis). Talking in Yiddish and writing in Hebrew, the rabbis expressed … concern over the future of Judaism in America … They worried about low standards of Jewish education, inadequate observance of the Jewish Sabbath, improper supervision of kosher food, lax observance of Jewish marriage and divorce laws, and the like. Their solution … was to reinvigorate the authority of European-trained rabbis (like themselves), who would work to solve these problems collectively … The only Orthodox rabbis they

were prepared to recognize were those trained in traditional Talmudic academies, known as yeshivot, and personally ordained by an East European rabbinic luminary. They also promoted a strategy of resistance to Americanization, opposing English-language sermons and advocating Yiddish as the preferred language of instruction in Jewish schools.

Sarna, *American Judaism* pp. 191-192

Margolies was president of Agudath Harabbonim for some years, and, per his *New York Times* obituary, was honorary president at the time of his death. So he was not some left-wing rabbinical 'radical' like Mordechai Kaplan.[34]

Despite this, Margolies and Friederman developed different worldviews, particularly with respect to how Judaism should respond to new American and Zionist social forces.

This is something highlighted in Seth Farber's *An American Orthodox Dreamer: Rabbi Joseph B. Soloveitchik and Boston's Maimonides School.* Farber pictures Margolies as a progenitor of modern Orthodoxy, while Friederman was old-world haredi:

> Conflicting perspectives regarding their new environment existed between the rabbinic leadership of the new Orthodox immigrants and the more traditionalist rabbis. Rabbi Moshe Zevulun Margolies (Ramaz), who lived in Boston until 1902,[35] saw opportunities for religious growth within his new

---

[34] Indeed, Margolies was hired by Kehillat Jeshurun to provide a senior conservative rabbinical presence to offset the 'left-wing' resident 'minister' -- Mordechai Kaplan. Kaplan was jealous of Margolies, saying the following in his dairy: "October 29, 1914: Margolies rose to speak. I can surmise by this time what he has to say on occasions such as these. I have heard him repeat these speeches so often that I know them backwards. There is absolutely no connection in what he says, his language – i.e. his Yiddish is interspersed with English words, and he tries to make up for the lack of sense by being vociferous, getting red in the face and sometimes even stamping with his foot. These tricks ill accord with his general makeup and with his well combed white long beard. His followers listen to him with what might be called a sacramental attitude. They expect nothing new; what he says is a sort of liturgy with them and they are perfectly satisfied with whatever he says." (*Communings of the Spirit: The Journals of Mordecai M. Kaplan*, 1913-1934)

[35] The *New York Times* obituary says 1906, which is supported by *Boston City Directory* listings.

> society and attempted to Americanize European Orthodoxy. Ramaz preached to immigrants who had abandoned Orthodoxy, attempting to win them back to a more modern form of traditional Judaism. Rabbi Zalman Ya'akov[36] Freiderman [sic], by contrast, rejected Americanism and sought to reduce its attractive power over American Jews, even though he himself was forced to adopt certain elements of the new cultural environment, such as the English language. While the Freiderman-type rabbis, like their counterparts in Europe, tended to idealize their European past, Ramaz and his colleagues focused their sermons and their writings on the promising future for Orthodoxy in America, Ramaz shared a common mode of old-world dress with Rabbi Freiderman, but each related differently to his new surroundings.
>
> Farber, *An American Orthodox Dreamer*, p. 4

Thus, while Friederman became the senior Orthodox rabbi in the North and West Ends[37] after Margolies left for greener pastures in New York, he would be out of touch with an increasing fraction of his congregants and his synagogue lay leadership.

The effect would be seen in the time period between 1905 and 1925 with respect to the types of rabbis who were hired by The Boston Synagogue's predecessor shuls. Few of them engaged Friederman clones.

Rabbinical Infighting

In addition to conflicts over ideology, the rabbis in this era fought for control of the newly established Boston Orthodox community (a good example is Friederman's use of the title "Rabbi of the United Congregations"). Kashrut became a key venue for infighting, since it was a lucrative income source. Here is a discussion by Lisitzky, who clearly was a Margolies loyalist. One suspects that one of the rabbis

---

[36] Zalman is Yiddish for 'Solomon'; Yaakov is Hebrew/Yiddish for Jacob. So Zalman Yaakov Friederman is the same name as Solomon Jacob Friederman.

[37] Aside from Pinchas Horowitz in the Chassidic niche.

he is attacking is Friederman:

> [Ramaz] was not the only rabbi in Boston. There were others – the same self-important braggarts as in other Jewish communities in America. For American rabbis had deserted the moral basis of their profession to foster Jewish learning. Instead, they converted Judaism into a kashruth cult. This cult they made the cardinal tenet of American Jewish life. Supervision of this cult yielded a material reward – the kashruth certification fee – to which everyone aspired. The result was ugly competition; what one rabbi declared kosher, another declared not kosher, all for the sake of profit, under the guise of piety.
>
> Ramaz was an Orthodox rabbi who would not and could not shirk the responsibility of kashruth, a fundamental of traditional Judaism. Nor could he avoid conflict with other rabbis. But his intentions were of the highest, and he was careful to keep his nature and that of the community unsullied.
>
> Lisitzky, *op. cit.*

Lisitzky's portrait of Margolies as totally altruistic and unconcerned about power and money arguably is overstated. As previously noted, Margolies was the listed rabbi for six shuls, he accepted honorifics like Chief Rabbi and the Ramaz acronym (something reserved for great rabbis), and he liked to dress elegantly with a top-hat. In addition, paying for a wedding with 2,000 guests was expensive. In the end, the major difference between Margolies and his rivals may be that he was more successful in asserting his authority.

In future years, the fight over control would continue, with some of the Boston rabbis (Moses Margolies and his successor Wolf Margolis) changing the venue to New York (see Chapter 5). In the 1930s through 1941, kashrut in Boston would become a major source of conflict between Rav Joseph Soloveitchick and the entrenched V'aad Harabonim (source: Farber, *op. cit.*). In 1965, litigation brought by the United Kosher Butchers Association against the V'aad would be decided in favor of the V'aad on First Amendment grounds.[38]

Shul Lay Leadership

Sharing power with the rabbis were shul officers and board members. For immigrants with minimal experience with political power, becoming part of lay leadership was a powerful affirmation of having 'made it' in American Jewish society. Only people with high social standing became officers or board members. Shul officers had the privilege of sitting next to the ark, in clear sight of the congregation.

Here is how Charles Angoff, a resident of the West End born in 1903, described the importance of his great-uncle Mottel, a vice-president of North Russell Street Shul:

> [The] vice president [of North Russell Street] was a great-uncle of mine, the son of my grandmother. He was the nabob in our family. He ran a soda and candy store on Leverett Street and did handsomely[39]....
>
> On Saturdays, before I was *bar mitzvah,* I was, so to speak, my Alte Bobbe's *Shabbes goy* (Sabbath gentile). I would go with her to the North Russell Street Shul, carrying her prayerbook... That relieved her from any possible charge of carrying something on the Sabbath, and hence performing manual labor. Now and then I would look upstairs at her, where she sat with the other women, and I saw on her face a joy and a delight such as I have never seen since. She looked at her son, the vice-president of the synagogue, and she was happy, as only a woman of ninety can be happy her son was a *gabbai* (important functionary) in a synagogue. What greater joy was there for a mother?
>
> Charles Angoff, "Memories of Boston" in *The Menorah Journal,* 1962 valedictory issue

---

[38]*United Kosher Butchers Asso*ciation v. *Associated Synagogues of Greater Boston,* 349 Mass. 595, 598 (1965). See further discussion of the case in Chapter 13.

[39] In the modern world, it is unlikely that a candy store owner would be considered a "nabob."

On one occasion, when Mottel faced a scandal that jeopardized his standing, an enemy argued that he no longer deserved the honor of sitting next to the Ark (*inter alia* showing how important an honor this was) [40]:

> Mottel was ... an officer in one of the most respected synagogues [North Russell Street] in Boston, the owner of a prosperous candy-and-soda store, and in general a man of eminence in the community.... [After his daughter became the mistress of a married man], Mottel came up for re-election as vice-president of his synagogue, and expected to be re-elected as a matter of course, as he had been three times before. But he sensed strong opposition. At first this opposition refused to come out into the open, but then a long-time enemy blurted out at a meeting of the Board of Trustees of the synagogue: "I don't think it is proper that we have sitting beside the Holy Ark every Saturday and every holiday a man whose daughter openly indulges in sin." Mottel was reelected by a large majority.
>
> Angoff, *Something About My Father*, pp. 130, 136

In this spirit, here are the leaders of CBJ in 1899, as listed in the *American Jewish Yearbook*:

- **Elias Kamberg** was President of the CBJ in 1899. Nothing else is known about him, aside from the fact that he was the start of a long series of Kambergs associated with the shul. In the 1940 incorporation papers for Beth Amedrish Agudal Beth Jacob (merging North Russell with Beth Jacob), his son Morris Kamberg is listed second in the list of officers.
- **A. Shine** was Vice President; nothing else is known about him.
- **J. Rathchkovsky** is listed as 'Assistant' to the rabbi. In the *Boston City Directory* for 1900 and 1910, he is listed as J.

---

[40] At Charles River Park Synagogue, officers like Allan Green continued to sit up on the platform by the ark into the 1980s. This is why there are four wooden chairs with armrests – for use upfront. In the shul's modern era, no one sits on the front platform any longer.

Rachkoosky, Sexton. Typically, the assistant/sexton/shammash was a poorly paid position.

Kambergs Associated With The Boston Synagogue Shuls

From: 1941 Mortgage Redemption Plaque	From: The Boston Synagogue Memorial Board	
Officers of the [Ladies] Auxiliary Mrs. D. Kamberg, Treasurer **Mortgage Committee** Mr. M. Kamberg, Vice Chairman Mr. D. Kamberg **Board of Directors** Mr. M. Kamberg **Mortgage Redemption Donors** Mr. & Mrs. M. Kamberg	Rose Kamberg Dora Kamberg Morris Kamberg Dr. Irving Kamberg	March 3, 1924 April 8, 1948 November 13, 1950 September 17, 1988

At the turn of the century, powerful rabbis such as Margolies and Friederman would largely control the policies of their synagogues. However, over time, socially and economically privileged lay leadership would assert control at the expense of the rabbis.

Shul Affiliations

Although all of the predecessor synagogues were Orthodox, there is no indication that they had formal movement affiliations. This presumably was because:

- The major Orthodox organization, Agudat Harabbonim (Union of Orthodox Rabbis), was an assembly of rabbis rather than synagogues.
- More generally, the predecessor shuls had no trouble finding rabbis (a typical reason for movement affiliation). There was therefore no reason to pay dues to an outside group.

Chapter 4

The Early Shuls and their Communities

Wieder, in *The Early Jewish Community of Boston's North End,* commented on the broader role of the immigrant synagogue beyond being a place of worship:

> To the early settlers the synagogue meant much more than just a place of worship. Before and after the services, worshipers discussed all matters that were vital to them in the new world. The stranger, whom a long business trip brought to Boston, stopped first at the synagogue to inquire about lodging in a Jewish home. Here they exchanged experiences gained in peddling, gave advice and encouragement to the newcomers, received news about home and about *landsleit* who dwelt in other cities.
>
> The synagogue was for a long time the only place where the immigrants' cultural needs could be satisfied. Many lectures and adult classes were held on its premises. For the learned, this was the place where their knowledge would be recognized and appreciated. Since Hebrew books were scarce, the synagogue's *sforim* (Hebrew volumes) purchased with great sacrifice, rendered an invaluable service to former students of European *yeshivas* and *chadorim*. An unskilled laborer or a struggling peddler would earn the esteem of his fellow Jews, if he was able to answer a knotty question of law or explain a difficult passage of the Talmud.
>
> Within the synagogues, small auxiliary groups were formed to satisfy specific religious or educational needs. Members of the Chevra Tehillim assembled at given times to recite certain portions of the Hebrew Book of Psalms. When one of their rank died, other members were on hand to read Psalms in unison at the home of the deceased or at the funeral chapel.

Wieder, *The Early Jewish Community of Boston's North End,* pp. 50-51

On the other hand, Lisitzky noted that while the immigrant shuls were transplanted versions of the world they were accustomed to in Eastern Europe, Jews in America were interacting increasingly with a secular world. This resulted in less overall observance – even if the shuls they attended continued to be Orthodox:

> At the time I immigrated to America the Jewish community there was in a state of upheaval caused by the clash of diverse elements, each striving for supremacy. The equilibrium which was bound to be established was postponed by the constant arrival of new groups. The most important group were the Orthodox, stable Jews who came to America and brought their tradition with them. They founded synagogues, schools, associations and fraternal organizations for the fostering of religion. These they maintained by donations, after the Old Country manner. The Orthodox had a great deal of vital energy. But their influence was limited both by their numbers and by their economic instability. Strict observance of the Sabbath and the Jewish festivals lessened their income! This, in turn, lessened their influence.
>
> The Orthodox were submerged in the mass which constituted the majority of the American Jewish community. This mass, which appeared united from the outside, was actually divided into several distinct groups. A significant part consisted of Jews who had sentiment for religious tradition and supported its institutions, even becoming their officers. But they were forced by economic circumstances to give up some observances of traditional Judaism. Another group of American Jews denounced all religious discipline gladly as a kind of emancipation from slavery. And then there were the spite-workers – those who belonged to the Jewish socialist movement, whose cardinal tenets then were: atheism, denial of all religious and national values, and disparagement of the Jewish cultural legacy. In this general mass, alienated from religious observances, the Orthodox element constituted a tiny, lonely and isolated minority.

To all outward appearances, my first days in Boston, when I was able to live as I had in Slutzk, were only a matter of change of locale: the synagogue where I prayed daily was always packed; the congregants gathered after the morning prayers to study the Mishna and between the afternoon and evening prayers to study the Well of Jacob; one group stayed on after the evening prayers to study the daily page of Talmud -- everything in Boston was just as it had been in Slutzk. But in Slutzk, the learned and the pious had been in the vast majority; here in Boston, they were a small minority; so I felt like an alien in Boston.

I particularly sensed the spiritual decline of American Jews on the Sabbath.... In Boston very few Jews observed the Sabbath.... Leaving the synagogue after the Sabbath Eve service, the observants were confronted by a tumultuous Jewish quarter: shopkeepers stood in their shop doorways, peddlers on their wagons shouted their wares.

Ephraim Lisitzky, op. cit., pp. 66-67

In *The Promised Land*, Mary Antin illustrated how rapid the process of Americanization, and with it, secularization, could be. Within a week of her arrival in Boston:

We exchanged our hateful homemade European costumes, which pointed us out as "greenhorns" to the children on the street, for real American machine made garments....

With our despised immigrant clothing we shed also our impossible Hebrew names. A committee of our friends, several years ahead of us in American experience, put their heads together and concocted American names for us all. Those of our real names that had no pleasing American equivalents they ruthlessly discarded,

The Antin Sisters in European Clothing

content if they retained the initials. My mother, possessing a name that was not easily translatable, was punished with the undignified nickname of Annie. Fetchke, Joseph, and Deborah issued as Frieda, Joseph, and Dora, respectively. As for poor me, I was simply cheated. The name they gave me was hardly new. My Hebrew name being Maryashe in full, Mashke for short, Russianized into Marya (Mar-ya), my friends said that it would hold good in English as Mary; which was very disappointing, as I longed to possess a strange-sounding American name like the others.

Antin, *op. cit.*, pp. 187-188

A further illustration of assimilation is the fact that in the balance of Antin's book, she does not discuss religion aside from mentioning that her father sent her to school on the High Holidays. She ended up marrying the son and grandson of German-born Lutheran ministers.

As a result of progressive Americanization/secularization by the Jews of the West End, this would put increasing pressure on support for the shuls in the neighborhood.

Role of the Synagogue in Social and Political Issues 1888-1905

As a center for the Jewish community in the West End, CBJ and the other predecessor shuls played a role in helping its congregants deal with social issues. Here is an article from the *Boston Evening Transcript* dated Nov 13, 1903, showing that the North Russell Street Shul was used as an auditorium for discussing community social welfare issues. The topic proved controversial, resulting in mud being thrown through the windows. (Note the references to James J. Storrow of Storrow Drive fame.)

> **NEW EDUCATIONAL CENTRE**
>
> **Jewish Meeting Held in North Russell-Street Synagogue**
>
> Mud was thrown through the open windows of the North Russell Street Synagogue last evening, disturbing a meeting of Jewish residents of the West End held in the interests of the new educational centre to be opened Nov. 16 in the Mayhew School at Poplar and Chambers streets. Mrs. Lina Hecht, who was speaking, seized upon the incident as a practical example of conditions in the West End and of the great need of just such education as the educational centre is expected to provide. The mud-throwing created considerable excitement in the synagogue, which was crowded with men, women and children. The disturbers were driven away, and a police officer kept them from interfering during the remainder of the evening.
>
> Addresses were made by Godfrey Morse, president of the Federation of Jewish Charities; David Ellis and James J. Storrow of the school committee; Leo Friedman, Ferdinand Strauss, chairman of the Baron de Hirsch Society; Louis Sonnabend and James Oppenheim, secretary of the Boston Educational Union. Mr. Morse advised his hearers to attend this school in order that they may learn to be better able to support themselves and to progress in the affairs of life. Mr. Ellis emphasized the idea that people are not accepting charity in going to this school. It is a place where they have as much right to go as to a synagogue or to a club. Mrs. Hecht said that the broader the centre can be made the better it will be for the people. They must not let it become a fad, but make it a success by earnestness and enthusiasm. Mr. Storrow briefly outlined the history of the educational centre movement and its practical operation.

As Jewish emigrants felt more secure in America, they also began to assert their political rights. The following 1905 article from a paper called *Our Paper* (Massachusetts Reformatory, Concord Junction) refers to a mass rally at North Russell Street Shul protesting Theodore Roosevelt and his Secretary of State's failure to deal with Russian atrocities (presumably the Odessa pogrom during the Revolution of 1905).

> **News of the Week.**
>
> **FRIDAY**
>
> Senator Morgan of Alabama will lead the debate, from the Democratic side of the Senate, on the rate question. He will oppose the President's policy from beginning to end.
>
> President Roosevelt and Secretary Root were criticised for their neglect to protest against the present Russian atrocities, at the Jewish mass meeting held at the North Russell street synagogue, Boston.

Life Cycle Events 1888-1905

With respect to weddings, here is a charming narrative by a woman who was married at North Russell Street Shul on a Friday afternoon. She and her new husband went home instead of on a honeymoon (to save money), and then immediately got pregnant. One can hear the Yiddishisms in her grammar:

I got married just like all girls. I got married a Friday afternoon in North Russell Street Shul. In the West End is a North Russell Street Shul, and I got married there. And I was dressed. I got pictures, you saw, like all brides, everything. In a Friday afternoon, June. At the supper I had from New York an uncle, and my mother was yet living then.

Minnie Kasser and Joseph Needle, Engagement photo, 1911

I took an apartment before I was married. My sister says, "So what do you want to go to an apartment? Go on a honeymoon."

I says, "Where am I gonna come home then when I go for a honeymoon and spend the money I have?" I says, "No, I've got to have a home to come back. That will be my honeymoon." So I had an apartment and I furnished it and everything, and that night I went home to my home in the West End.

[My daughter] was born nine months to the day.

Minnie Kasser Needle/Jewish Grandmother. Excerpt from *First Generation: In the Words of Twentieth-Century American Immigrants* by June Namias

In the same vein, here are two pieces from the *Boston Globe*. One is about a wedding conducted by Rabbi Friederman in 1903 which already shows signs of creeping Americanisms such as maid of honor, best man, ushers – even in a Friederman wedding! The other is an amusing account of a 1906 wedding with some last-minute documentation problems, held at the Anshei Libavitz synagogue on Joy Street/Smith Court:

Mittel-Rubin

The wedding of Miss Linna Rubin, daughter of Mr. and Mrs. J. Rubin, and Morris Mittel took place last evening at Minot Hall. The ceremony was performed by Rabbi Friederman in the presence of a gathering of relatives and friends that filled the spacious hall. The bride's only attendant was Miss Mary Rubin, her sister, who was the maid of honor. Solomon Rubin, brother of the bride, was the best man. The ushers were Messrs. Henry and Joseph Mittel, A. Albaum and Isaac Rubin. The ceremony was followed by a reception and wedding supper.

March 30, 1903 *Boston Globe*

*   *   *

Wedding Delayed (Yaffe-Glaser)
Groom Mislaid License, He Forgot Where.
Ceremony Set for 5 is Performed at 9 for West End Couple

Miss Lena Yaffe, daughter of Mr. and Mrs. Max Yaffe of the West End, was married last evening to Israel Glaser of the same district, by Rev. M. Kopelowitz of the Joy Street synagogue, after a delay of several hours, because of the groom mislaying the marriage license

The ceremony was to have taken place at 5 o'clock, but owing to the tardiness of the guests it was about 7 when the officiating clergyman asked to be shown the marriage license. It then transpired that the groom had left the document behind and he could not remember just where he had put the precious paper.

Several messengers were sent to hunt for the paper and when at last one appeared with it the clock had registered the hour of 9.

The groom was attended beneath the canopy by Mr. and Mrs. Isaac Glaser, Mr. Glaser being a brother of the groom, while the bride was escorted by Mr. and Mrs. Max Rubin, uncle and aunt of the bride. Miss Mary Rubin was maid of honor and Israel Yaffe, brother of the bride, was best man. The bridesmaids were Misses Eva Rubin, Etta Rubin, Lena

Cohen, Rose Rubin, Bessie Mosner, Ida Levitsky, Sarah Kaplan and Tillie Sacks. The ushers were Israel G. Rubin, P. Bolansky, H. Paul, Samuel Moletzky and Israel Gellerman.

The wedding feast was served in one of the lower halls, after which there was dancing until an early hour this morning.

June 20, 1906, *Boston Globe*

Cemeteries

Moving to the other end of the life cycle, it is often said that for immigrant Jews, having a cemetery was more important than having a shul. Perhaps this was because it was easy to get ten men together for a minyan, but much harder to buy a plot of land for a cemetery.

The first Jewish cemetery in Boston was established in 1733 in the West End – although obviously not by the late 19th century Eastern European immigrants. From Isaac Fein's *Boston—Where it All Began*, "The records show that on February 22, 1733 two Jews, Michael Asher and Isaac Solomon, partners in a tobacco enterprise, bought a lot (now 15 and 17 Chambers Street), setting aside a section of this lot, 100 square feet, as a burying ground for the use by the 'Jewish Nation'.... there is no definite proof that it was ever used, but it remained intact until 1790."

In more modern times, Beth Jacob, North Russell and Anshei Lebavitz each had cemeteries located in Woburn and Everett[41].

---

[41] *Bridging Past, Present and Future: History & Guide: Massachusetts Jewish Cemeteries.*

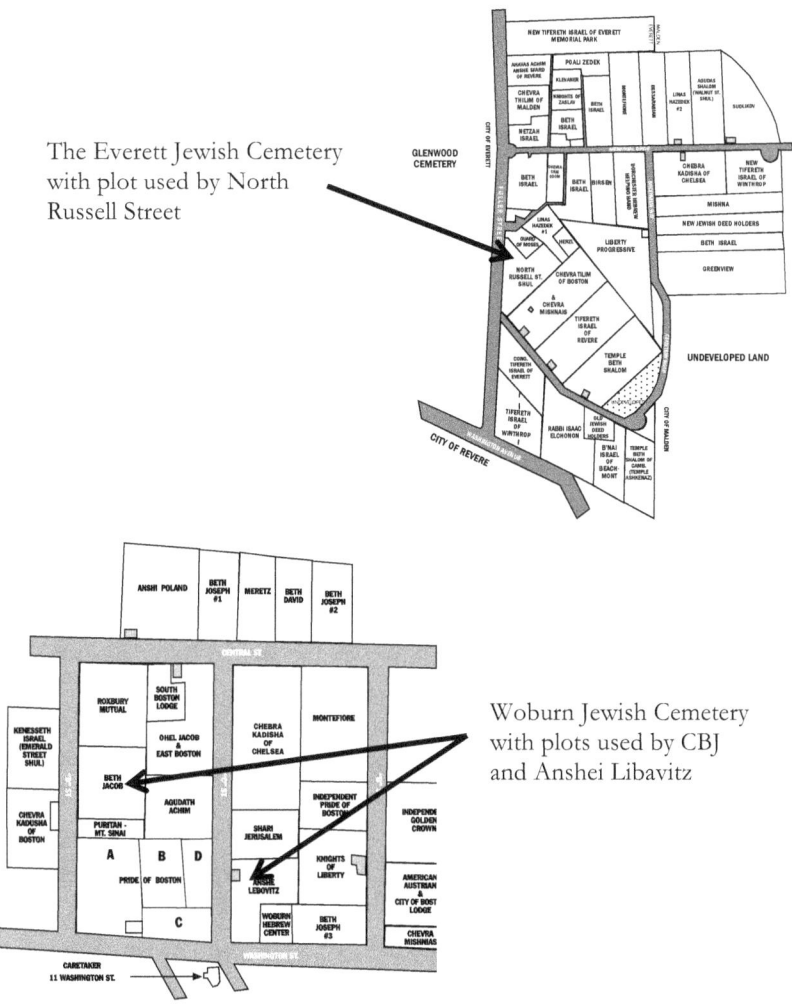

The Everett Jewish Cemetery with plot used by North Russell Street

Woburn Jewish Cemetery with plots used by CBJ and Anshei Libavitz

Christian Impressions, 1913

The West End synagogues of this era were immigrant shuls with practices that would have seemed strange to Christians. Here is one set of impressions based on a visit to an unidentified immigrant congregation, circa 1913 (while this chronologically belongs in the next chapter, it is reminiscent of the immigrant era, so is included here):

Synagogue Service in Boston Ghetto:
Impressions of a Gentile Visitor There

The spectator is wondering why, for all his unquenchable interest in the people of the Ghetto, he has waited these many years visiting an Orthodox Jewish Synagogue at the time of service. It was in Boston that, strolling through Salem Street on a Saturday morning, he noted at the foot of a blind alley the ugly, dingy-yellow, spireless old church which serves the faithful of this Ghetto.

The door stood wide. Not without misgivings on the score of a welcome, he ventured in. As he climbed the stairs to the audience room an indescribably stirring sound smote his ears - a singular hubbub, a surge of male voices, the wild, rhythmless babel of Hebrew prayers. The spectator paused in the doorway, surveying the congregation rocking on their feet as, with no attempt at unison, they fervently intoned the ancient ritual.

Amazingly picturesque was the scene before him. The congregation of black-bearded men, robed in the broad stripes and mellowed ivory hues of venerable prayer-shawls, might have been an Oriental group out of a painting by Tissot but for the over-large derby or, in the case of the dignitaries, silk hats worn low over their ears. There, where the pulpit of a Christian church would be, rose the impressive curtained niche of the Ark of the Law, with the carved lions of Judah supporting the tables of the law, mounted over all.

Just then the excited "Bub-ba-ubba-bubba-bub!" of the congregational responses died down and a single voice, a glorious baritone, took up a recitative. The spectator's eyes came to rapid focus upon the singer. Upon a low platform in the center of the floor of the synagogue, leaning upon a reading desk draped with rich Eastern fabrics, he stood - a big man in a high black cap of fur, his prayer shawl, gold-banded at the neck, enveloping him like a robe. The cantor, beyond a doubt.

Behind him a little group of white-haired men in silk hats were busy over something which one of them held in his arm. The Spectator caught the flash of blue and the gleam of silver. Then the group separated and he saw that they held the Scroll of the Law. The reading was over. They were adjusting the "shirt" or robe of blue plush, securing the broad silver clasp and preparing to replace it in the Sacred Ark.

And now an old man, apparently a mere member of the congregation rose with the sacred scroll in his arms, the tall silver ornaments on the rollers reaching above his head, and descending the aisle, began a slow progress to the Ark. At every step worshipers crowded round him to touch and kiss the mantle of the Scroll. The curtains of the Ark were drawn back, the Scroll reverently set up among its fellows, the synagogue thrilling meanwhile to the wonderful music of an ecstatic hymn of praise.

For dramatic intensity the intoning of the poems of the Hebrew liturgy, the congregation alternating with the cantor, surpassed any religious music it has been the spectator's fortune to hear. At times quaintly plaintive, at times soul-stirring, at times fiercely joyful, at times the jubilance quenched in sobbing agony - it needed no Yiddish to understand that.

And then the outbreak of the passionate chorus of the people, rushing, hurried, wild - there was in it the whole thrill of the National experience, the joy of the chosen people, the triumph of Israel, the despair of the carrying away into Babylon, the long patience of the persecution.

All this time the spectator had been standing unnoted in a pew by the door. Instinctively, on entering he had removed his hat. Now a late comer stopped beside him and said courteously: "Excuse me, sir, but it is the Orthodox custom to wear the hat in the synagogue. Would you like a better seat?"

So the spectator, feeling as if he were breaking something, replaced his hat and followed down the aisle. Coming to anchor in a bare pew in the transept from which his eye was free to range the whole room, he shortly discovered the women segregated in a gallery running round three sides of the building - a black-habited, negligible element in the scene.

A Yiddish-English prayer book he had purchased before coming in bore eloquent testimony as to the place of a woman in the synagogue. For do not all the men say: "O Lord God, Eternal King of the Universe, I thank thee that thou hast made me according to thy will."

Vainly the spectator strove to reconcile with the primitive grandeur of the service, the apparent informalities all about him. There were the Jewish boys in their little blue-striped talliths staring coldly about or even parading guilelessly from pew to pew unrebuked of their elders. And this although a bulletin in the vestibule commands that no one shall walk about or talk "during the speaking."

The elder Hebrew, too, arriving late, betrayed none of the self-consciousness and guilty slinking of a Gentile who gets to church after the first prayer. They marched unconcernedly to their places, leisurely extracted their prayer shawls from their velvet bags, adjusted them robe-fashion, looped the folds over their arms, found the place in the service book, and began the curious rapid, rocking bob with which the Orthodox Hebrew accompanies his intoning.

All this without any special manner of Sabbath sanctity, but with a business-like directness. From time to time in similar nonchalant fashion such as were impelled flung off the tallith, carefully folding the great striped fringed square, stowed it in its bag, and informally departed.

The Outlook, January 5, 1913, *Boston Globe*

Chapter 5

Developments in the West End 1905-1925

During this period, there were three major developments:

- The West End Jewish population and shul count peaked and then began a rapid decline, resulting in shuls merging, moving or dying. The North End continued its decline from the previous period.
- There was a new wave of rabbis who replaced Margolies and Friederman in the predecessor shuls, some of whom then moved to New York. The net result was consolidation of power by lay boards.
- This period also saw the emergence of Beth Hamedrash Hagadol (the North Russell Street Shul) as one of the major shuls in the West End.

The balance of Chapter 5 deals with overall West End trends. Chapter 6 will focus on the history of the North Russell Street Shul. Chapter 7 will discuss shul building and architectural topics.

Demographics

1915 was the high water mark for Jewish population in the West End, as it was for the overall West End population. After this, the population declined rapidly as Jews began moving to Dorchester and Mattapan.

The population decline (including non-Jews) is seen in Massachusetts state population censuses for Ward 5, which includes Beacon Hill, Back Bay, the North End and the West End.

The results show that from 1915 to 1925, Ward 5's population fell by half. Given that Back Bay and Beacon Hill were relatively stable, the population loss in the West End presumably was greater.

Boston Ward 5 Census

Year	Ward 5	Index (1915 = 100)
1895	12,986	17
1905	12,653	16
1915	**77,573**	**100**
1920	**63,267**	**82**
1925	**37,036**	**48**

Massachusetts State Census

The West End remained heavily Jewish despite the population loss. Gans, in *The Urban Villagers,* says that based on library card registrations, Jews represented 75% of the West End population by 1926. If so, then the Jewish population in 1925 was approximately 19,000 (down 52% from 40,000 in 1910).

Synagogue Count & Mergers 1905-1925

As a result of this population decline, the glory days of the North and West End shuls were ending (with the exception of North Russell Street, at least for some years). In the North End, the five shuls existing in 1905 dropped to four by 1925. In the West End, after the number of shuls grew from 20 to 24 at the end of World War I, the count dropped to fifteen by 1925.

Examining the West End shul decline in detail, three shuls simply shut down. In one case (Agudath Achim), the shul decided to move from the West End:

> Agudath Achim, a group that described itself as strictly Orthodox, reported that it had moved its synagogue out of the West End in the 1910s because "most of its members had already gone to live" in Roxbury.
>
> Gamm, *Urban Exodus*, p.116

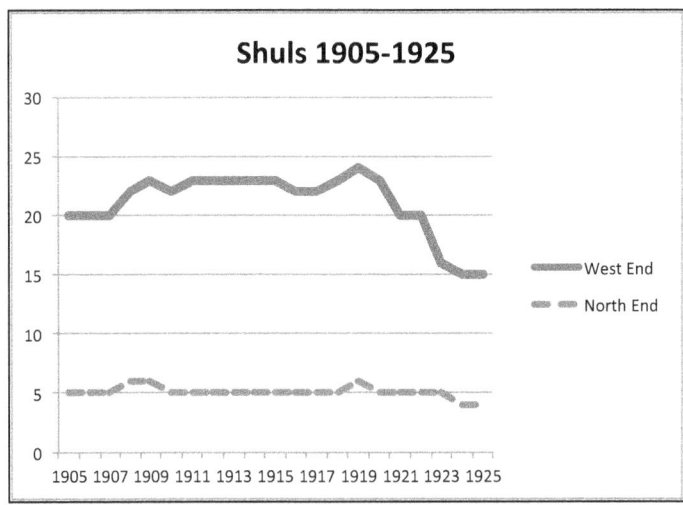

Clingan Spreadsheet and Boston Synagogue analysis

The greatest driver of West End shul loss, however, was merger, with nine shuls combining into three surviving entities. Of these one involved CBJ, which absorbed two other entities:

- In 1916, Anshei Slavuta and Anshei Zoslave merged into the combined 'Anshe Slavuta and Anshei Zoslave.' This made sense, since Slavuta and Zoslave were neighboring towns in the Ukraine.
- In 1919, Anshei Sfard, Russian Sfard and Linas Hazedek merged into Tifereth Israel.
- In 1923, CBJ merged with Ein Jacob and Mishkan Shlomo to form United Congregation Beth Jacob, located at CBJ's Wall Street building.

And one 'rising' shul that did not merge in this period, North Russell Street, doubled down by building a large new synagogue center in 1923.

The West End shuls' approaches (Agudas Achim excepted), contrast with those of the South End shuls. Although the South End shul count shows similar declines after World War I, the driving factor for large synagogues like Ohabei Shalom, Temple Israel and Mishkan Tefila in the South End was the imperative to grow by moving to up-and-coming neighborhoods.

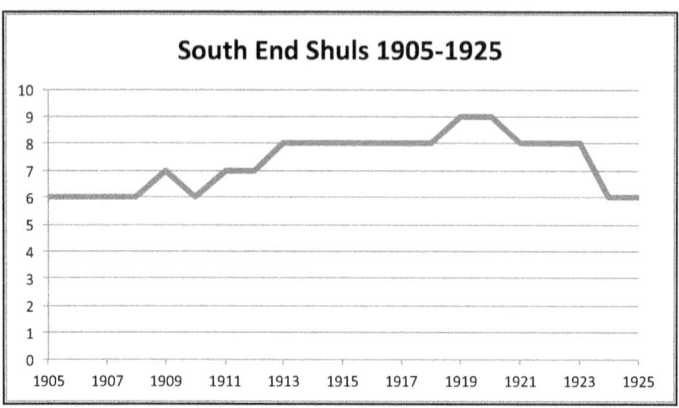

Source: Clingan Spreadsheet and Boston Synagogue analysis

The West End shuls' decision to stay put was in conflict with the conclusions of a 1921 demographic study commissioned by the Federated Jewish Charities of Boston and titled *The Trend of Jewish Population in Boston*. This report recommended that a planned new Jewish communal building be placed in Dorchester or Mattapan, where the Jewish population was growing:

> Of the many tragic affairs daily obtruding themselves upon those interested in communal affairs, one of the saddest is the anarchic location of communal buildings. In every large city of the country stand buildings, the use of which is seriously limited by reason of their original inept location. The relatively rapid shifts in population, in addition to causing communal buildings to lose some of their effectiveness, serve also to uncover quickly the mistakes made in original locations...
>
> The North End is today practically no longer a Jewish community. The West End, South End and East Boston are gradually losing their Jewish population.
>
> Ben Rosen, *The Trend of Jewish Population in Boston*, Federated Jewish Charities of Boston, 1921

Rabbis in the North and West End 1905-1925

Increasing Rabbi-to-Shul Ratio

Based on Boston city directory data, there was a substantial increase in the number of rabbis in the North End/West End relative to the number of shuls. This reflects the fact that the West End's increasing prosperity allowed more shuls to support a full-time rabbi – or even two.

To illustrate: In 1900, there are listings for five rabbis who in total served eleven congregations, with most rabbis working on a part-time basis for any individual shul. Margolies of Beth Jacob was listed as rabbi for six different shuls, while Friederman at Ein Jacob was listed twice.

By 1910, there are listings for eleven rabbis who in total served ten shuls; growing in 1920 to thirteen rabbis serving eleven shuls.

As a result, the number of rabbis per shul grew from 0.45 in 1900 to 1.18 by 1920.

West End: Rabbi-to-Shul Ratio
Based on Boston City Directories

	1900	1910	1920
Shuls	11	10	11
Rabbis	5	11	13
Rabbis Per Shul	0.45	1.10	1.18

Source: *Boston City Directories* and Boston Synagogue analysis

Rabbis in The Predecessor Shuls

During this period, there were substantial changes in rabbinical support at the predecessor shuls. A summary listing of the rabbis in each shul is shown here, followed by an in-depth review of Rabbis Margolis, Yudlevitz and Lifland. North Russell Street rabbis Rubinovitz, Hillman and Sharfman will be discussed in greater detail in Chapter 6.

Beth Jacob (CBJ)

In 1907, Beth Jacob replaced the by-now departed Rabbi Margolies with Rabbi Harry Epstein, who lived at 59 Spring Street. In 1914, Epstein was replaced by Rabbi Simon Price.

By 1919, Beth Jacob had two rabbis, Aaron Mancovitz and Morris Levin.

The reason for the rapid rabbinical turnover is unclear, but it indicates substantial board versus rabbinical leadership.

North Russell

The North Russell Street Shul hired D.M. Rubinovitz during the 1904-1906 period as its first listed rabbi.

In 1908-1909, Rubinovitz was replaced by Rabbi Marcus Hillman.

In 1910, North Russell Street added a second rabbi, Hyman Sharfman. By 1913, Sharfman became the sole rabbi, where he remained through 1923.

There will be a more detailed discussion of Rubinovitz, Hillman and Sharfman in Chapter 6; as with Beth Jacob, the velocity of change indicates a shul in which the lay board was in control.

Ein Jacob

Ein Jacob, which in 1903 had employed Rabbi Friederman part-time, replaced him in 1910 with Isaac Baritz. Baritz remained through 1923, when Ein Jacob merged with Beth Jacob. He followed the Margolies multiple-congregation model by serving 2-5 shuls simultaneously (see Appendix 6).

There is limited information on Rabbi Baritz, although he was sufficiently prominent to be asked to address the Jews of Plymouth, helping them raise an additional $1500:

> The orthodox Jews of Plymouth, numbering 40 families, are to have a new synagogue. At a meeting, which was addressed by Rabbi Baritz of Boston, they subscribed an additional $1500.
>
> *Our Paper* by Massachusetts Reformatory (Concord, MA), Volume 23; May 18, 1907

Anshei Libavitz

Anshei Libavitz, which had listed Margolies as rabbi through 1903, employed Rabbi M. Kopelowitz in 1906.[42] There then is no listing until 1918, when it hired Joseph Lifland from 1918-1923. This

---

[42] Source: the previously quoted 1906 *Boston Globe* article about the Yaffe-Glaser wedding.

suggests that the shul was relatively small and could not afford continuous rabbinic support.

Adath Jesura Nusach Ari

Adath Jesura, replaced the departed Moses Margolies in 1908 with Rabbi Wolf Margolis (no direct relationship to Moses). This was a part-time position; Margolis's primary affiliation was the Baldwin Street Shul in the North End.

By 1913, after Wolf Margolis left for New York, he was replaced by Rabbi Abraham Yudlevitz.

In 1920, Yudlevitz also left for New York, reinforcing the concept that promising rabbis from Boston tended to be lured away by wealthier congregations from the Big Apple. Rabbi Simon Lefland (of whom little is known) replaced him.

* * *

This is not to say that Friederman left the Boston scene entirely. During this period, he continued to be Shaari Jerusalem's rabbi in the North End, where he remained for many years. As previously noted, in 1914 Friederman wrote *Nachalat Yaakov* and in 1927 *Shoshanat Yaakov*. And he was listed as a "leading rabbi" who presided at the dedication of the Adams Street Synagogue in Newton in 1912:[43]

> The Synagogue, which is to be erected on a plot of land situated at 114 Adams St., Newton, is to be a two-story, half cement, tile and smooth red brick finish structure.... Leading Rabbis and Cantors of Boston and vicinity will officiate at the exercises in the afternoon.... Rabbi Friederman will also be prominent during the services.
>
> *The Newton Times*, July 31, 1912

In sum, as a result of the growing Jewish population in the West End and growing community affluence, The Boston Synagogue's leading predecessor shuls, Beth Jacob and North Russell, were able to afford full-time rabbis – in some years, two rabbis.

---

[43] Another participant in the dedication was Rabbi Rabinovitz, who previously had been the rabbi at North Russell Street

The balance of this chapter discusses three prominent rabbis associated with Adath Jesura Nusach and Anshei Libavitz: Wolf Margolis, Aaron Yudlevich and Joseph Lifland. The history of these rabbis shows a clear transition, from rebbe-type traditionalists like Margolis and Yudlevich, to less-controlling Orthodox rabbis like Lifland.

Rabbi Wolf Margolis

Wolf Margolis served as the rabbi of Adath Jesura Nusach Ari from 1910-1911, as well the Baldwin Street Shul in the North End. Since the latter was the leading shul in the North End, this made Margolis one of the leading Orthodox rabbis in Boston.

Photos of Rabbi Wolf Margolis.
http://search.ancestry.com/cgibin/sse.dll?gl=allgs&gsfn=Wolf&gsln=Margolis&gss=seo&ghc=20

According to Joshua Hoffman, a Yeshiva University-educated rabbi who wrote a master's thesis on Margolis, Wolf was invited, as a senior prestigious European rabbi, to come to Boston to replace Moses Margolies:

> Rabbi Gavriel Zev Margolis, or Rav Velvele,[44] as he was popularly known.., came to the United States in 1907 at the age of 59, after having previously served as rabbi of Grodno for twenty-seven years…. When Rabbi Moshe Zevulun

---

[44] Zev is Hebrew for Wolf; Velvel is Yiddish for Wolf.

Margolies, widely known as RaMaZ, decided to leave Boston in 1906 to take a rabbinic position in New York, the community there decided to bring in another prestigious European rabbi to replace him as spiritual leader of several congregations in Boston, and they invited Rav Velvele to come. He accepted the invitation and arrived in Boston in 1907, remaining there until 1911…

Joshua Hoffman, "The Changing Attitude of Rabbi Gavriel Zev Margolis Towards RIETS"

Despite the reference to "several congregations," Wolf Margolis in the 1910 *Boston City Directory* is listed only as the rabbi for Baldwin Street and Adath Jesura Nusach Ari. He then moved to New York in 1911.

Wolf's 1911 departure from Boston was discussed in this piece in the *Boston Evening Transcript* (September 14, 1922), where he expressed dissatisfaction with the way in which he had been treated (presumably by his shul boards; echoing Rabbi Friederman's complaints). By way of a comparison, the $7,000 that was offered to Margolis in 1911 "to keep the rabbi here" is equivalent to $162,000 today, so some wealthy congregants badly wanted him to stay.

In New York, Wolf Margolis became rabbi of Adas Yisroel on the Lower East Side, where he quickly fought with other rabbis over control of Kosher supervision in New York. This led to serious conflict with the establishment Agudath HaRabbanim (founded in part by Moses Margolies):

FAREWELL WAS NOT HARMONIOUS
Discordant Note Sounded at Good-by Meeting for Rabbi Margolis

All was not harmony at the meeting in the synagogue Beth Israel in Baldwin place, held as a farewell to Rabbi Wolf Margolis, who is going to New York. For a few minutes the gathering, which packed the synagogue to the doors, became much excited and almost everyone was on his feet, but Rabbi Margolis spoke to his friends and they became quiet. The trouble came when Nathan Pinanski, president of Temple Adath Jeshurun of Roxbury, accused some Boston Jews of conspiring with the New York committee to have Rabbi Margolis go to the latter city to wage a campaign against certain interests there. Mr. Pinanski also found fault with members of the committee which raised $7000 to keep the rabbi here.

Although every effort had been made to return the rabbi to Boston, and it had been thought that he might change his mind and remain, he announced emphatically last night that he would not break his promise to go to New York under any circumstances. He took occasion to say that his teachings had not been followed here and that there had been too much politics and business among the people with whom he

> After the death of Rabbi Jacob Joseph, the first ever and only chief rabbi of New York, in 1902, chaos and corruption in [Kosher] slaughter houses increased. There was no centralized system in place, and this applied to Orthodox Jewish life in general, as well. Adas Yisroel hoped to bring in a prestigious, scholarly rabbi who would serve as chief rabbi of New York, and bring the various factions together to end the disorganized state of affairs that currently existed. Rav Velvele, then, was the man they chose for this task.
>
> The grandiose scheme of Adas Yisroel was doomed to failure, partly because there was already another Orthodox organization in place, based in New York, the Agudath HaRabbanim of America, or the Union of Orthodox Rabbis, begun in 1902 directly after the death of Rabbi Jacob Joseph. Rav Velvele did not accept the authority of that group, considering himself to be of greater stature than any of its members, and he constantly accused them of being more interested in monetary gain than in the maintenance of halakhic standards in kashrut. Over the years, Rav Velvele challenged the Agudath HaRabbanim in many areas, particularly in regard to its standards of kashrut supervision... In one protracted conflict, in 1918, the Agudath HaRabbanim put him into cherem [excommunication] for opposing their support of a strike of kosher chicken slaughterers. Rav Velvele... continued to accuse the Agudath HaRabbanim of being interested in monetary gain rather that in improving the halakhic standards in the community...
> Hoffmann, op. cit.

One arena for Margolis' conflict with the Agudath was Prohibition, which began in 1919. According to Hoffman, "The Agudath HaRabbanim... tried to have [Wolf Margolis] thrown into jail through implicating him in the biggest sacramental wine scandal of the entire prohibition era." The accusation was that Wolf issued fraudulent certificates that illegal wine producers were abusing the Kosher wine production loophole. The issue rose to the level of a *New York Times* denial by Wolf.

DENIAL BY RABBI MARGOLIS.

Says He Had No Part in Deal in Sacramental Wine.

Rabbi G. Wolf Margolis of 203 East Broadway, New York City, who was mentioned in an article in The Providence Journal on a sacramental wine deal, parts of which article were reprinted in THE NEW YORK TIMES, has written a letter to The Providence Journal denying that he had any part in the deal. He states:

"I never had any business relations with Mr. Musher, never had anything to do with his wine and never O. K.'d his wine or the wine of the Menorah Wine Company or the Continental Distributing Company."

He further adds that he was never, and is not now, a Hebrew teacher, as stated in the article, but was "Chief Rabbi of Grodno, Poland (then part of Russia) for twenty-seven years." "Thereafter," he says, "I received a call from the Jewish Community of Boston to become their rabbi, and about this time of the year in 1907 I arrived at Boston and received a public welcome which included some of the highest officials. I was in Boston for about four and one-half years, when I received a call from the Hebrew Community of New York, where I have been rabbi for the past ten and one-half years. The Hebrew Community of New York is a body of Jews having a membership of over 8,000."

The New York Times
Published: January 15, 1922
Copyright © The New York Times

In a further area of conflict with other rabbis, Wolf strongly opposed the establishment of secular studies at RIETS and Yeshiva University:

> In 1919, Rav Velvele wrote that he disapprovingly learned, a year earlier, from Isaac Travis, father-in-law of Rabbi Dr. Bernard Revel (rosh yeshiva of RIETS), that he planned to create a rabbinical seminary uptown, with Dr. Revel as its head. The curriculum in that seminary, Travis told Rav Velvele, would include "*haskalah ivrit,*" or Hebrew enlightenment, which Travis thought was necessary for American rabbis. Rav Velvele wrote, in that essay, that the proposed seminary reminded him of the Vilna Rabbinical Seminary, which was imposed on the Jewish community there by the Russian government, and produced highly unqualified rabbis.... In a further essay, in 1924, Rav Velvele

again wrote... that Dr. Revel had launched a campaign to raise five-million dollars to create a rabbinical seminary uptown, where philosophy and other secular topics would be taught... Besides the danger that he saw in the study of some of the topics he mentioned, Rav Velvele felt that, in general, the time devoted to these studies would take away from time that should be devoted to Torah studies, so that the rabbis emerging from RIETS would not be qualified for their positions, thus replicating the situation that existed in the Vilna Rabbinical Seminary. Rav Velvele wrote, in fact, that the yeshiva was moving uptown in order to hide its activities from the Orthodox community of the Lower East Side, and that the rabbis it would produce did not warrant its continued association with the name of Rabbi Yitzchak Elchanan Spektor. In 1925, three years before Yeshiva College opened, Rav Velvele wrote a letter in which he criticized the Agudath HaRabbanim for its continued support of RIETS which had, he wrote, become a "semikha factory."

Rabbi Aharon Soloveichik once remarked that although, today, there are many "kana'im," or zealots, on the Orthodox Jewish scene in America, in those days, Rav Velvele was "the kanai."

Hoffman, op. cit.

Clearly then, Wolf Margolis and Solomon Friederman had similar views toward adapting to (or resisting) American secular norms, putting them at odds with Moses Margolies – a key supporter of expanding RIETS into secular studies.

Rabbi Abraham Yudlevitz

Rabbi Abraham Aaron Yudlevitz (as spelled in the *Boston City Directory*), or Yudelovitch as spelled by New York's Eldridge Street Shul, replaced Wolf Margolis at Adath Jesura Nusach Ari and Baldwin Street. He served there as rabbi for five years from 1913-1918. Like Margolies and Margolis, he had substantial rabbinical experience in Europe before coming to America. Also like them, he ended up in New York City; in Yudlevitz's case, as rabbi of the Eldridge Street Synagogue on the Lower East Side. On the Eldridge Street Synagogue's website, there is the following biography of Yudlevitz:

> A kindly-looking, gray-haired, white-whiskered old gentleman, Abraham Aaron Yudelovitch was a famous Talmudic scholar and a preacher that served as a rabbi at the Eldridge Street Synagogue…
>
> Born in Novardok, Russia in 1850, Yudelovitch was recognized as a child prodigy. After studying under the tutelage of his uncle, he attended the Volozhiner Yeshiva. In 1871, at the age of 21, he published his first sefer, entitled *Olim Lemivehon* (Page Proofs). This was a compilation of halachic responsa and sermons. He served twenty-six years in Russia and ten years in England. Rav Tzvi Hirsch Orliansky, the Maggid of Skidell, described Yudelovitch's memorable preaching style:
>
> *In 1878, when I was learning in Sokolka, I heard a lot about the Rov of Kuzhnetza -- that he is a Torah giant who studied constantly and over and above that, is a wonderful preacher whose mouth produces pearls of wisdom. Erev Shabbos Chazon the word got out that Rav Avrohom Aharon, the Rov of Kuzhnetza, was coming to Sokolka for Shabbos, and the gabba'im of the New Beis Hamidrash (where all the finest scholars and the wealthy men davened) invited him to preach there. By 3 p.m. on Shabbos the new Beis Hamidrash was full, with people standing crowded, waiting for the darshan to begin. (…) His powerful voice and the tune through which he poured out his soul, as well as his lofty ideas and extraordinary explanations of the verses of Eichah -- I will never forget as long as I live.*
>
> While in Manchester, England, Yudelovitch criticized the plan to establish Uganda as a safe haven for Jews though he was an ardent advocate of Zionism. He came to the US around 1908 to serve American Jewry and filled rabbinical

Rabbi Abraham Yudlevitz

charges in Boston, New Haven, Bayonne and New York. He served as the rabbi of the Eldridge Street Synagogue from 1918 until his death.

http://www.eldridgestreet.org

From the following comments by Yudlevitz's grandson, it appears that Yudlevitz was not immune to the desire for control. One of the attractions of Eldridge Street was that its rabbis held substantial power relative to lay boards. The new position also allowed him to be named "Chief Rabbi of the U.S." (a title not generally acknowledged by others).

> In the early history of the [Eldridge Street] congregation, lay leadership held power. However, by the late 1910's the balance of power had shifted to rabbis. By 1918, Eldridge Street's congregation combined its appreciation of wonderful speakers with its respect for scholarship by hiring Rabbi Dr. Avrum Aharon Yudelovitch as its rabbi. Yudelovitch, a brilliant speaker and scholar who was descended from a family of noted rabbis dating back to the 12th century, was made Chief Rabbi of the U.S. in 1919.

Barry, Yood, "Zayde's Shul Revisited," December 5, 2008

Margolis/Yudlevitz 1925 Photo

This photo of the Rabbis Margolis and Yudlevitz was taken in 1925 in Washington D.C. According to the Eldridge Street Shul website, the purpose of the trip was "to thank President Calvin Coolidge for his 'Omaha Tolerance Speech' in which he pointed out the importance of providing youth with a religious education. Additionally, the rabbi asked the president to ease immigration restriction."

Rabbis Margolis and Yudlevitz in Washington, DC, 1925

The title of the photograph is "Chief Rabbis G. Wolf Margolis and Abraham A. Yudelovitch, 11/10/25," suggesting that both men thought that they were more important than 'regular' rabbis.

Rabbi Lifland

In comparison to Margolis and Yudlevich, Rabbi Joseph Lifland of Anshei Libavitz (listed as rabbi for 1918-1923) had a less grandiose self-image. In the forward to his book *Converts and Conversion to Judaism* (published posthumously), there is an interesting biography of Lifland:

> In 1914 Rabbi Lifland went to Massachusetts [from New York City] at the behest of his nephew, Gershon Wilcher. In addition to serving as a pulpit rabbi, he officiated at weddings and funerals, functioned as a ritual slaughterer (*shohet*), and served on rabbinical courts for divorces and conversions. He enlisted in the U.S. Army, but due to poor health was asked to

sell bonds rather than serve actively as a rabbi. After holding the pulpit in the prestigious Joy Street Synagogue in Boston, he spent a year in Chicago leading the Sephardic Synagogue. Upon returning to Massachusetts, be became rabbi of the Agudat Achim Synagogue…

Though he continued to occupy a pulpit, Rabbi Lifland also worked in real estate. He was a founder of the New England Hebrew Academy, helped implement a five-day work week so that public schools would be closed on Shabbat, and established standards for Kosher-for-Passover food certification, all the while maintaining his scholarly endeavors…

There also is this interesting snippet about Wilcher and Lifland from *The Libin Family: From the Chernigov Country* [Ukraine]; Yehoshua Buch, editor. Apparently, Lifland was separated from his family for ten years (due to a combination of war and lack of money) before he could bring them to America.

> During 1913/4, due to the deteriorating political situation in Europe, another Jewish wave came to the US. Gershon Wilcher and his family came in 1913. In many cases, the husband immigrated to the U.S. alone planning to save some money to bring the rest of his family. … Rabbi Yosef Lifland came in 1914. Unfortunately, due to the outbreak of World War I, his wife and children came to the U.S. ten years later.

From these, one can observe several things distinguishing Lifland from Margolis or Yudkowitz:

- Lifland did not come to Boston to be 'Chief Rabbi.' He left to escape persecution, and had to leave his family behind in Europe for a decade.
- His nephew Gershon Wilcher was not a *macher* (big shot) in the Boston community, having only emigrated with his family the year before, in 1913.
- Lifland had what presumably was a part-time job in the small Anshei Libavitz shul, where he had to supplement his income by working in real estate and education. His scholarly efforts appear to be something that he did in his free time.

- Given that Chabad founded the New England Hebrew Academy in 1944, this suggests that Lifland either was Chabad himself or a sympathizer.

In other words, Lifland was a 'regular' Orthodox rabbi without pretensions of being a Chief or Grand Rabbi of Boston. Yet his helping to found the New England Hebrew Academy in Brookline (which exists today) was an important accomplishment.

Regarding his book on conversion, Lifland notes that its impetus was the emotional impact of the following incident, which led him to revisit the conversion laws from square one:

> Here in America when a Gentile approaches us requesting conversion, in most cases we unfortunately suspect that intermarriage is a factor, i.e., that he wants to convert so he can marry a Jewish woman (or she wants to marry a Jewish man). Today we rarely deal with a case of a *ger tzedek* [a 'righteous' convert acting from a sincere desire to be Jewish]. Thus we encounter a dilemma – if we refuse to activate conversion, some would maintain that we are adding to assimilation and perhaps even encouraging apostasy from Judaism, G-d forbid.
>
> I myself have experienced this. A number of years ago a Gentile named A.Y. came to me requesting that I convert him. I declined because I suspected his motives were marriage-oriented. Consequently, the object of his desire – a Jewish girl from a respected family – abandoned her Jewish heritage and converted to Catholicism, bringing grief and obloquy to her family. Then her mother, a devout woman all her life, cursed the Rabbi [e.g., Lifland] who caused her daughter to become an apostate. She did this shortly before she passed away, as a result of the anguish she suffered from the episode.
>
> Lifland, *Converts and Conversions to Judaism,* p. 14

Reading this, one sees a scholarly rabbi who was tortured by the consequences of his halachic ruling and sought comfort in study.

Summary Observations: Rabbis 1905-1925

Looking at the records of the rabbis who served at predecessor shuls during this period, one can observe two rabbinic models.

The first was a continuation of the Margolies/Friederman Old Country 'grand rabbi' approach, as characterized by Wolf Margolis and Abraham Yudlevitz. In these rabbis' world views, they would rule Boston as 'chief rabbi' from the 'central' Baldwin Street Shul in the North End,[45] with control over subsidiary shuls such as Adath Jesura Nusach Ari. This model did not work well (the Jews moving out of the North End did not help), with Wolf Margolis leaving after a few years, complaining bitterly about his congregants. While there is not the same level of written vitriol from Yudlevitz, he too left for a pulpit in New York, where he would have greater control.

During this period, the only predecessor shul that followed this model was Adath Jesura, and only until 1918, when Yudlevitz departed for New York.

After Yudlevitz's departure, the West End would not see a continuation of the grand rabbi model – the exception being Rabbi Pinchas Horowitz, the Bostoner rebbe who founded Machzike Torah on Poplar Street in the West End in 1915.

A second model, which prevailed in this period, was for the lay board to assert control. As a key demonstration of power and determination to break away from the grand rabbi model, the predecessor shul boards either: (a) never hired Moses Margolies at all (Mishkan Shlomo; which instead chose Isaac Baritz in 1904); (b) if they had hired Margolies initially, decided not to replace him with his linear successor Wolf Margolies (CBJ, Anshei Libavitz); or (c) if they had hired traditionalist rabbis like Friederman or Rubinovitz, terminated them (Ein Jacob, North Russell). Going forward, as previously noted, they then made frequent staffing changes.

---

[45] Relying on Baldwin Street as the center of power ignored the fading demographics of the North End, which was already apparent to CJP in its 1921 study.

Continuing Non-Affiliation

Despite the increasing role of lay leadership at the expense of rabbinical control, there was no change in the predecessor shuls' non-affiliation stances. For one thing, all of the shuls remained Orthodox, which, unlike Reform or Conservative synagogues, typically did not affiliate with national groups. In addition, since the predecessor shuls were located in a major Northeastern city with a sizeable Jewish population, they did not need affiliation to gain access to a pool of rabbinical candidates.

This would continue in the period between 1930 and 1958, when the declining Jewish population made the idea of paying dues to a national organization problematic.

Chapter 6

North Russell as Leading West End Shul

The 1905-1925 period saw the emergence of Beth Hamedrash Hagadol (Anshe Sfard), the North Russell Street Shul, as the major synagogue in the West End. At its peak, it had over 1,000 members.[46] Prominent members of the shul included the Kirstein family, who endowed the famous Kirstein Library in downtown Boston, and Elihu Stone, a prominent Zionist.

According to Clingan, Beth Hamedrash Hagadol began in 1896, with Massachusetts records showing that it was incorporated six years later on April 5, 1902 as "Beth Amedrish Agudal Anshi Sfard," located at 30 Poplar Street. By 1904, it had moved to its permanent location at 30 North Russell Street (making it the North Russell Street Shul).

The shul's name is an unusual and perhaps unique transliteration from the Hebrew.[47] The typical 'modern' Israeli-Sephardic transliteration would be Beth Hamedrash Hagadol, as Clingan used in her spreadsheet. Alternatively, there are several Ashkenazic synagogues named Beth Hamedrosh Hagodol. When asked about this, Dr. David Fishman, professor of Modern Jewish History at Jewish Theological Seminary and a Yiddish expert, commented that 'Amedrish' is consistent with Polish Ashkenazic pronunciation. On that basis, however, the transliteration for the second word should then be 'Agudol' or 'Agodol,' not 'Agudal.'

Since "Amedrish Agudal" in Hebrew means 'great study house,' this suggests that the incorporators had big plans. They were not thinking about creating a small *shtibl*. Instead they wanted their shul to be one of the major synagogues in the city – something they succeeded in accomplishing.

---

[46] *Beacon Hill Times*, August 4, 1998

[47] An Internet search failed to surface any other shul using this transliteration spelling.

As previously noted, the "Anshi Sfard" part of the name refers to the founders' intent to follow Chassidic nusach sfard. One tangible manifestation would be the shul's choice of Chassidic D.M. Rubinovitz as its initial rabbi in 1904-1906 (more on him in the next section of this chapter).

In contrast to the heterogeneous background of CBJ's founders, most of Beth Hamedrash Hagadol's twenty incorporators had Eastern European names. One exception (with a Sephardic name) was Joseph Sondon, who presumably was related to Luis Sondon at CBJ. Due to their relatively nondescript names, nothing else is known of the founding officers, and the only last name repeating on the 1941 Mortgage Redemption Plaque is Wasserman.

Officers and Board Members:
Beth Amedrish Agudal Anshi Sfard, 1902

President	David Stern
Treasurer	Simon Magur
Vice President	David Feinzig
Recording Secretary	Abraham Castleman
Financial Secretary	Joseph Sondon Israel Kites
Board Members	Jacob Maranis David Wasserman Morris Frankel David H. Platisnky Samuel Sheinfeine Orsi Shapiro Morris Ableman Samuel Rotman Nathan Rovanrnick Joseph Tenenblatt Joe Jetzer William Rosenblat Louis Coretsky Hyman Schneiderman

Beth Amedrish Incorporation Papers, 1902

Despite its relatively late start, North Russell Street by 1910-1920 had become one of the leading shuls in the West End – as illustrated by the fact that it included two rabbis on staff (Hillman and

Sharfman) in the 1910 *Boston City Directory*.

Key to North Russell Street's success was its emphasis on parties and music. As an example of the former, the shul held a Chanukah party in December 1905 that attracted 3,000 children[48]

With respect to music, North Russell's reputation was based on its high-quality cantor and male choir.[49] It also was known for hosting concerts by famous touring cantors.

Illustrating the shul's emphasis on music is a 1912 leaflet from the Adams Street Shul dedication in Newton noting that "Cantor Emanuel Shafer and Choir from the North Russell Street synagogue of Boston ... will entertain us." This attests to North Russell Street's leading role in the Jewish community at that time, and that this reputation was based on music, rather than its rabbis.[50]

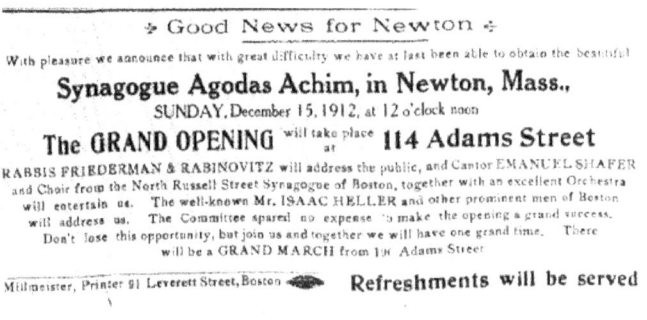

Adams Street Shul dedication leaflet, 1912

Musically, two things separated North Russell Street from small shuls like Vilna: (a) it had a choir that performed 52 weeks a year, and (b) as a result, it was able to recruit high-quality singers. As recounted by one prospective young choir candidate:

---

[48] *Boston Advocate* December 29, 1905 p.6; quoted in Kleinstein, "Echoes of the Old West End Boston, 1900-1914."

[49] Sarna, in *American Judaism,* notes that the use of cantors and choirs was a general trend in Orthodox shuls at the time to attract attendees; see pp. 176-177.

[50] By 1912, Rabinovitz, who was part of the ceremony, was no longer associated with North Russell.

In preparation for our singing careers [my friend] Curly and I planned to apply for the choir at the Wilner shul on Philips Street. The Wilner shul was a modest synagogue and employed a choir only on Rosh Hashonoh and Yom Kippur. Subconsciously, I imagine, we assumed that we stood a better chance of being accepted at this shul than at a more affluent one, such as the North Russell Street shul. Of course, we were not going to tell our parents about this until the cantor or the head of the choir at the Wilner shul had accepted us. This was May and the High Holidays didn't come until September, so there was plenty of time.

But we didn't plan on wasting the intervening time. We were going to visit the North Russell Street shul on Saturdays to hear the choir there, so that we could pick up some pointers. Fortunately, there was choir singing at North Russell Street every Saturday throughout the year, and, what was even better, there was no charge for admission there at any time except on Rosh Hashonoh and Yom Kippur.

Angoff, *Something About My Father*, pp. 130, 136

The author of these comments about the North Russell Street choir was the famous editor and writer Charles Angoff,[51] editor of *The American Mercury*, where he succeeded H.L. Mencken. He was born in 1903 and lived in the West End as a child. In 1962, Angoff wrote an article called "Memories of Boston" for the final issue of The *Menorah Journal*,[52] in which he describes some of his

Charles Angoff

---

[51] In 1977, the Charles River Park Synagogue held a dinner in honor of Charles' brother Sam Angoff, a leading labor lawyer.

[52] The *Menorah Journal* was published by the Menorah Society, a pre-Hillel Jewish inter-campus society (founded at Harvard) that focused entirely on Jewish culture rather than religion. Its first issue in 1915 featured articles by Louis Brandeis and Harry Wolfson. As Hillel became more established, the Menorah Society shut down in 1962.

experiences as a pre-bar mitzvah and bar mitzvah boy in the West End (this would have been circa 1913-1916). As seen in the following vignette, Angoff viewed North Russell Street as the rich Jew's establishment synagogue, known for holding large cantorial concerts:[53]

> In [the North Russell Street's] days of glory it was one of the great synagogues of America. To me it has special significance on various counts. First of all, its vice president was a great-uncle of mine. ... This great-uncle of mine offered to get my parents into his synagogue on the High Holy Days at a reduced rate, but my father refused....
>
> But my father did accept my great-uncle's invitations to come to the North Russell Street Shul to hear great cantors. When the word went around that one was coming, the synagogue naturally filled up quickly, and that's when my great-uncle came in handy. He took my father and me into the synagogue with him, and father and I had, so to speak, orchestra seats. It was there that I got the full meaning of what it meant to get *"dem emessen nigun"* ("the true melody") into a prayer. Never will I forget Sirota singing *Lecho Dodi* (Come, My Beloved) on Friday night, and Quartin singing *Ovinu Malchaynu* (Our Father, Our King), and Rosenblatt singing *Adon Olam* (Lord of the Universe). I once heard Sirota chant the *Kiddush* on Friday night with such profound sincerity that I felt shivers of delight pass up and down my spine. I was only a boy, under thirteen, but intuitively I grasped what was being done by these great cantors. I grasped, for all time, what Jewish prayer meant, and in a vague way I understood why the Jews have lasted all these years and will last to the end of time.
>
> Charles Angoff, "Memories of Boston," *The Menorah Journal* 1962

---

[53] Given that Angoff wrote this piece forty-plus years after the fact, some of these concerts may have occurred years later. Cantor Sirota gave a US concert tour in 1907, which fits with Angoff's recollection. Quartin's tour was in 1920; Rosenblatt immigrated to New York in 1912, but his major concert tours were in the 1920s.

The cost of High Holiday tickets at North Russell Street meant that only wealthier Jews could afford the performances. Poorer Jews instead set up storefront shuls:

> I have been thinking a great deal about a temporary shul that my father and I went to. The poorer Jews of the neighborhood, who could not afford to pay the price of the tickets even to the modest synagogues, would rent [a] store for the High Holidays and turn it into a place of worship.

Angoff, *Something About My Father*, p. 70

The Rabbis of North Russell Street 1905-1925

As previously noted, North Russell Street's first listed rabbi was D.M. (David Mayer) Rubinovitz for 1904-1906, followed by Rabbi Hillman in 1908-1910. In 1910, Rabbi Hyman Sharfman joined Hillman as second rabbi.

D.M. "Rubinovitz" turns out to be a different transliteration of the rabbi's more frequently used D.M. Rabinovitz (there also are some references to "Rubinovits"). D.M Rabinovitz was born in 1863 and was one of the first Lubavitcher rabbis in America, arriving in Boston in 1896 at the age of 33.[54]

In 1904 (eight years after his arrival), Rabinovitz was hired by North Russell Street as its first listed rabbi in the *Boston City Directory*. As previously noted, hiring a Chabad rabbi was consistent with the "Anshi Sfard" part of the shul's formal name.

Unlike other rabbis in that era who served multiple congregations, Rabinovitz's only listing in the 1904 *Boston City Directory* was as rabbi for North Russell.[55] Given that Rabinovitz only lasted for three

---

[54] Ira Robinson, *Translating a Tradition: Studies in American Jewish History*, p. 192

[55] A Lubavitch website claims that "The Rebbe Rashab [the 5th Lubavitch Rebbe] … sent Rabbi Dovid Mayer Rabinowitz to Boston, Massachusetts, where Rabbi Dovid Mayer became the Rov of a large Nusach Ari Shul"
(source: http://www.collive.com/show_news.rtx?id=20646&alias=the-miracle-in-springfield). This is questionable, since the only Nusach Ari shul in downtown when Rabinovitz arrived was The Boston Synagogue's predecessor shul Adath Jesura Nusach Ari, whose rabbis through 1923 were Moses Margolies, Wolf Margolies, Abraham Yudlevitz and Samuel Lefland. Perhaps the website meant North Russell, although North Russell was nusach Sfard, not nusach Ari.

years,[56] a reasonable supposition is that the North Russell's board decided that Rabinovitz was not a good fit and terminated him – if so, showing the supremacy of the board over the rabbi.[57]

Little is known about Rabinovitz's replacement, Rabbi Hillman (who began in 1908), aside from the fact that he lived near the shul at 22 North Russell Street.

However, in "Memories of Boston," Angoff discusses two rabbis. He begins by mentioning the rabbi of North Russell Street by title (a.k.a. "The Rabbi") rather than by name, and he then describes him as formal and unapproachable:

> The rabbi at the North Russell Street Shul seemed aloof to me. I'm sure he wasn't that way actually. My great-uncle said some very nice things about him to my father. Yet I would not have dared to smile at this rabbi. I wouldn't have dared to come up to him and say how nice a day it was, or ask him a question about some puzzling matter in the Bible, or about a matter of ritual or custom.

Given that North Russell's first listed rabbi (of two) in the *1910 Directory* is Marcus Hillman, one suspects that Angoff is referring to him.

Angoff then praises Rabbi Sharfman by name and at length – although he identifies Sharfman as rabbi of the Vilner Shul, not North Russell Street:

---

[56] After 1907, Rabinovitz does not appear in any Boston *City Directory* listings. So he did not find a major replacement pulpit.

[57] Rabbi Rabinovitz would continue to appear in Boston Jewish circles for many years. As previously noted, Rabinovitz participated in a 1912 Newton shul inauguration with Rabbi Friederman. In the 1920s, Rabinovitz was asked by Rabbi Pinchas Horowitz (along with Rabbi Friederman) to defend him in a beth din proceeding involving Horowitz's charges that a Kosher sausage company was using non-Kosher meat. In 1938-1940, D.M. Rabinovitz served as part of the Boston V'aad Harabonim (the establishment Orthodox rabbinical establishment) when it fought a kashrut war against Joseph Soloveitchik. (See Farber in *An American Orthodox Dreamer* pp. 60-63).

Rabbi Sharfman in the Vilner Shul was different. .... He was horny,[58] he was quiet and intimate. He was approachable. Indeed, he was often the first to approach others, young and old... He was a man of mysterious feelings and powers and insights. He was capable of sorrow, and he was capable of joy... The rabbi had a synagogue face. He had a synagogue gait -- slow, quiet, deliberate. He had a synagogue voice. His *droshes* (sermons) were brief, gentle, to the point. He pointed out to his small congregation that the Bible was very much up to date; that the principles of Deuteronomy and Leviticus were the abiding principles of mankind and of the United States in particular; that the labor laws in the Bible were the freest in all human history -- truly human, truly democratic, truly kind. He pointed out that it simply wasn't true that the New Testament was a document of love and the Old Testament a document of strict duty and strict justice, that in fact the doctrine of loving kindness appears in Micah and in Isaiah and in Samuel and in all the other books of the Jewish tradition. He pointed out time and again that it was no accident that the words inscribed around the Liberty Bell came not from the New Testament but from the Old Testament, Leviticus (25:10): "Proclaim liberty throughout the land and to all the people thereof." He quoted parables and other sayings of the Sages. I was astonished, in my early youth, at how well read he was, how well he had digested what he read, how unfanatical he was despite his orthodoxy. I remember well what he used to say when people brought up the fact that this or that Jew didn't always go to *shul* when he should, or observe too many of the *613 mitzvahs* (good deeds). He said, "Eh, I don't know. A man should observe. Of course a Jew should observe. But we must remember that it is an *avayreh* [transgression] to cast aspersions upon any man who performs deeds of charity. Such a man is good in the eyes of God. A charitable man in

---

[58] By "horny," Angoff presumably meant "tough and calloused," rather than "sexually aroused."

the eyes of God, is like all the 613 *mitzvahs* put together." Rabbi Sharfman was more than a spiritual leader. He was a job hunter and an apartment hunter, he was a lay analyst, a home saver, a social worker, and a doctor. In our poor neighborhood, people generally made use of the "lodge doctor" for ordinary ailments, but when a family was large the permitted number of doctor calls was pretty much used up by the early winter. Then the lodge doctor would be called anyway. He would be paid first with Passover wine, then with Passover wine and *lekach* (honey cake), then with boiled eggs and home baked bread. Then the doctor would not be called any more. The poor were just ashamed. So they went to the rabbi, and the rabbi went to the Talmud, which is full of medical lore. I remember my father asking the rabbi for a remedy for a sour stomach. The rabbi thought and then said, "It says in the Talmud that a man's stomach is made up of three parts: one for liquid, one for solid foods, and one has to be empty. Maybe, Reb Yid, you have put something in the part that has to be empty? So eat a little less bread, a little less herring, and if you skip a meal, it won't hurt so much. Try it for a couple days, maybe three days, don't starve yourself, just eat a little less, and then let me know." My father did as he was told, and it helped. Of course, when there was a serious illness the rabbi told the man to see a doctor, and when the man said he had no money for a doctor or he had used up the lodge doctor calls, the rabbi would get in touch with a neighborhood doctor, who would visit the man and charge him nothing: "Eh, pay me when you can." Or the rabbi arranged for the sick person to go to the clinic in the neighborhood.

Charles Angoff, "Memories of Boston," *The Menorah Journal* 1962

A major problem with this account is that it does not tie to contemporaneous *Boston City Directory* records. Given that Angoff was born in 1903 and is describing his pre-bar mitzvah days here, the relevant dates are 1913 to 1916. During these years, and for the entire period from 1910 through 1923, the directories show that Sharfman was either co-rabbi with Hillman at North Russell (1910 to

1912), or sole rabbi (1913 to 1923). For the Vilna Shul, there is no listing of any rabbi during this period.

One possible answer to the discontinuity is that Sharfman, like Margolies and Friedman before him, earned a living by working part-time at multiple shuls. This is supported by comments by a Vilna Shul writer, Thomas Lyman: "The [Vilna] congregation being poor, was unable to hire a full time rabbi, thus a senior male congregant led the services. At important holy days, the shul would hire a rabbi or cantor."[59]

Alternatively, Angoff may simply have forgotten the correct timeline (he wrote "Memories of Boston" in 1962), so that by 1913-1916, Sharfman was the rabbi for North Russell, not Vilna. In this scenario, North Russell had the same favorable reaction to Sharfman that Angoff had, and used its greater financial resources to recruit Sharfman full-time -- in a manner analogous to the way that wealthy baseball teams like the Yankees or Red Sox today recruit free agents from small-market teams. The lack of Vilna listings in the city directories suggest that this may have been what happened.

One important difference between Sharfman and rabbis like Friederman was his accommodation to the realities of making a living, and his sympathy for Jews who had to work on Shabbat to feed their families:

> One of the problems frequently placed before Rabbi Sharfman by members of his congregation was whether they should work on the Sabbath. The poor Jews of the West End slums struggled heroically to make ends meet by not working on the Sabbath, but it was extremely difficult, especially in times of depression, when every half day of work meant the difference between having regular meals at home and skipping a few (the parent alone did the skipping)... Rabbi Sharfman was heartsick whenever he was called upon to offer advice on this subject. He knew how badly his flock needed the money, and he also knew what working on the Sabbath would do to them internally – very

---

[59] Thomas K. Lyman, "Vilna Shul: A Remnant of Beacon Hill's Jewish History," Fall 1996.

few of those who desecrated the Sabbath ever felt spiritually whole again. Rabbi Sharfman would say to one seeking his advice: "I cannot, of course, tell you to work on the Sabbath. But neither can I tell you not to, for then I would be telling you to force your wife and children to starve, and, God forbid, perhaps to get sick – and ... you know. God is not an executioner. God is merciful. He understands. All I can say is that if a doctor may desecrate the Sabbath to save a life ... then, well, isn't food a medicine, too? And doesn't that make you, as the provider of food, a sort of doctor? I'm not telling you what to do, and I'm not telling you what not to do. It is a terrible choice, and I feel ashamed that you ask for my advice, since I do not have to make such a choice, and so do not really know the suffering involved. But always remember that our God is even kinder than the kindest judge." The import of Rabbi Sharfman's words did not escape anyone, and all were grateful to him for making it easier for them to do what was so horrible. As my father said: "Sometimes he talks like a mother."

Angoff, *Something About My Father*, pp. 194-195

In sum, Sharfman of North Russell Street was an extremely empathetic rabbi who is worthy of recognition alongside Margolies and Friederman.

Observations: North Russell Street Rabbis

The stories of Rubinovitz, Hillman and Sharfman reinforce basic themes developed previously. Like CBJ and the other shuls that moved away from authoritarian rebbes to rabbis controlled by lay boards, North Russell started off with a traditionalist rabbi – in this case, Chassidic (Rubinovitz). However, like the other predecessor shuls (or perhaps even more rapidly), the lay leadership of North Russell asserted itself and made multiple rabbinical changes, moving from Chassidic traditionalist to Hillman's aloofness to Sharfman's understanding that some Jews needed to work on Shabbat to feed their families. As a result, control was left with boards, not rabbis.

Postscript: the North Russell Mishnah Study Group

One of the most interesting (and beautiful) archival finds of The Boston Synagogue history project is the 1909-1910 ledger book of the North Russell Street Mishnah study group. The inside front cover is hand illuminated with an additional eight pages of Torah-quality Hebrew calligraphy containing the constitution and bylaws of the organization. After this, there are 62 pages of illuminated names of the members (one of whom is Rabbi Sharfman). For some of the names, there is a date or indication of death with cemetery information.

The bylaws (see Appendix 3) lay out a set of substantial obligations on the members. They must study 26 chapters of Mishnah each month.[60] If they miss a meeting of the study group or fail to do their assigned studies, they must pay a fine to the gabbai. If they miss three meetings, the gabbai and two other members can expel them from the study group.

Also of interest is that one of the group members, Nettie Feltsman, was a woman – showing that women's interest in learning Talmud is not a recent thing.[61] Given her later listing in the book and the lack of gold paint around her name in the register, Nettie was not one of the original members.

---

[60] There are 523 chapters in the Mishnah, so it would take 20 months (1 year, 8 months) to complete a cycle.

[61] Having one woman in a study group of 62 is reminiscent of the role of Beruria, the only female scholar mentioned in the original Talmud. Interestingly, unlike the men's names, which are in the traditional 'ABC' ben or bar 'XYZ,' format, with the last name then appended in Yiddish, here the listing is R' (for Raba) Nettie Feltsman in Yiddish with no 'bas XYZ' Hebrew name – perhaps reflecting the gabbais' discomfort in acknowledging her gender explicitly.

 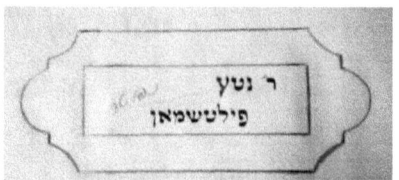

Left: Listing for Rabbi Hyman Sharfman with Cemetery Information.
Right: Listing for Nettie Feltsman (With No Gold Painting).

The existence of this document and the effort to create a beautiful illuminated document highlights the value that the members placed on Talmudic study.

*   *   *

A Charles River Park era document from the 1980s refers to the document as a "historical treasure," and states that "a lithograph of the original will be permanently exhibited in our synagogue lobby." This was never done, but thanks to the help of the American Jewish Historical Society, The Boston Synagogue has obtained a high-resolution digital copy of the front page that it will use to fulfill the vision of the unknown 1980s author.

Chapter 7

Shul Buildings and Architecture

The North Russell Street Shul, 1923

The period between 1905 and 1925 was one in which the increasingly prosperous West End Jews were able to afford new buildings – in particular the North Russell Street shul, built in 1923.

In 1917, the synagogue owned 28 and 30 North Russell Street, which only gave it a narrow frontage. To build the 1923 facility with a 40-50 foot wide frontage, the shul also purchased 24 and 26 North Russell.

Based on information prepared by a consulting engineer in 1959 (for purposes of obtaining eminent domain compensation from the City of Boston), the new shul had 94 men's pews and 46 women's pews.[62] Accordingly seating capacity was approximately 600 (376 men and 222 women).[63]

Despite the tradition that Jewish shuls in the West should have their arks facing east toward Jerusalem, the North Russell Street ark was located on the western wall. This reflected the fact that the main entrance on the North Russell Street side faced east, making an east-facing ark impractical (unless the shul had decided to place its main entrance on the north side, facing Russell Court).[64]

---

[62] Source: Thomas F. McSweeney Associates valuation study.

[63] As previously noted, the 1903 Wall Street Shul had seating capacity of 950.

[64] The same is true of Anshei Libavitz at 8 Smith Court, where the ark wall faced south. In the case of CBJ, the building was located on the north side of Wall Street, with the entryway facing south. Accordingly, the CBJ ark wall faced north. Clearly, for Jews building shuls with geographical constraints, having an ark on the eastern wall was secondary to having a shul at all. In a more modern era, the ark wall at The Boston Synagogue indeed faces east.

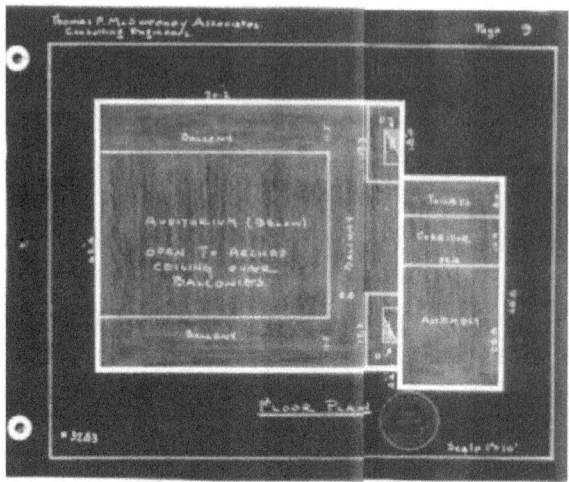

Floor Plan, North Russell Street Shul

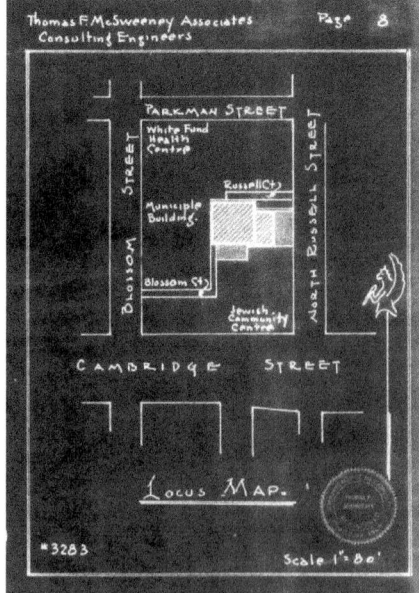

Street grid for the North Russell Street Shul block (Showing Russell Court to the north). McSweeney Associates study, 1959

Observations on Shul Architecture

At the same time that North Russell Street was building its new shul, so were a number of other synagogues:

- In the West End, the Vilna Shul's new facility was inaugurated in 1919, and the Chambers Street Shul dedicated an elaborate new ark by Sam Katz in 1920 (Katz also built Vilna's ark).
- Ohabei Shalom and Temple Israel, which had started out in the South End, were building new facilities in Brookline and the Boston Fens -- as was Kehillath Israel in Brookline.

The West End shul exteriors were relatively plain. The major difference between North Russell and Vilna is that North Russell had a neo-classical pediment and entryway archstone (making it a low budget version of the former Museum of Natural History building built in 1862 and located at 234 Berkeley Street in Boston). North Russell also was much larger than Vilna.

West End Shul Exteriors. Left: North Russell Street Shul. Right: Vilna Shul

Comparable Neo-Classical Design, 234 Berkeley Street, Boston, Massachusetts (1862)

In contrast to the exteriors, the West End shul interiors were ornate, with old-fashioned arks that could have belonged in a 200-year-old shul from the Old Country. North Russell's ark was twice as tall as Vilna's and more elaborate. A detailed description was included in the McSweeney Associates 1959 valuation analysis:

> At the west end of the room is an elaborate painted and illuminated altar with an arch over a wood cupboard, wood free standing decorated columns, dentil moldings, symbolic lions holding tablets and three free standing gilt eagles, among other symbolic moldings. The altar is elevated on a three foot platform up four steps from the floor, the platform being surrounded by a two foot high railing. On either side of the altar, in the west wall, is a stained glass window with a semi-elliptical head.
>
> In front of the altar is a bim[a] (a pulpit-like structure) flanked by chairs for the elders of the congregations. This is on a platform two feet high with a wooden rail. The platform floor is covered with linoleum; the platform measures 12'.1 x 10'.1.

North Russell Street Shul interior photos

Left: Vilna Shul interior. Right: Chambers Street 1920 ark dedication

In contrast, the Brookline/Boston Fens synagogues embraced a modern Art Deco style incorporating neo-Byzantine and Classical design elements. This put them at the cutting edge of architectural design:

- There are striking similarities between the façades of Kehillath Israel, built in 1925, with the Théâtre des Champs-Élysées in Paris, built in 1913.
- Ohabei Shalom's art deco ark design and vault (built in 1925) has clear similarities with the entry door to the Canadian Bank of Commerce in Toronto (1930), and is radically different from the traditional 1920 Chambers Street Shul ark.

Art Deco Design Comparisons

Upper Left: Théâtre des Champs-Élysées (1913), Paris, France. Upper Right: Kehillath Israel, Brookline, Massachusetts (1925).

Lower Left: Canadian Bank of Commerce Toronto, Canada (1930).
Lower Right: Ohabei Shalom, Art Deco ark (1925).

Maintaining the Shul

From Anshei Libavitz records found in The Boston Synagogue's files,[65] the following is the translator's summarization of and observations about the details of taking care of the synagogue, including installing electricity in 1908 and taking out a second mortgage in 1912 to pay for repairs.[66]

1907-1908

The earliest available minutes include bills for gas and coal among their expenses. The board of trustees decided to institute electricity at its meeting of May 17, 1908; the electric lighting was installed during the summer. There is a drop in the gas bills after the installation of electricity, but the former do not disappear (e.g. November 11, 1907 - $6.10 vs. December 20, 1908 -$3.04).

There was a $20 plumbing job in January 1908, but no details are given.

1909

A year of varied repairs and alterations: a $15.00 roofing job in March; sidewalk repairs in July, total of $10.15; windows fixed in September.

Two major structural changes of the year: First, a major repair of the sewage system in August totaling $81.00. Second, part of the yard on the east side of the Synagogue was sold for $500.00 to Mr. Murray Siegal, a building developer. The deal was finalized at the meeting of October 6.

1910

The minutes of June 19 refer to decisions on several repairs: to fix the floor in the hallway, the sewage system, and to build a fence across from the "new building." What this new building was is not clear to us. It may simply refer to the new boundary between the Synagogue and the property sold to Mr. Siegal. The floor and fence

---

[65] Original in Yiddish, translated by Dr. David Fishman; originals held by the US National Park Service.

[66] $1.00 in 1910 is the equivalent of $23.40 today.

cost $30, reported July 3.

1911

More extensive repairs. A total of $30 spent on roofing; a total of $105.81 on fixing the electrical system. This must have been a major overhaul or extension of the system.

1912

The minutes of this year are enigmatic and frustrating. It is clear that work of major proportions was going on in the building. What that work was cannot be ascertained.

The Board of Trustees appointed a separate committee to supervise all building repairs, transferred Synagogue funds to the committee, and gave it free rein over the disbursement of funds.

A second mortgage was taken out to finance the repairs.

The work on the building went on throughout the summer and fall of 1912. The only related bill registered in the Congregation minutes, $37 for carpentry, was listed on July 21. The minutes on November 10 note that all repairs were completed.

1913

The platform for the Cantor and the reading of the Torah, the Bimah, was reconstructed during this year. (Note that this probably followed extensive work on the interior of the building.) The meeting on February 2 lists bills for lumber totaling $48.15, and a carpentry bill for $45.

March 30, $9.59 for Bimah. May 4, $101.15 for Bimah. This makes one wonder whether more than the platform was involved in these repairs. $20 paint job for Bimah.

1914

Bills for coal reappear after a two-year absence. $15 window repair reported on November 1.

Chapter 8

Developments in the West End 1925-1945

Demographics

Published Jewish population figures for the West End do not exist for this period, presumably because of limited communal interest in downtown Boston.

It is possible, however, to estimate Jewish West End population by starting with the 1910 population figure of 40,000 from Chapter 2 and then extrapolating from other datasets.

The first dataset is the Boston Ward 5 census. In 1915, Ward 5 population was 77,573. By 1930, the population declined 61% to 30,571 (growing slightly to 32,962 in 1945).

The second dataset is Jewish share of West End population. Herbert Gans in *The Urban Villagers* estimated that Jewish population share dropped from 75% in 1926 to 20% by 1936. This was a decline of 73% in a single decade. Given that Gans also indicated that the Italian share grew from 35% in 1936 to a majority in 1945, the Jewish share by 1945 presumably was less than 20%.

> Around the turn of the century, the Irish were replaced by the Jews, who dominated the West End until about 1930. During this era, the West End sometimes was called the Lower East Side of Boston. In the late twenties, Italians and Poles began to arrive, the former from the North End, and they joined a small Italian settlement that had existed in the lower end of the area since the beginning of the century. Throughout the 1930s and early 1940s, the Italian influx continued until eventually they became the largest ethnic group in both the upper and lower portions of the West End. The changes in population are reflected in data taken from library registration cards. In 1926, the area was estimated to be 75 per cent Jewish. In 1936, however, the library users were 35 per cent Italian, 25 per cent Polish, 20

per cent Jewish, and 20 per cent "miscellaneous." By 1942, the Italians were in the majority.

Gans, *Urban Villagers*, p.7

Combining these datasets, a reasonable estimate for 1935 Jewish population is 4,368, based on:

- 1910 Jewish population of 40,000; times
- Ward 5 population ratio for 1935 versus 1915 ($31,767^{67}/77,573^{68}$); times
- Jewish population share ratio for 1936 versus 1926 ($20\%/75\%^{69}$).

Assuming that by 1945, the Italian share grew to 60% and the non-Italian share dropped proportionately, the 1945 Jewish share was only around 12%, with a Jewish population of 2,620.

North End and West End Population Trends

Year	North End Jews	North End Italians	West End Jews	West End Italians
1880	500	1,000	100	125
1895	6,200	7,700	6,300	1,100
1905	4,700	18,000		
1910			40,000	
1920	Negligible			
1925	Negligible		19,097	
1935	Negligible		4,368	
1945	Negligible		2,620	

Jews of Boston and Boston Synagogue analysis

Synagogue Count

This sharp Jewish population drop, along with the impact of the Great Depression, led to a dramatic decline in the number of shuls in the North and West Ends:

---

[67] Average between the 1930 and 1945 census figures.

[68] Assumes no Ward 5 population change from 1910 to 1915.

[69] Assumes that the 1910 Jewish population share was 75% (same as in 1926).

- The North End went from four to two shuls by 1931. By 1941, no shuls were left.

- The West End went from fifteen to six shuls by 1931. By 1941, there were four shuls left.

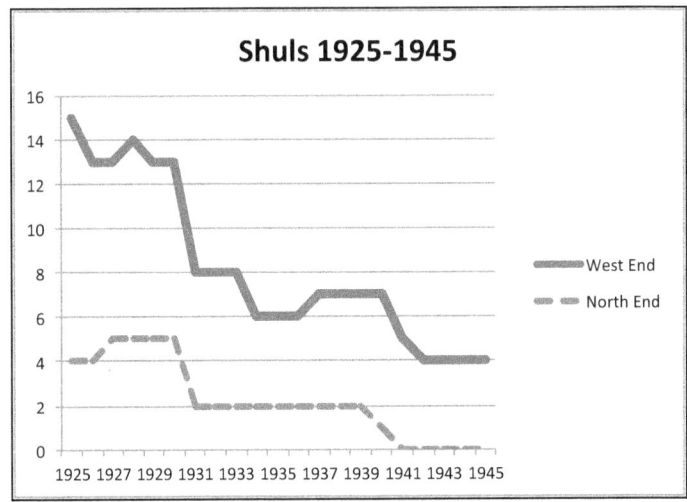

Clingan Spreadsheet and Boston Synagogue analysis

There was a parallel drop in Jewish communal resources:

> The Hecht House ... moved from the West End to Dorchester in 1936. Even the West End YMHA left the West End, relocating to Roxbury in the late 1930s.
>
> Gamm, *Urban Exodus*, p. 138

1940 Merger

In response to a collapsing community, United Congregation Beth Jacob and Beth Hamedrash Hagadol (Anshe Sfard) merged in 1940, forming Beth Hamedrash Hagadol/Beth Jacob.

Based on a 1987 recollection by Israel Alpert when he was Treasurer for the Charles River Park Synagogue, the merger was caused by severe building repair problems at Beth Jacob:

> ... way back the name of the synagogue was Beth Hamidrash Hagodal Beth Jacob, and that Beth Jacob refers to a time when a synagogue that was on Wall Street in the West End

had dissolved, threw in the sponge, and joined the North Russell Street Synagogue, and I was very young then and my recollection is that their building was in deplorable condition and rather than spend money fixing up the building, they joined with the North Russell Street Synagogue, because shortly after they joined us, the building collapsed and the City had some troubles with it.... I don't think there was any sale of the land. The City had the problem of moving it. But there were things like the Torah [that] came to the Charles River Park Synagogue.

Israel Alpert deposition, March 16, 1987[70]

The incorporation papers for "Congregation Beth Amedrish Agudal Beth Jacob," as the merged shul was called, were filed on October 19, 1940, for the purpose of "the maintenance of a place of worship according to the Orthodox Hebrew Rite..." This is in contrast to the predecessor shuls' 1888 and 1902 incorporation papers, which refer only to "Hebrew worship"[71] or "place of worship where persons of the Jewish faith may attend."[72] By 1940, Jewish sectarian lines had clearly been drawn.

The new entity was located in Beth Hamedrash Hagadol's building at 28 North Russell Street.

As a sign of the merger, a new cornerstone was commissioned. The inscribed Jewish year 5701 is 1940-41, with the name of the shul Beth Hamedrash Hagodal Beth Jacob written in Hebrew. The cornerstone was later installed in The Boston Synagogue's current building.

---

[70] Israel Alpert gave this deposition testimony in 1987 as part of legal proceedings related to the disposition of the Vilna shul estate assets (discussed in Chapter 12).

[71] CBJ

[72] North Russell Street

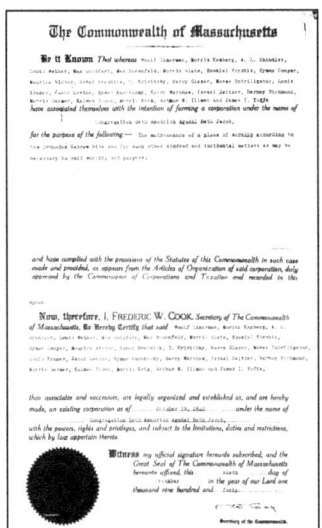 

Left: 1940 Beth Amedrish Articles of Incorporation. Right: 1940-41 Cornerstone (reinstalled at The Boston Synagogue)

The shul consolidation was celebrated with a gala dedication dinner held on Sunday, March 2, 1941 at the Dorchester Manor. The Dedication card (front and back) reveals a number of things about the shul, its leadership and its members:

- There is no listed rabbi or cantor. This was a lay-led synagogue.
- The name of the synagogue in English is spelled "Beth Hamedrosh Hagodol Beth Jacob," despite the fact that the 1940 incorporation papers were for "Beth Amedrish Agudal Beth Jacob." The shul leadership was still transliteration-challenged.
- There was an active Ladies Auxiliary, showing the important, albeit subsidiary, role that women played. The shul's bylaws adopted on September 22, 1940 restricted membership to "Jewish male persons of good moral character." However, an unsigned and undated addendum stated that "Officers of Ladies Auxiliary... [are] members for all purposes." Presumably, some of the women officers complained about their second-class status, which led to the addition.

- The deep commitment of families to the shul is seen with Morris Kamberg serving as First Vice President and Dora Kamberg serving as Treasurer of the Ladies' Auxiliary (Elias was the Beth Jacob president in 1899)
- This was a pre-dieting age, so people stuffed themselves when given the chance. Each attendee was served a full half-broiler, on top of multiple other items.
- The alcohol of choice was beer, not wine. For Jews of that generation, wine was a tumbler of sweet Concord grape for Kiddush, not something to drink as a main beverage.
- The stereotypical African-American servers are regrettable.

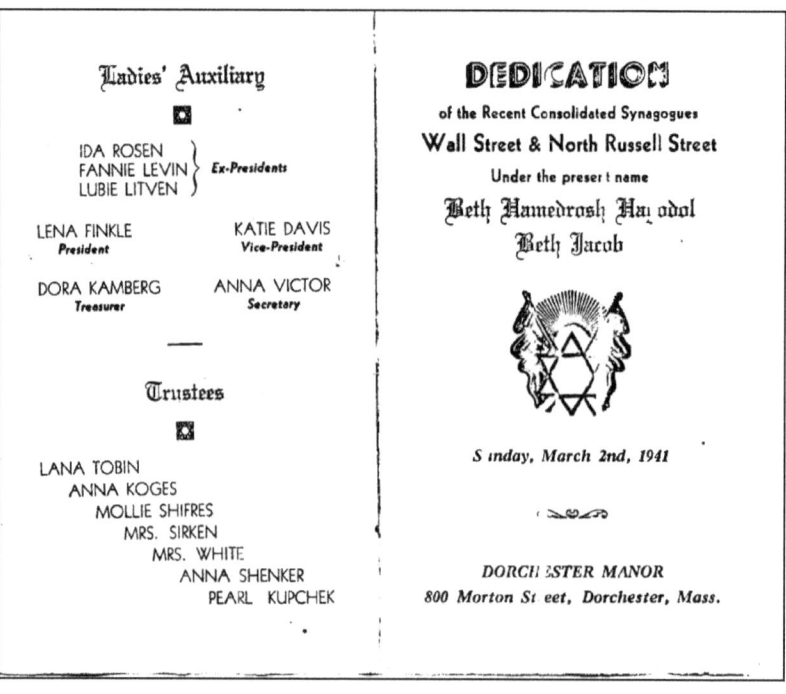

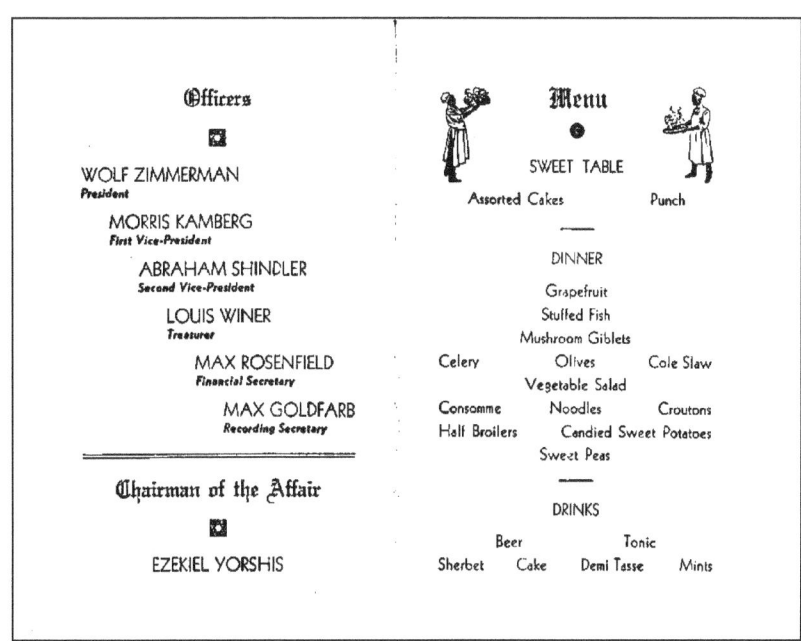

1941 Dinner Celebrating the North Russell/Wall Street Shul Merger (Front and Back)

An impressive memento of this age is the *Beth Amedresh[73] Agudal Beth Jacob Mortgage Redemption Plaque*, which today hangs in the entryway of The Boston Synagogue.

The apparent age and old-fashioned style of the plaque led many people at the shul to believe that the plaque dated to the early 1900s. However, given that the merger of Beth Jacob and Hamedrash Hagadol only took place in late 1940, it clearly was created after this.

---

[73] The plaque's spelling of "Amedresh" is different from the 1902 and 1940 incorporation spelling, both of which use the form "Amedrish."

Beth Amedresh Agudal/Beth Jacob Mortgage Redemption Plaque

A review of the officer and donor lists leads to the following observations:

- As with the dedication dinner card, there is no listed rabbi or cantor. North Russell Street was controlled by lay people, not rabbis.
- There is no segregation of donors by contribution level, e.g., Platinum, Gold, Silver, Bronze. Every donor is treated equally.
- There are 266 unduplicated names on the list (two names were listed twice). Of these, fourteen are corporate or institutional names, with the remaining 252 being families or individuals. While not all of the donors are necessarily members of the combined congregation, this number is twice the size of Beth Jacob's 125 members in 1899. Therefore the merger resulted in a congregation of a size that was economically viable,

assuming no continuing declines.

- At the top of the plaque, there are eight officer/board member groups, with a total of 77 names (58 unduplicated). This is a large number compared to The Boston Synagogue's current nineteen-member board.

- Of the donor list, one name that generates particular interest by shul visitors is Mr. and Mrs. M. Nimoy. Max and Dora Nimoy lived in the West End, where Max was a barber. In 1926 they had a son Melvin, who went to Boston Latin and MIT and became a chemical engineer at Johnson & Johnson. In 1931, they had a second son, Leonard. Leonard Nimoy later achieved fame as Mr. Spock in the original *Star Trek* series.

1948 West End Playground; Leonard Nimoy in upper right. Fisher and Hughes, *The Last Tenement*

The existence of a Mortgage Redemption Plaque suggests, of course, that there was a mortgage to be redeemed. This leads to questions about when this mortgage was taken out, for how much, on what terms and when it was redeemed.

After conducting research, the Archival and Historical Committee was able to determine that on December 10, 1940, two months after the merger incorporation papers were signed, the congregation took out a $20,000 ten-year mortgage at an unspecified interest rate, consolidating two prior mortgages.[74] The Charlestown Five Cents Savings Bank was the lender. Four years later, on November 16, 1944 during World War II, the mortgage was redeemed – six years earlier than necessary. Hence, the Mortgage Redemption Plaque in the entryway of The Boston Synagogue probably dates to 1944 or 1945. Once the mortgage was paid off, the shul held a gala party similar to the 1940 merger celebration.

The 'official mortgage redemption: From Boston city records

Recollections By Leonard Nimoy

For The Boston Synagogue's history project, Leonard Nimoy graciously agreed to be interviewed about his recollections of his parents and the North Russell Street Shul during this period.

Max and Dora Nimoy knew each other as children in the town of Zaslov, Ukraine and became reacquainted in Boston, marrying in 1925. Max, who was a barber in Zaslov, emigrated after World War I,[75] first to Buenos Aires, then to New York. He then moved to Boston when he learned of a barber in the West End who was looking for a partner. Leonard's mother Dora Shpanger (Spinner post-immigration) came to America with her parents and brothers (one of whom was turned away with an eye infection). Dora's father Samuel was a leather cutter and her brother Meyer was a house painter. Eventually, three generations would live together on Chambers Street.

---

[74] The prevailing rate in those days appears to have been 3%.

[75] Due to the large-scale killings of Jews in the Ukraine that were a result of the Russian Revolution.

Leonard Nimoy's grandmother Sarah Spinner (on left): 87 Chambers Street. Jules Aarons

The Nimoy household initially spoke only Yiddish. As a result, Leonard's older brother Melvin's first language was Yiddish. By the time Leonard was born in 1931, his parents had become reasonably fluent in English, so that Leonard's first language was English (although he spoke Yiddish in order to communicate with his Yiddish-speaking grandparents).[76]

While the home was kosher (in deference to Leonard's grandmother), Max Nimoy needed to work on Saturdays and the family did not attend shul services regularly. Initially the family joined Tifereth Israel on 99 Chambers Street because it was near their home (in the following 1952 photograph, the Nimoy family lived three buildings to the right). However, when Leonard neared his bar mitzvah, his father had a dispute with Chambers Street over High Holiday seating and joined North Russell.

Leonard, who went to Hebrew School on Poplar Street, had his bar mitzvah in 1944 at Chambers Street,[77] where he recalls davening Shaharit, reading the entire Torah portion and haftarah, and then davening Musaf (something that today would only be done by someone attending yeshiva or Jewish day school). A week later, he partially reprised his performance at the North Russell Shul, davening Shaharit.

---

[76] As a young actor in Los Angeles, Leonard Nimoy found part-time work with touring Yiddish theater troupes.

[77] Chambers Street was not a predecessor shul of The Boston Synagogue – in 1958, it merged with Vilna.

Chambers Street Shul (Nimoy house on the extreme right). Source: Leonard Nimoy

After his bar mitzvah, Leonard stopped attending shul except for High Holidays. However, one now-famous event occurred at North Russell Street's High Holiday services, when a young Leonard was fascinated by seeing five to six Cohanim blessing the congregation. This later became the basis for the now famous Vulcan "live long and prosper" salute. As he recounted in his autobiography *I Am Spock*:

> For what would soon become known as the Vulcan salute, I borrowed a hand symbol from Orthodox Judaism. During the High Holiday services, the Kohanim (who are the priests) bless those in attendance. As they do, they extend the palms of both hands over the congregation, with thumbs outstretched and the middle and ring fingers parted so that each hand forms two vees. This gesture symbolizes the Hebrew letter shin, the first letter in the word Shaddai, "Lord"; in the Jewish Qabala, shin also represents eternal Spirit.
>
> The ritual made an extraordinary impression on me when, as a young boy, I attended those services with my family in an orthodox synagogue. The women sat separately in the balcony, and I sat near the front with my father, grandfather, and older brother, Melvin. The special moment when the Kohanim blessed the assembly moved me deeply, for it possessed a great sense of magic and theatricality. In Hebrew, they would chant:

"May the Lord bless you and keep you. May the Lord turn His face upon you, and give you peace..."

In approximate unison, their voices rose and fell in loud, piercing shouts-fervent, impassioned, ecstatic.

"Don't look," my father whispered. "Close your eyes. You mustn't look."

Being a child, I of course asked, "Why?"

"Because this is the moment that the Shekhinah- the holy essence of God-enters the sanctuary ."

I had heard that this indwelling Spirit of God was too powerful, too beautiful, too awesome for any mortal to look upon and survive, and so I obediently covered my face with my hands.

But of course, I had to peek.

And I saw the priests enrapt in religious ecstasy, their heads and faces hidden by their shawls, spreading their arms out over the congregation. As they invoked the essence of God, their hands were fixed in representations of the letter shin.

So it was that, when I searched my imagination for an appropriate gesture to represent the peace-loving Vulcans, the Kohanim's symbol of blessing came to mind.

Nimoy, *I Am Spock*, pp. 67-69

Rabbis 1925-1945

The 1930 *Boston City Directory* shows rabbis for each shul, but stopped afterwards. By 1930, the impact of the Depression as well as local Jewish population decline was evident. Instead of the thirteen rabbis listed in 1920, there are only two in 1930.

- Rabbi Friederman, who was still at Shaari Jerusalem in the North End was in his late 60s (he died in 1936). At this point, he no longer was affiliated with any of The Boston

Synagogue's predecessor shuls.[78]

- Morris Levin was the rabbi at Congregation Beth Jacob. He lived at 1 Russell Place, near the North Russell Street Shul. Contradicting this, however, a biography listing for Levin's daughter in *The Encyclopedia of Cleveland History* suggests that by 1918 (when she presumably graduated from high school), Levin had relocated to Cleveland to run the Community Hebrew Schools there.

    BRAVERMAN, LIBBIE LEVIN (20 Dec. 1900 - 10 Dec. 1990) was a teacher, educational consultant, and writer. Braverman was born in Boston, Massachusetts, to Rabbi Morris A. and Pauline Drucker Levin. She and her brothers, Sol and Harry, attended school in various locations. When her father became director of Community Hebrew Schools in Cleveland, she came to this city and graduated from Central High School..."
    The Encyclopedia of Cleveland History
    http://ech.case.edu/cgi/article.pl?id=BLL1

At North Russell Street, Rabbi Sharfman's tenure ended in 1923. The shul then hired Rabbi Jacob Shohet for 1927-1928. Shohet was

---

[78] Here is a poignant postscript on Friederman: Rabbi Yosef Goldman, upon immigrating to American in the early 50s, decided to become a Jewish bookseller (this became the basis for the Goldman Collection of American Jewish Books and Manuscripts in Flatbush, Brooklyn). As recounted by Goldman to Dr. Yitzchok Levine in *Hooked on American Jewish History*: ""I always liked old things… I ran an ad in the paper looking for old furniture. An old woman in Boston responded telling me that she did not have any furniture for sale, but that she did have bookcases to sell." Upon arriving at her home Yosef found that her bookcases were filled with many seforim. She told him that her husband, who had passed away, was the son of Rav Zalman Friederman, Z"L. …The son had inherited these seforim from his father. So, I not only bought the bookcases, but I also bought most of the books she had."

Yosef then realized that there was a market for such books. He began to run ads in newspapers saying that he was interested in buying old Jewish books. In the late 1960s there were a number of people, the children of rabbonim who had passed away, who had inherited seforim from their fathers. Many of them, sadly enough, had no interest in these seforim and were happy to sell them.

-- posted at http://personal.stevens.edu/~llevine/Hooked%20on%20American%20Jewish%20History_v4.pdf

64 years old,[79] somewhat mature for a new hire. He appears to have been selected based on political connections, given that he was related to Rabbi David M. Shohet of Dorchester's Temple Beth El. Not only were the two related directly, but David also married Jacob's daughter.

> **Mrs. David M. Shohet In Boston Hospital**
>
> Mrs. David M. Shohet, wife of Rabbi Shohet of Congregation Agudas Achim, is convalescing from two operations performed Wednesday, at Beth-Israel Hospital, Boston. She will be in the hospital for about two weeks more.
>
> Mrs. Shohet went to New England three weeks ago to visit her parents, the Rev. and Mrs. Jacob Shohet of Roxbury, Mass., when she was taken ill.

Yonkers Herald Statesman September 9, 1941

After Shohet in 1928, there is no record of any rabbis at North Russell Street. This is supported by Oscar Epstein, who became bar mitzvah there in the 1930s. Oscar said that in the 30s, the shul was lay-led with hired cantors for the High Holidays (more on Oscar later):

> The North Russell Street shul did not employ a salaried rabbi. The lay leadership ran the shul very effectively. However there was a shamus (sexton), who took care of the operations of the shul. There were people in the congregation from Eastern Europe who were very learned in Talmud, Mishna, reading the Torah, etc. They were very well qualified to ensure that the services were carried out in accordance with the Orthodox tradition.

Oscar Epstein oral history interview, February 2013

* * *

There was one additional rabbi in this period, 'hired' under unusual circumstances. In December 1938, Anshei Libavitz signed a contract

---

[79] Source: 1940 U.S. Census

to employ a rabbi (Vilem Schreiber) who appears to have been a refugee from Europe and probably Czechoslovakia.[80] Schreiber was to receive $1,500 per year for a two-year period; equivalent to $25,000 today – with the proviso that he obtain permanent U.S. residency:

> WHEREAS the said CONGREGATION ANSHEI LIBAVITZ is desirous of engaging the said RABBI VILEM SCHREIBER (LEIBER)[81] to occupy its pulpit and to render such services as are usually rendered by a Rabbi in an orthodox synagogue, and
>
> WHEREAS, the said RABBI VILEM SCHREIBER (LEIBER) is now a temporary resident of said Boston, but is endeavoring to become a permanent and legal resident of said Boston, and is desirous of accepting said pulpit…
>
> … That for and in consideration of the fulfillment of the agreements, promises and engagements of the said RABBI VILEM SCHREIBER (LEIBER), said CONGREGATION ANSHEI LIBAVITZ hereby engages said Rabbi to perform the work and professional services of an Orthodox Rabbi and hereby agrees to pay a salary of Fifteen Hundred ($1500.00) Dollars per annum for a period of two (2) years from the time of said RABBI VILEM SCHREIBER (LEIBER) is legally admitted in this country…

One suspects that the document's real purpose was to provide Rabbi Schreiber with papers allowing him to escape from the Nazis. This is based on: (a) the surprisingly formal nature of the contract; (b) the fact that it was done in English and not Yiddish, in an era when the Anshei Libavitz records were kept in Yiddish (for an example of a more typical Yiddish contract, see the North Russell cantorial contract in the next section); and (c) the fact that Rabbi Schreiber's English language signature looks more like the calligraphy of a clerk

---

[80] Vilem is a Czech variant of William. Presumably Rabbi Schreiber was desperately trying to escape Czechoslovakia after the Munich agreement was signed on September 29, 1938.

[81] Presumably, the Lieber name in parentheses refers to American relatives who were sponsoring Schreiber for permanent residency status.

than the handwriting of a European rabbi (there also is no accent mark on the 'e' in Vilém). In all likelihood, this document was meant to impress some State Department functionary rather being drafted for normal commercial purposes. Confirming this, Anshei Libavitz's cash ledger shows no payments to Rabbi Schreiber in 1940-1941.

One hopes that this apparently fraudulent contract allowed Schreiber to escape the Holocaust.

Descriptions of North Russell Street Shul 1925-1945

With the 1940 merger of Beth Hamedrash and Beth Jacob, North Russell became by far the largest shul in downtown Boston. It remained this way until urban renewal in 1958.

During this period, North Russell Street continued to be THE shul that hosted concerts by major cantors, large holiday parties and extravagant High Holiday services.

The following photograph shows the Ladies Auxiliary of the North Russell Street Shul, putting on a Purim Play in 1931. Unlike today's norms, where Hebrew School children perform the Purim play for adults, here, adult women were taking the opportunity to dress in costumes.

Ladies Auxiliary North Russell Street Shul Purim Play 1931

However the Ladies Auxiliary did much more than Purim parties. Oscar Epstein recalls that they ran a series of functions to raise money for the shul.[82]

> I know that the shul had a very devoted Ladies Auxiliary which would run functions on Sunday nights to raise money for the shul. They had somebody who performed as a one-man band and he would play klezmer music. Since this would go on until late in the evening, I remember that neighbors would yell that they were unable to fall asleep because of the loud music coming from the open windows of the shul's hall.
>
> Oscar Epstein oral history interview, February 2013

In addition to local musical talent, the shul's tradition of holding concerts with famous cantors (and young prodigies) continued:

> The North Russell Street Shul particularly is remembered by some for its guest cantors and its Jewish holiday parties. One of the many visiting cantors was Yossele Rosenblatt [died 1933].
>
> Michael A Ross, from Boston Walks *The Jewish Friendship Trail*, p41.

Yossele Rosenblatt

* * *

> Thirteen-year-old Shloimele youngest cantor in Boston, sang services last night at the North [Russell] Street Synagogue before a congregation of more than 600. He will sing at the same synagogue this morning ... and tomorrow at the 8 o'clock services.
>
> *Boston Globe*, August 1, 1931

---

[82] The Ladies Auxiliary used some of the proceeds in 1934 to buy a Torah for the shul, which is still used regularly today.

Aside from periodic concerts, having high quality cantors and choirs continued to be a major focus for the High Holidays. Oscar Epstein recalled that:

> Cantors were usually hired from New York. They had to come to Boston to perform in front of a committee appointed by the congregation. Usually three cantors would come and the one with the best voice was eventually hired for the High Holy Days. They all had to be able to perform with a local choir group. As you would walk by the shul on a hot summer evening, you could hear the beautiful, inspiring melodies from the cantor and his choir coming through the shul's open windows.
>
> Oscar Epstein oral history interview, February 2013

Here is a 1933 Yiddish-language contract between North Russell and a choir for Selikhot and the High Holidays. Abraham Rubin, conductor, alongside Sholom Leker, tenor and lead-singer, led the seven-person choir. The shul paid $400 to Rubin and Leker who made the financial arrangement with the other singers. This is equivalent to $7,064 in 2012 dollars, showing that the shul was prepared to spend large sums of money on major events like the High Holidays.

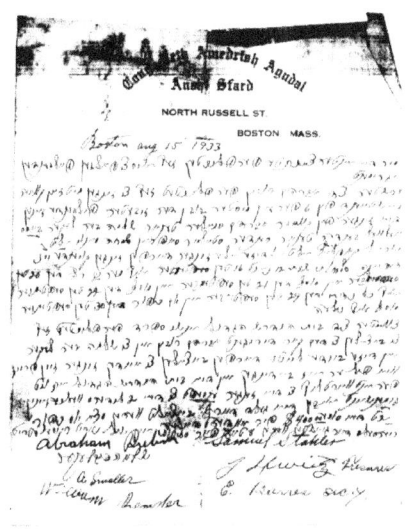

1933 High Holidays Cantorial Contract. Translation by David Fishman

To pay for this type of extravaganza, the shul sold seats. Here is a copy of a High Holiday ticket for North Russell Street for the year 1931. The $5.00 seat is equivalent to $76 today. So 80 tickets would pay for the aforementioned $400 choir. This was easily covered in a shul that could sell hundreds of seats.

In the 1940s, Leonard Nimoy recalls hearing that North Russell Street was able to engage a famous cantor named Pinchik from New York. He was prominent enough to have a recording contract with RCA. To promote Pintchik's High Holiday appearance at North Russell, there were posters on the streets with his picture. [Clips of Pierre Pintchik's singing can be found on YouTube.] People evidently said on the street, "Pintchik is coming! Pintchik is coming!" -- in a Jewish version of Paul Revere's "The British are coming!"

Pierre Pinchik, Cantor

From *The Last Tenement*, there is a photo of one High Holiday attendee (circa 1941):

"Mrs. Anne Victor carrying prayer books for High Holy Days as she is leaving the North Russell Street Synagogue, 1941"

The Last Tenement, p.12

At the same time, North Russell Street supported the needs of ordinary people in the middle of the Depression. A good example is Oscar Epstein, who was previously quoted in this chapter. Oscar, at age 89, is the oldest active employee of the Government of Massachusetts. He works as an engineer for the Department of Transportation's Highway Division and was the subject of a December 2012 *Boston Globe* profile.

As a child, Oscar lived at 18 North Russell in a $30 per month four-room rental apartment. His family spoke only Yiddish at home and his mother observed kashrut and Shabbat, although his father worked on Shabbat. He and his friends took off from school for Jewish holidays.

> Yiddish was the only language my parents and grandfather spoke at home. However they did understand English. When they spoke to us, I would sometimes answer in English. When I spoke to my grandfather, I would only use Yiddish. My mother was very observant with kashrut and kept the Sabbath. She would leave a stove burning all day from Friday evening through Saturday until the Sabbath was over. However, to support the family, my father did work on Saturday but he would never smoke on Saturday
>
> Both my brother and I would put on tefillin every day before we ate breakfast and went to school. But we were

really pressed for time because we were always afraid of being tardy for school. So we only did this for about two years.

Oscar became bar mitzvah at North Russell Street Shul in 1936. He used a private tutor, since the North Russell Street Shul did not have a Hebrew School. He delivered his bar mitzvah speech in Yiddish.

> Of course my bar mitzvah took place on Saturday morning. I made the blessings and read the entire Haftorah.
>
> As far as my bar mitzvah speech, I remember the opening line, which would read in Yiddish as follows: 'Liebe elteren un geschetzte versammlung' ['Dear Parents and Honored Assembly']. I remember that the speech was very short and was mostly about promising to live a Jewish life and do all that is expected of young Jewish boys. I know that the old ladies in the balcony were very impressed and smiled as I presented my bar mitzvah speech in the Yiddish language.

Oscar Epstein oral history interviews, February-March 2013

Oscar Epstein from *Boston Globe* article, December 29, 2012

A 'celebration' at the North Russell Street Shul at the time of Oscar's bar mitzvah, he noted, consisted of not much more than *nahit* (chickpeas), wine and a bit of cake – with, of course, glasses of schnapps!

> There were no gala parties for either of us. Just a small kiddush in the shul followed by a supper on Sunday night in our dining room.

Oscar Epstein oral history interviews, February-March 2013

Chapter 9

Developments in the West End 1945-1965

Demographics

The most important factor affecting the North Russell Street Shul in this period was the City of Boston's population decline. As seen in the following Boston Redevelopment Authority (BRA) chart, Boston reached a peak population of 801,444 in 1950. By 1980, its population would drop 30%, to 562,994. Even premier neighborhoods like Beacon Hill and Back Bay were declining, with Yankee Brahmins leaving for upper class suburbs like Wellesley and Beverly Farms. Working class neighborhoods like the West End were in worse shape.

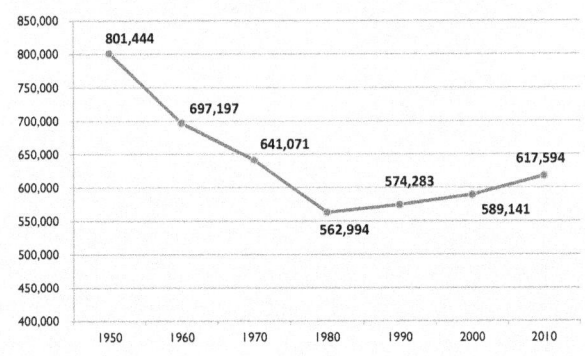

With respect to the West End specifically, Gans in *Urban Villagers* states that prior to the urban renewal evictions in 1958, only 7,000 people were living there. In *The Last Tenement,* Fisher and Hughes found that the population declined from 12,000 in 1950 to 7,500 by 1957.

If Jews still had the 12% population share estimated for 1945 in the previous chapter, this means that the Jewish population was down to 900 by 1957, from a peak of 40,000 in 1910.

The following photograph by Jules Aarons shows the kosher West End Meat Market circa 1947 to 1953,[83] at the tail end of the life of the old West End.

West End Kosher Meat Market. Jules Aaron

Another view of the decline of the Jewish West End is seen in this 1956 Charles Angoff description:

> Whenever I am in Boston I try to spend some time on Leverett Street, if at all possible. I used to roam that street as a young boy. It used to hold romance for me. It was filled with Yiddish bookstores, English bookstores, stores that sold religious articles such as prayer shawls and phylacteries; there was Schwartz Hall, where my father's lodge used to hold its installation of officers, an event that made me very happy, for ice cream and candy and popcorn used to be served to the young folk; and there was a second-hand

---

[83] "I began photographing in the West End, a vital neighborhood with kids and adults playing and living in the streets. At the time I photographed there, (1947-1953), the West End was an integrated area where people seemed to get along." Jules Aarons, *Into the Streets 1947-1976*

furniture store… Leverett Street is no more what it used to be. There are now only two or three bookshops, and they do so little business that they also have to sell "notions," which is the polite phrase for toys and candy and such patent medicines as aspirin and various brands of mouthwash. Schwartz Hall is still there, but it is now dilapidated, and the B'nai B'rith lodge doesn't meet there any more. I am told the Ancient Order of Hibernians now uses it for its headquarters.

Angoff, *Something About My Father*, p. 117

Synagogue Count 1945-1965

In this environment, the only solution for the remaining four shuls was merger.

- In 1960, Anshei Libavitz effectively merged into Beth Hamedrash Hagadol/Beth Jacob (with North Russell 'renting' the building and using the main chapel; more on this below).
- In 1958, Tifereth Israel (the Chambers Street shul) merged into the Vilna Shul.

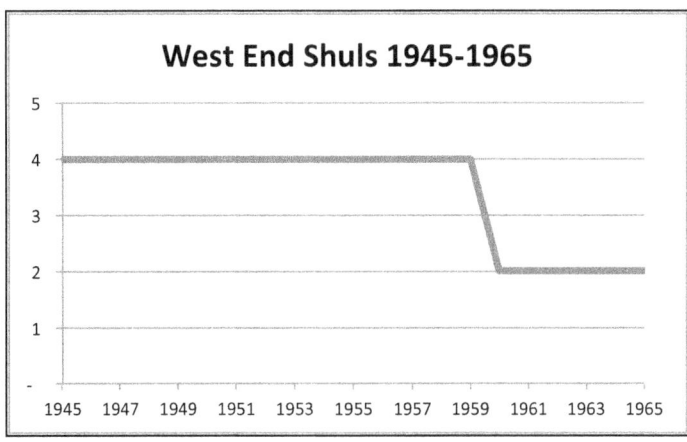

Clingan Spreadsheet and Boston Synagogue analysis

Anshei Libavitz

The following review of Anshei Libavitz in this era highlights the difficulties that even the surviving shuls had during this era.

Anshei Libavitz (the Joy Street Shul) always was much smaller than Beth Jacob or North Russell Street. As a result, it had to find low-cost talent for its High Holiday services. One colorful cantor used in the 1940s and 1950s was a local street person with substantial Yiddishkeit and a terrific voice – Al Tabashnick.

Nimoy remembers Tabashnick as an erratic gentleman who was troubled mentally and was always drinking alcohol. However he had a "glorious voice," was very observant and would frequently be singing in the street in Hebrew. A sympathetic man who owned a big liquor store near North Station would give him around $5 a week to pay for rent and living expenses. Then for the High Holidays, the Joy Street shul, which was a "very small congregation" that could not be as picky as other shuls, would hire Al as its cantor. Al would then go to the liquor store owner and use the money to pay off his debts. This went on for some years.

A similar Tabashnick recollection comes from Sammarco in his book *Boston's West End*: "Al Tabashnick was a well-known character who seemed to fit right into the West End. Though an obvious street person, he often was asked to cantor at religious holidays in the neighborhood temples, appearing in flowing robes and singing in a deep voice. The next day, he would be walking the streets and picking trash."

Sammarco, *Boston's West End;* photo by Jules Aaron

In the end, saving money on High Holiday cantors was not sufficient to sustain Anshei Libavitz – something that is seen by observing the shul's minute books for 1955-1964.[84] In late 1955, the shul had $5,200 of liquid assets (cash plus savings; equivalent to $40,000 today). By 1956, it appeared to be in liquidation mode, giving away Torahs to Israel, a new shul in Miami and a synagogue on Nantasket; as well as 25 prayer books to the Lebavitz Yeshiva.

> A motion was made by Brother M. Hootnick to give one Torah to Mr. Jacobs for the different services which he has rendered the congregation who in turn intends to donate it to Israel. Seconded by Brother M. Barr and unanimously approved.
> Libavitz minutes June 3, 1956

* * *

> A communication was received from the Nantasket synagogue headed by Brother P. Golov, requested a Torah for their local community center. This was generally discussed and a motion was made by Brother M. Barr to charge $50.00 for the Torah. An amendment was then offered suggesting $200.00 and still another amendment to give two Torahs for $200.00. This was unanimously passed.
> Libavitz minutes December 2, 1957

Much of the discussion on operations in 1956-57 instead focused on a costly renovation of the shul's cemetery:

> The cemetery committee discussed the rebuilding of the cemetery; such as the removal of the beds, and falling in of graves, which have been neglected over the years. This matter was generally discussed and will be acted on in the near future.
> Libavitz minutes August 4, 1957

* * *

> The cemetery committee reported that a contract had been made ... to regrade and eliminate all beds from the cemetery,

---

[84] The minute books are now held by the American Jewish Historical Society in Boston.

at a cost of $2,000. A motion to accept this contract was made... As the commitment had already been signed the schull is therefore obligated to go along and fulfill the terms of the contract, the body approved this motion.
Libavitz minutes November 3, 1957

* * *

The rebuilding of the cemetery was discussed and Brother Ricen questioned the cost of the rebuilding.
Libavitz minutes December 1, 1957

The cost of the cemetery project and the need for ceiling repairs helped to wipe out the shul's meager cash reserves. On January 5, 1958, the cash plus savings balance was $6,327.69. On January 13, 1959, someone added a comment (in pencil) that after $3,500 was paid out for a "permit" (apparently related to cemetery renovation costs), the balance would only be $1,961.56 ($1,361.56 excluding a non-liquid Israel bond). Matters got worse in 1958, when the shul needed to pay for a repair of the upstairs shul costing $2,235.00.

A communication was received from the Washington Construction Co. relative to repainting and redecorating the upstairs schull. In view of the fact that some members were in doubt as to the contract and in order to get a few more bids for the work a special meeting was called for on Aug 10, 1958.
Libavitz minutes August 5, 1958

* * *

... there were 2 contractors for the job and after the committee discussed the job with each of them a motion was made by Brother Barr to accept a contract with the Washington Construction Co. for $2235.00... Terms of payment are to be $700 to be paid after plastering and rear wall are finished $700 more to be paid when the job is concluded and final payment is to be made 60 days on completion of the entire job. The vote was unanimous to do the job complete.
Libavitz minutes August 10, 1958

As a result of impending cash insolvency, the shul began to look into sale and merger options. On June 1, 1958, "a Mr. Cassidy addressed the members regarding the sale of our synagogue and will mail us an offer by mail in the near future." In November 1958, after the BRA moved to seize the North Russell Street by eminent domain, there was hope that Anshei Libavitz would gain new members. However, time was running out. On November 30, 1958, the shul's cash balance was down to $1,038.13.

As a result, the shul considered different options. On February 1, 1959, "a communication was received from Hunneman & Co relative to the purchase of our schull." No decision was made.

On March 1, 1959 (with a cash balance of $340.86), a board member proposed a merger with the Vilna Shul. A committee of three members was authorized to negotiate by the next monthly meeting. In that meeting, held on April 5, 1959, "the Vilna schull committee reported that they had met with Mr. Kaufman [of Vilna] and could not come to any agreement and suggested that we drop the matter." Despite this, talks continued until on August 2, 1959, when the board secretary reported that "Mr. Kaufman of the Vilna schull wants $100.00 monthly." This ended the talks permanently.

As a result of its cash position, Anshei Libavitz fired its Torah layner (reader) and custodian.

By June 7, 1959, "a committee from the Lebavitz Yeshiva came with a request for our congregation to turn over to them our schull in the event that we should desire to sell it."

At this point, a group from the North Russell Street Shul approached Anshei Libavitz about working together. This is discussed in Chapter 10.

North Russell Street Shul

From an oral history interview conducted with David Wizansky, it appears that in the 1945-1959 time frame, North Russell Street Shul also had declined substantially and did not have sufficient funds for a cantor or rabbi. The Wizanskys[85] saw the neighborhood degrading and moved out in 1956.

> David Wizansky, a Brookline-based social worker, was born in Dorchester in 1938, the son of Max and Sarah (Artenstein) Wizansky, and became bar mitzvah at the North Russell Street Shul in 1951, eleven years after his family moved to a modern building in the West End, at 3 Blossom Court, and whose living room window abutted the Cambridge Street side of the shul. His father operated a kosher butcher shop with his grandfather. In a November 2012 oral history interview, he recalled his Hafetz Chaim Hebrew school (at the Chambers Street Shul) as well as the "eclectic" West End neighborhood with its different ethnic communities. His recollection of the North Russell Street Shul [in marked contrast with the Angoff description of an earlier age] was of a "very democratic" institution, with much membership "participation" from the floor and no formal cantor or hazzan. The Wizanskys, like other Jewish families at the time, became aware of significant social change in the West End and moved away from the neighborhood in 1956.
> Wizansky interview, November 29, 2012

Oscar Epstein has provided the following photos of the North Russell Street Shul that were taken around 1952,[86] long after he moved out of the neighborhood. From these, one makes the following observations:

- The "No Trespassing" sign in the upper right hand photo (put on top of a corroded older sign) suggests a neighborhood in

---

[85] In Wieder's book *The Early Jewish Community of Boston's North End*, 1962, there is the following vignette of the extended Wizansky family: "I started telling you about Henry Wyzansky. He was one of eight or nine brothers. One of his brothers had a butcher store in the South End when Henry came. In 1869 or 1870 he bought (or perhaps hired first) a house on 5 Stillman Street and opened downstairs a butcher store of his own. Many of the newcomers came to his house when they arrived. Many immigrants lived with him for a considerable period of time. They paid him three dollars a week for room and board. Most of them were not relatives."

[86] The car in one of the photos is a 1952 Chevy Belair.

decline. Oscar says that the gate was typically kept locked.

- The roof in the lower right photo appears warped and in need of replacement. In 1952, a building constructed in 1923 would be 29 years old.[87] The fence for the parking lot, which opened out onto Cambridge Street, has barbed wire on an angled support at the top. This is something that one expects to see in dangerous neighborhoods, not across the street from Beacon Hill.

Photos of North Russell Street Shul, 1952. Source: Oscar Epstein.

---

[87] Despite the photographic evidence, the McSweeeney 1959 study states that "both buildings were in good physical condition. There were no evidences of any structural deterioration to be found in a careful examination. The maintenance had been good; the plaster and painting had been kept up in good condition; the altar, the bim[a], and the decoration in the main temple auditorium were like new."

Finally, as a memento of this era, here is a hand-drawn Lifetime Certificate of Membership in the Ladies Auxiliary given to Bessie Rosenberg in 1951. On the Mortgage Redemption Plaque, Bessie was listed as Chairman of the Ladies Auxiliary, President of the Purim Club and mortgage redemption donor.[88] The Boston Synagogue honors Bessie as one of many people who devoted considerable time and energy to maintaining the shul (and note with fondness the misspelling of Auxiliery).

Bessie Rosenberg Life Membership Card, 1951

---

[88] Babette (Bessie) Rosenberg was born in Boston in 1884. She was married in 1905 at age 21 and had three children. She died at age 95 in Mamaroneck, NY. One of North Russell Street's Torahs was donated to the shul by the Rosenberg family.

Chapter 10

Urban Renewal and Survival

The Decision to Tear Down the West End

As seen in the Chapter 9 Boston Redevelopment Authority (BRA) population chart, Boston city population continued to decline until bottoming out in 1980.

In response, the Boston Planning Board (predecessor to the BRA) decided in 1950 to demolish the entire West End (which it called "An Obsolete Neighborhood"), replacing it with what would become Charles River Park. The project was managed by the Boston Housing Authority (BHA) until the BRA's formation in 1957.

In the plan, the two shuls in the redevelopment zone, North Russell Street and Chambers Street, were slated for demolition. However, this was not a foregone conclusion. For one thing, there was an eight-year period from initial plan until execution, which provided time for challenges. Secondly, geography favored North Russell. As seen in the 1950 Boston Planning Board map, the North Russell Street Shul was located at the edge of the development zone (shaded dark grey in the map), unlike St. Joseph's Roman Catholic Church, which was more centrally located. Chambers Street was in the center, so also was at greater risk.

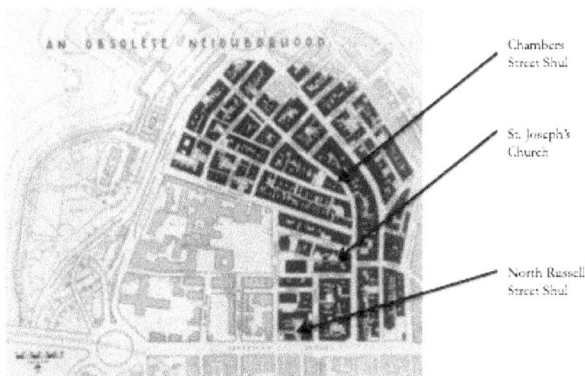

General Plan for Boston, 1950, map titled "An Obsolete Neighborhood," Boston Planning Board and Boston Synagogue analysis

On April 25, 1958, West End residents received notices from the city of Boston that it would take over the neighborhood, including houses of worship -- except for St. Joseph's, which was exempted, despite its location in the center of the zone. Among the residents were Max and Dora Nimoy, who still lived on Chambers Street and whose barbershop was on Leverett Street. Demolition occurred by 1960, in what is now generally considered a major error. From a Pulitzer Prize-winning *Boston Globe* column written 35 years later, in 1995:

> It was in the summer of 1960, 35 years ago, that the bulldozers of the city of Boston wiped out a living community on this site as brutally as if it had been bombed. That was the old West End. The narrow crowded streets simply disappeared. So did the residents. In their place arrived classier tenants, housed in the antiseptic high-rise apartments of a new development called Charles River Park. Slum clearance, they called this process. Urban renewal. Today the very words sound like groans from the Dark Ages.
>
> Charles Campbell, "Charles River Park at 35" in *Boston Globe* May 26, 1995; 1996 Pulitzer Prize Essay for Criticism

"Parking lot on what was... North Russell and Chambers Streets, 1961," *The Last Tenement* and Boston Synagogue analysis

Given that in the end, St. Joseph's survived and North Russell Street did not, an obvious question is how and why this occurred.

Catholic Versus Jewish Response

The answer appears to be the result of the very different stances that Catholic and Greater Boston Jewish communal leaders took regarding the West End.

The Catholic Church agreed with the BRA on the need for urban redevelopment as a means for revitalizing Boston. Its main concern, therefore, was to ensure that Catholic institutions remained in the zone post-redevelopment. Cardinal Cushing did this by arranging for his right-hand man, Monsignor Joseph Lally, to become an inaugural member of the BRA in 1957 and Chairman three years later. By doing this, Cushing was able to influence BRA decision-making from the inside. As described in *Catholics in the American Century: Recasting Narratives of U.S. History* (R. Scott Appleby, editor):

> [A] major commitment that [Cardinal] Cushing's Boston Catholic Church made that was crucial to launching the city's urban renewal was delegating his close adviser Monsignor Francis J. Lally to serve first as one of the original members and then, in 1960, as chairman of the Boston Redevelopment Authority (BRA), a new administrative entity created in 1957 as an independent public authority to deal exclusively with redevelopment, particularly federal urban-renewal funding. Lally had been Cushing's right-hand man in matters of civil rights and interfaith relations, and it was a progressive act to name him editor of the archdiocesan weekly newspaper, the *Pilot*, in 1952 and to promote him for the BRA post in 1957. When [urban planner Ed] Logue arrived in Boston from New Haven in the spring of 1960 at the invitation of recently elected Mayor Collins with big plans to revitalize the city, Lally's enthusiastic support made his appointment and his proposals possible. Without it, Logue would never have been approved by a divided BRA Board because the old-guard Irish pols were dead set against

Logue, an outsider, coming in to remake their city. Lally's – and through him the cardinal's – endorsement, communicated through leadership on the BRA, editorials in the *Pilot*, archdiocesan instructions to parish priests, and many other kinds of support, remained critical throughout Logue's tenure in Boston.

Catholics in the American Century: Recasting Narratives of U.S. History (R. Scott Appleby, editor), p. 56

Leveraging its inside player position, the Catholic Church, in addition to preserving St. Joseph's, obtained a $1.2 million BRA grant to develop the adjacent land parcel as the Regina Cleri home for retired priests.[89] The street in front of St. Francis was named Cardinal O'Connell Way.

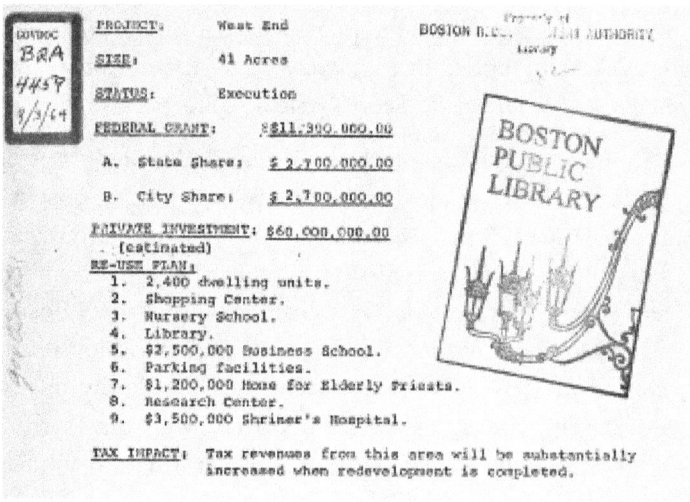

$1.2 Million BRA "Home for Elderly Priests" allocation September 3, 1964

---

[89] Source: 1964 Boston Redevelopment Authority document at Boston Public Library. Downloadable at:
http://ia600602.us.archive.org/30/items/westend9364bost/ westend9364bost.pdf
Accessed: March 2013

Regina Cleri Home in Charles River Park

In contrast to the Catholics' activist stance, there is no published record of Combined Jewish Philanthropies' predecessors, Associated Jewish Philanthropies (AJP) and Combined Jewish Appeal (CJA), seeking to help the local shuls.[90] This conclusion is based on a review of available secondary sources as well as two primary source autobiographies.[91] [Since AJP was the major operational group and CJA was more of a fundraising entity, AJP will be used henceforth in this chapter to refer to the Greater Boston Jewish community.]

As a result, the North Russell and Chambers Street Shuls were left with minimal political support.

Underlying Drivers: Jewish Communal Response

At issue is why AJP did not try to do more on behalf of the downtown shuls. One reason was a substantial difference in power. Catholics had much more influence than Jews in Boston generally, and the West End of the 1950s was majority Italian Catholic. However this alone does not explain the absence of Jewish communal efforts, particularly given the fact that one Jewish leader –

---

[90] Combined Jewish Philanthropies was formed by the merger of AJP and CJA in 1960.

[91] Referenced secondary sources include Gerald Gamm's book *Urban Exodus: Why the Jews Left Boston and the Catholics Stayed*; Gamm's article, "In Search of Suburbs: Boston's Jewish Districts, 1943-1994," in *Jews of Boston*; as well as an Internet search. The two autobiographies are Lewis H. Weinstein's *Masa: Odyssey of an American Jew* and *My Life At the Bar*.

Lewis Weinstein – also had substantial 'insider' power.

In the 1950s, Lewis H. Weinstein was one of the most important Jewish communal leaders in Greater Boston. He was president of the Combined Jewish Appeal in 1954 to 1957 and Campaign Chair for Associated Jewish Philanthropies in 1957. In addition, he was president of Hebrew College in the 1950s.

Professionally, Weinstein was an attorney and senior partner at Foley Hoag and Elliot. His area of expertise was housing, and his clients primarily were government housing agencies.[92] By the mid-1950s he was a leading exponent of using eminent domain for the purpose of urban renewal.[93] As an indication of his stature, Presidents Kennedy and Johnson appointed him to the Committee on Equal Opportunity in Housing.

In addition to his general expertise in eminent domain law, Weinstein had important professional relationships with the specific Boston government entities that were managing the West End redevelopment process. With respect to the Boston Housing Authority, which managed the West End urban redevelopment project until 1957, Weinstein served as BHA's General Counsel in the 1930s until he joined the U.S. Army in World War II. In the 1950s, Weinstein continued to represent the BHA as outside counsel.[94]

Weinstein also had close ties with the BRA, which was created in 1957 and absorbed the functions of the Boston Housing Authority. In 1958 he (successfully) recommended that incoming Boston Mayor Collins hire Ed Logue, New Haven's urban planner, as BRA director. Logue reciprocated by hiring Weinstein as outside Special Counsel in

---

[92] This is highlighted in his autobiography *My Life At The Bar* (1993).

[93] *My Life At the Bar*, p. 135.

[94] For example, Weinstein represented the BHA in 1955-1956 in an eminent domain case (Mcauliffe & Burke Company vs. Boston Housing Authority & Another, 334 Mass. 28, Dec. 27, 1955 - April 2, 1956, Suffolk County). In 1958, he defended John Carroll, Chairman of the Boston Housing Authority, in a case brought against him by Old Colony Construction Company (*My Life At The Bar*, p. 168).

With respect to BRA legal representation on West End matters, it appears that most of this work was done in-house. In the North Russell Street Shul lawsuit against the BRA, John C. Conley, in-house Counsel, represented the agency. Conley handled another West End damages case, Francis J. Ramacorti vs. Boston Redevelopment Authority, 341 Mass. 377.

1959. Weinstein then represented the BRA in eminent domain matters related to the creation of the Prudential and Government Centers.[95]

So Weinstein (and AJP) was in an excellent position to help North Russell and Chambers Street be exempted from takeover; or failing this, receive sufficient land and money to replace their facilities. This apparently was never attempted. Since Weinstein did not discuss the West End in his autobiographies, the explicit reason for inaction is unknown.[96]

Reading between the lines, however, it appears that a central driver behind this inactivity was the perception that the downtown Boston Jewish community was a lost cause that did not warrant expending political capital. Weinstein's belief that Jews needed to leave declining neighborhoods is seen in his role as President of Hebrew College, where he was responsible in 1951 for moving the College from Roxbury to Brookline on similar grounds. At that time, AJP staff challenged Weinstein and failed; by the time of the West End eminent domain taking in 1958, the staffers presumably fell into line:

> The location of [Hebrew] College was beginning to undergo population changes, with Jews moving out of Roxbury and Dorchester to Brighton, Brookline, Newton and other areas in the Boston suburbs, and with blacks moving in. The college had little in the way of general community acceptance....
>
> Property of the Gordon College of Theology and Missions in Brookline became available to us... We had an uphill battle getting the approval of the Boston Federation, the Associated Jewish Philanthropies (AJP), for the move from Roxbury. The staffs of the AJP and the Bureau of

---

[95] *My Life At the Bar*, pp. 139-145.

[96] Disclaimer: More research is needed to determine Weinstein's role vis-à-vis CJP's stance. To date, the Committee has uncovered no information that Weinstein participated in or affected any Jewish communal deliberations in the 1950s regarding North Russell Street Shul – or even that there were deliberations. A complete investigation would require review of the extensive archival materials for the key parties. The Archival/Historical Committee considered this to be beyond the scope of its mandate.

Jewish Education were unanimously opposed, because they claimed our move would pronounce doom on the Roxbury Jewish community and accelerate its demise. I countered with charts based on my studies for the National Jewish Community Relations Advisory Council (NJCRAC) which were published in a booklet titled *Changing Neighborhoods*. These studies showed in detail how a neighborhood, in five years, could change from predominantly white to considerably black and that the inevitable future was a completely or very heavily black area. My charts showed the specific area (including the Roxbury site of the Hebrew College) as it then existed, what its condition had been five years earlier and how it would look five years later, applying development standards I had helped establish at various other local areas through our national study. We agreed to maintain our Roxbury building with a reduced staff, so long as there was need for its use by residents of Roxbury and Dorchester. The AJP board voted approval of the new site. We closed our Roxbury school in a year…

Masa: Odyssey of an American Jew, pp. 204-205

This 'divestment-from-decaying-neighborhoods' thinking was supported by the Jewish community's demographic research. In 1967, CJP published *A Community Survey For Long Range Planning: A Study of the Jewish Population of Greater Boston*.[97] The results suggested that 'mid-Boston'[98] had a small and declining Jewish population of 16,500, 7.9 percent of total Greater Boston. The group was aging, had a low level of synagogue affiliation and there were no Jewish children – therefore it presumably was not worth saving:

> The 17,000 Jews living in Central Boston tend to live in the smallest households; almost one-third live in one-person households. There are virtually no Jewish children living in

---

[97] In 1960, AJP and CJA merged to form CJP. While CJP's 1967 study was published after the demolition of the West End, the findings arguably reflect views of downtown consistent with communal views held in the 1950s.

[98] Defined as Roxbury, Hyde Park, Roslindale, Back Bay, Downtown and Jamaica Plain.

this area. Most (79 percent) are renters... Almost one-third of the adults are over 65 – the higher rate in the metropolitan area.... a third of the adults are immigrants, one-fourth of the heads are blue collar workers, and the area has the second highest incidence of people who have not finished high school (47 percent)....

Perhaps the most marked characteristic of this group is their low level of participation. Synagogue membership is below average, as is synagogue attendance, despite the number of immigrants and Orthodox in the population here. With the exception of Cambridge-Lexington the rate of membership in Jewish organization is lower than anywhere else in Greater Boston...

CJP 1967 Survey, pp. 181-182

As a result, leaders like Weinstein were strong advocates of urban renewal, and included the West End in the list of needed redevelopments:

Twenty-six hundred years have elapsed since the prophet Zaphaniah decried the filth and decay of the city.[99] Today the goals of our Commonwealth as well as of the Nation include the eradication of slums which attack "the moral and physical fibre" of the nation's mankind and womankind, the development of "bright and orderly" homes and neighborhoods, efficient, attractive and productive. The Governor and state officials, as well as the President and leading diplomats, emphasize the long-range economic, social and political aims in urban renewal and its influence upon our reputation at home and abroad. Our courts have not interfered with these goals.

---

[99] Weinstein presumably is referring to the following passage: "Is this the gay city that dwelt secure, that thought in her heart, 'I am, and there is none but me'? Alas, she is become a waste, a lair of wild beasts! Everyone who passes by her hisses and gestures with his hand. A sullied, polluted, overbearing city!" (Zaphaniah 2:15-3:1; *JPS Tanakh*). A more complete reading of the Book of Zaphaniah suggests that this degradation was due not to the physical state of the city but the moral state of its inhabitants. Zaphaniah therefore was calling for moral renewal, not urban renewal.

* * *

There are now some 60 urban renewal projects at various stages of development in 27 municipalities throughout the Commonwealth. Examples of redevelopment under Chapter 121 are the high-rise apartment project, Charles River Park, in Boston's West End...

Louis H. Weinstein, "Urban Renewal in Massachusetts," in *Massachusetts Law Quarterly*, March, 1962, vol. 47:1, pp. 9-10, 22

One final contributor to AJP's passivity may have been a belief that involvement in local synagogue issues was outside its mandate. As noted in Gamm's *Urban Exodus* regarding later demographic issues in Roxbury,

> Jewish ... institutions were largely on their own through the middle 1960s. Not until 1967 did leaders of ... Boston's Jewish community begin to take coordinated and conscious action to assist residents and institutions in upper Roxbury and Dorchester. To be sure, the Associated Jewish Philanthropies ... had provided subsidies to Hebrew schools ... but these actions were ... entirely unrelated to the emerging crisis in Dorchester and Roxbury

Urban Exodus, pp. 258-9.

Synagogue Council: If AJP assumed a hands-off stance on local synagogue issues, what position did the Synagogue Council of Massachusetts's (SCM) take?

The answer appears to be that there was limited tangible involvement. The only available document is a February 1955 letter from SCM to the BHA using its previous organizational name, Associated Synagogues of Greater Boston (ASGB). In this letter, ASGB expressed interest in obtaining an option on a new shul site.[100] The letter is not explicitly linked to any North Russell or Chambers Street efforts, says nothing about requesting fair compensation for North Russell or Chambers and implicitly accepts the impending

---

[100] Boston Housing Authority, "Supporting Documentation To The Redevelopment Plan: West End Land Assembly And Redevelopment Plan," u. R. Mass. 2-3 (1955)

eminent domain as a *fait accompli*.

> ASSOCIATED SYNAGOGUES OF GREATER BOSTON
> 177 Tremont Street, Boston 11, Mass.
>
> February 8, 1955
>
> Mr. Herbert L. Bogen, Design Planner
> Boston Housing Authority
> 230 Congress Street
> Boston 10, Massachusetts
>
> Dear Mr. Bogen:
>
> In accordance with our recent telephone conversation, I am pleased to inform you that the Associated Synagogues of Greater Boston has given consideration to your letter of December 2, 1954.
>
> It is our judgment that we will be interested in taking an option on a synagogue building site, and shall be pleased to hear from you when your plans have received final approval.
>
> In accordance with your request, I am returning to you the West End Urban Redevelopment Study and Land Use Plan.
>
> Thanking you for your kindness, I am
>
> Sincerely yours,
>
> s/ Bernard Titlebaum
> Bernard Titlebaum
> Executive Director
>
> bt:vsc
> enclosures

Associated Synagogues Letter To BHA, February 1955

It is unclear if ASGB followed up the February 1955 letter with further actions. Alan Teperow's 2007 Synagogue Council history, *One Community, Many Branches*, says nothing on the subject of the West End; and Teperow has told the Committee that he is unaware of ASGB involvement.

On the other hand, Maurice Saval, who would lead the fight on behalf of North Russell Street (see Chapter 11), was a major contributor to ASGB (donating the Saval Chapel at its Tremont Street headquarters) and he served as president in the late 1960s and early 1970s. So ASGB presumably would have coordinated with Saval and North Russell Street. However the nature of any collaboration is unclear.

Three Congregations, Two Shuls

The result of BRA determination and the Jewish community's limited involvement was that by 1960, there were only two synagogue buildings left in the West End -- Anshei Libavitz and Anshei Vilna[101] -- both on the flat of Beacon Hill and therefore outside the BRA redevelopment area.

This set up a real-life version of musical chairs, with three marginal congregations (Vilna, Libavitz and North Russell) and two buildings in disrepair.

One potential combination – between Vilna and Libavitz – had already been discussed by the parties and rejected, in part because Vilna required that Libavitz contribute cash that it did not have. As a result, the real issue was which shul North Russell would partner with.

North Russell chose to work with Anshei Libavitz. Discussions began when, as recorded in the Libavitz board minutes for July 5, 1959, "Mr. Seltzer and a committee of four from the North Russell St. Schull petitioned us to consider renting our facilities to them as a separate unit. President Brother Sandler and J. Entin will try to work out a satisfactory arrangement and present it at the next meeting."

The continuing negotiations were mentioned in Libavitz board minutes for August 2 and December 6, 1959, with Libavitz President Sandler saying that he "is still trying to bring about a merger."

Finally on March 10, 1960, North Russell President Israel Alpert wrote a proposal letter to Anshei Libavitz, in which he laid out the idea of a 'space rental' (as opposed to a complete merger):

> Gentlemen:
>
> We appreciate your Congregation inviting us to hold our services in your Synagogue in Smith Court.
>
> We feel you would prefer that we outline the conditions.

---

[101] According to the Clingan spreadsheet, Tiffereth Israel, which had its Chambers Street building taken in 1958 as part of the West End urban renewal effort, merged into Vilna. However, by 1960 it appears to have disappeared as a factor in negotiations, since it is never mentioned in Anshei Libavitz records during its negotiations with Vilna or North Russell; or by Special Master Alan Dimond in his 1987 Vilna receivership report.

Our Ark which is presently on our first floor containing four Torahs with silver will be taken to your Synagogue, together with prayer books, Tefillin, Tallith, benches and such other personal property and such other personal property as may be useful in conducting services. Ownership of the above will remain at all times in our Congregation and used as we direct. An inventory list will be made out.

We understand there will be no charge. But we shall be pleased to donate one hundred dollars a year.

We also understand we shall be permitted to place a sign with the name of our Congregation on the outside of your Synagogue.

Any and all of the above Torahs, prayer books, Tefillin, Tallith, benches and other personal property will be promptly returned to us when requested by a vote of our Congregation.

We wish to thank you again and would appreciate you advising us as to acceptance of all of the above terms.

Obviously, Alpert's offer varied substantially from Libavitz's hope for a full merger. It appears that the board of North Russell Street hoped that it ultimately would be in a position to build its own new shul. It therefore crafted a 'rental' plan that avoided long-term entanglements with Anshei Libavitz. Presumably the North Russell board also was aware of Libavitz's financial problems and felt that it could cut a 'tough' deal.

This raises the question as to why Libavitz accepted the deal, since North Russell's $100 donation offer was woefully insufficient to cover repair bills and operating costs. However Libavitz could still hope that North Russell Street would make 'voluntary contributions' for repairs and expenses -- since once North Russell moved in, it would be in its interest to have a well-maintained building. While this was not spelled out in Alpert's letter, both sides apparently understood the need for additional contributions; and North Russell ultimately did pay for some expenses.[102] In addition, the Vilna option was worse, involving cash outlays. So Libavitz approved the deal on March 13, 1960.[103]

With respect to how this arrangement worked, it appears that North Russell rented the upstairs chapel, while Libavitz used the downstairs floor.[104]

News of the agreement was announced in a March 24, 1960 *Boston Globe* article, with the shul keeping the name "North Russell Street," even though it was physically moving to Joy Street. This dichotomy also is seen in the shul's 1962 High Holiday tickets, which used the North Russell Street Synagogue name with an 8 Smith Court address.

North Russell Street 1962 High Holiday Ticket (Using 8 Smith Court Address)

---

[102] North Russell became more willing to pay for expenses after it received a $311,000 award from the City of Boston in Massachusetts Superior Court on November 21, 1960 – giving it 100 times Libavitz's cash reserves. On March 5, 1961, President Sandler of Libavitz told his board "that the No. Russell St. schull group expect to get their money in the near future and would like to make some improvements in our building." As another example from the Libavitz board minutes for October 1, 1961, "Discussion on fixing of the toilets and general area, said to cost in the vicinity of $1000.00 and the North Russell St. group suggested that we have the work done, after which they can give us a donation to cover this work."

[103] A final agreement was signed on December 4, 1961 between Louis Sander, President of Congregation Anshei Libavitz and Hyman Slate, President of Congregation Beth Amedrish Agudal Beth Jacob.

[104] The Libavitz minutes refers to heated discussions about a $2,575 bid to "redecorate and rebuild the downstairs chapel" (January 5, 1964) – presumably for its own use. On June 7, 1964 "a general discussion relative to the repairs in the lower chapel… erupted into a general name-calling and concluded with no final action."

THURSDAY, MARCH 24, 1960

No. Russell St. Shul Notes Interim Move

The North Russell Street Synagogue of Boston, which held services since its inception in 1895 and which was taken by the Boston Redevelopment Authority, has moved its quarters to Joy Street Synagogue, also of Boston.

The Board of Directors of the North Russell Street Synagogue through Harris Altman, Hyman Slate and Harry Goldfarb, issued the following statement:

"The holding of services and the uninterrupted reading of the Torah are the firmest pillars of the Jewish religion. Despite the taking of our physical facilities by redevelopment authorities, our spiritual resources remain undiminished. We are pleased that we have so planned this period of transition and our religious activities, that with the cooperation of the Joy Street Synagogue, we shall continue our services.

"Ultimately and by a vote passed by the members of our congregation, we plan to build a new synagogue which we fervently hope will be in the best traditions of the North Russell Street Synagogue."

Over time, the extent of the collaboration expanded. By late 1962, North Russell agreed to pay half of repair costs. By 1963, the shuls were doing joint financial planning and splitting of donations. By 1964, North Russell was willing to pay most of the costs for a High Holiday rabbi from New York (*inter alia* suggesting that by then, the congregations held joint High Holiday services):

> President Brother Sandler stated that in the future a fund will be started between our congregation and the No. Russell St group which will pay all expenses for oil, lights, gas, etc., and all monies remaining will be split in half.
>
> Libavitz minutes September 9, 1962

* * *

President Brother Sandler reported that a meeting will be held Sunday Nov 11, 1962 by the N. Russell St group and that he will try to arrange a group meeting between them and ourselves in order to adjust monies which come into the schull in the form of donations.

Libavitz minutes November 4, 1962

*   *   *

A report by President Brother L. Sandler on the general income from both synagogues was generally discussed.

Libavitz minutes December 2, 1962

*   *   *

Brother Sandler reported that a shamus had been hired to serve both the N. Russell St group and ourselves. Also that we will pay $15.00 weekly towards his salary. This matter was generally discussed.

Libavitz minutes May 5, 1963

*   *   *

President Brother Sandler reported that the N. Russell St. group were desirous of having a Rabbi from NY for the High Holidays and have agreed to donate $425.00 towards this, our share to be no more than $75.00.

Libavitz minutes July 5, 1964

Finally, a March 10, 1968 letter from President Freedman of Anshei Libavitz to the North Russell Street Shul suggests that the two congregations would negotiate an agreement by which North Russell "will take over management of the synagogue" (source: The Boston Synagogue archives).

The collaboration between North Russell and Libavitz raises a question as to why North Russell instead did not collaborate with Vilna. The answer seems to be that Mendel Miller, the man who ran Vilna, was a strong-willed and controlling individual with whom North Russell could not (or did not want to) deal.

This is suggested by the already referenced difficulties that Libavitz had negotiating a merger with Vilna during the same period. It is reinforced by testimony during the 1980s Vilna dissolution proceedings that Mendel Miller discouraged anyone from becoming a member of his shul[105] or helping it to grow – so that considering a full merger would have been even more problematic:

> On March 11, 1986 David Glater of Boston... filed a ... motion to intervene. Mr. Glater alleged that he had been "affiliated with The Vilner Congregation" since approximately 1970, that he had "repeatedly expressed an interest in more active membership with the Congregation and in greater administrative involvement" but had been "repeatedly rebuffed"... Occasionally, during the 1970s, he told Mr. Miller that he would like to become "involved" in the Congregation. "Why?" Mr. Miller asked, adding, "Just come and bring your friends."
>
> * * *
>
> A second would-be intervenor... is Richard D. Wimberly of Brookline... Although not a member of the Congregation, Mr. Wimberly attended its services at various times in the 1970s, but not after 1979... In 1981, in a chance meeting with Mr. Miller, he made some suggestions for an educational program to increase attendance at the Congregation's services but Mr. Miller showed no interest. Since 1975, Mr. Wimberly has been a member of Charles River Park and since 1981 a vice-president of that congregation.
>
> Alan J. Dimond, Master; *Master's Draft Report* April 28, 1987, The Vilner Congregation vs. Attorney General of the Commonwealth, Massachusetts Supreme Judicial Court for Suffolk County No. 85-290

---

[105] While at first glance, discouraging membership seems counterproductive and even fatal, because ultimately a shul with no members cannot continue. However, since Vilna only had 3-4 members in the early 1970s (Source: *Vilna Master's Draft Report*, 1987), admitting new members soon would have resulted in their gaining majority control of valuable real estate and Torahs, potentially displacing Miller. So from a short-term perspective, Miller's anti-membership stance made sense.

Negotiating For a New Synagogue

Despite the arrangement with Anshei Libavitz, the North Russell Street congregants still hoped to have their own building. However, the BRA initially offered compensation of $60,000, then $70,000, not enough to build a new shul.

At this point, Morris Saval, a wealthy congregant from Back Bay intervened. As he later noted in a *Newsweek* article:

> "I hadn't been very active in the [North Russell Street] synagogue until my mother passed away," admits insurance executive Maurice Saval. But the shock of seeing the neighborhood shul obliterated prompted Saval and several other younger members of the congregation to do something about it. "I felt we were the caretakers of a precious jewel," says Saval. "I felt the Jews of the city would support the memories of their families."

"The Exodus," in *Newsweek*, March 13, 1972

With the help of others like Hyman Slate, the President, and one of a series of Slates with an association with the Shul,[106] Beth Hamedrash Hagadol Beth Jacob sued the BRA in Suffolk Superior Court for damages and negotiated for the purchase of a new building site.

On November 21, 1960, the court found that "as a result of the taking, this court does assess the total damages at $281,395 plus interest at 4% per annum from April 23, 1958 to November 21, 1960." The total award, including interest, was $311,407.01.

---

[106] Hyman Slate and his wife Rose died in a fire on September 20, 1971, on Rosh Hashanah after the first evening's service – which coincided with the official resumption of services at the new Charles River Park Synagogue building. The story sounds eerily like Moses not getting to the Promised Land, except that Hyman Slate at least was able to attend Erev Rosh Hashanah services at the new shul.

Slate Family Members With A Boston Synagogue Association
[Later: Jonathan Slate as Vice Chairman]

From: 1941 Mortgage Redemption Plaque	From: Boston Synagogue Memorial Board	
Mortgage Committee Mr. M. Slate [Morris][107]	Myer Slate	3-Oct-12
	Dora Slate	31-Jul-53
	Bessie Slate	10-Jul-55
Board of Directors Mr. M. Slate [Morris]	Morris Slate	10-Nov-64
	Rose Slate	20-Sep-71
	Hyman Slate	20-Sep-71
	Israel Slate	5-Aug-77
Mortgage Redemption Donors Mr. & Mrs. M. Slate Mr. & Mrs. B. Slate	Lisa S. Slate	11-Apr-94
	Cara Slate	29-Sep-00

The importance of this achievement is highlighted when compared to the outcome for Tiffereth Israel, whose building on Chambers Street also was taken by eminent domain. Unlike North Russell, Chambers Street did not sue the BRA. It is unclear what remediation money it received, but the amount presumably was minimal,[108] since it was not mentioned by the Vilna Special Master during the Vilna asset disposition proceedings as a factor in Vilna's economic viability or assets. Had North Russell not sued the city and won, it presumably would have disappeared as well.

While the court award provided the shul with money, it took a further decade to acquire a suitable plot of land in the Charles River Park redevelopment zone (suggesting that the BRA and/or the Charles River Park developer did not want to facilitate the building of a new shul). Finally, on or about June 8, 1970, the shul purchased the current building site (12,326 sq. ft.) at Amy Court off Martha Road. The price was $1.35 per square foot, for a total of $26,640.10.[109]

---

[107] Morris Slate was Hyman's older brother, who died in 1964.

[108] Since Chambers Street was not a predecessor of The Boston Synagogue, the Archival/Historical Committee did not research this issue.

[109] The current City of Boston assessed land value is $1,297,800.00.

To Build Or Not To Build

By 1960 the shul had most of the necessary money, and by 1970 had the land. It seems today as though once funds were received, a new building was inevitable. However, the records reflect continuing disagreement through the 1960s, as expressed by board member and lawyer Louis Katz.

In a November 26, 1965 memo, Katz pointed out that while the Massachusetts Superior Court's decision of November 11, 1960 awarded the shul $311,407.01, "we are not obliged by this decision to build a synagogue – we may or may not build as we wish. We can spend the money in any way authorized by our Charter and By-Laws..." Reading between the lines, Katz was suggesting that the shul board consider alternatives to a new building.

Katz followed this up on January 14, 1967 with a letter in which he raised serious concerns regarding whether there was a sufficiently large group of people that would support an Orthodox shul in downtown Boston.

> To my fellow members of the North Russell Street Synagogue:
>
> We are now confronted with a very serious problem: "SHOULD WE BUILD A NEW SHOOL?" Our problem is not, "Do we want a new Shool?" Because everyone wants a new Shool. But many of us want a new Shool only if we can be reasonably sure that we can maintain and support a new Shool.
>
> So first we should estimate the expenses of operating a new Shool. These expenses would include a Rabbi, a Shamis, a janitor, insurance, electric, oil, building maintenance, and various other expenses, a total of at least $22,500 a year. Now, secondly. let's see how we can get $22,500 a year to meet these expenses. For the size of our proposed Shool, we can comfortably accommodate 100 family-members, or we can even squeeze in 125 family-members, which means that we will need 300 seats. So if we can get 125 family-members, each will have to pay $180 a year to cover the $22,500 (125 x $180 = $22,500). Yes,

maybe we will get donations of a few thousand a year, and that will cut the dues to $160 a year. In this figure I have given the benefit of the doubt in every way, and we will still need 125 family-members at $160 per year. We cannot figure on any income from sale of seats for the holidays, because our 125 family-members will need 300 seats, which will be more than our capacity.

"But," some people say, "We will not need a full time Rabbi at first or maybe we will get a part-time Rabbi." But how many members will you get at $160 a year, if you do not have a full time Rabbi? When a member pays $160 a year, he will expect the full time services of a Rabbi, or he will not be a member, with a few rare exceptions.

Yes, many new Shools are being built in the suburbs by young couples who have young families. And who want a neighborhood Synagogue and a Hebrew School for their children. But they are either reform or conservative Shools, with rare exceptions. The neighborhood Shools have become a social institution as well as a religious one, and young couples with families are willing to build and support them in their neighborhood. But in our own West End we have no young Jewish couples with children. Not one Jewish mother wants to live in the West End or on Beacon Hill with her children; she wants to live in a suburb if she can only afford it. And even if there are a few couples who do live in the West End because they cannot afford to live in a suburb, then they cannot afford to pay $160 per year for membership, and even if they could, there are no more than five or six such couples. We need 125 members to maintain the Shool.

And remember, ours is an Orthodox congregation, not Reform or Conservative. Anybody that says we can change to a Conservative congregation cannot possibly mean it. Even if most of us wish to do so, it would take five to ten years of legal litigation to accomplish, maybe!

So my dear fellow members. I beg you to face up to the facts. I am not asking that every penny be figured in advance.

I am not asking that we be absolutely positive that we can succeed. I just want a reasonable assurance that we can support a new Synagogue. I just do not want to jump into this expensive project with a blindfold. So let's all get together and find the solution."

APPENDIX: WEST END PROSPECTIVE MEMBERS
OLDER RESIDENTS

I am told that there are many well-to-do older couples in the new West End Project who would join our Synagogue at $160 a year. But, if these people are actually Synagogue people, they have been members of other Synagogues before they moved into the West End, and they will retain their allegiance to the other Synagogue such as the Temple Israel, Temple Ohabei Shalom, Kehilleth Israel and others where they have been members for many years. These other Synagogues have powerful Brotherhoods with many facilities and adult programs. It would take at least 15 years for us to develop such programs, if we had the man-power. And we must realize that 90% of these people are not Orthodox and would not go to Orthodox services. "But" I am told "we can later change to a conservative Synagogue!" In such a case there older people will say, "First make the change, and then we will see. But we will not get involved in a long battle to overcome the Orthodox element in the Shool." So think it over carefully, my friends.

Louis Katz letter January 14, 1967

The last opposition to a new shul came at a special membership meeting on January 12, 1969, in which an unsigned letter of opposition dated December 24, 1968 was read. While the referenced letter has not been found in The Boston Synagogue archives, one suspects that its arguments were consistent with Katz's January 14, 1967 letter, and perhaps came from Katz himself (as a board member, he would have had access to the membership mailing list):

The recording secretary read the un-registered, unsigned letter which was sent out to all members concerning this meeting. The letter was dated December 24, 1968. Later in the meeting, the chair ruled that because it had been specified that the letter as stated in the previous meeting, had to be registered and signed to be valid, no official business concerning the building of the new synagogue could be conducted. That is, no vote could be taken that would or could be valid....

By request of Mr. Maurice Saval, Mr. Robinson addressed the membership. Mr. Robinson stated that the money which the synagogue had in its possession had been appropriated for the construction of a new synagogue, and that there really should be no discussion otherwise...

Floor discussion continued with other main points being that the money the synagogue has should be spent in better ways such as contributing it to other existing Jewish organizations where the money will be put to good use. It was brought out that the building of the synagogue in the core city would serve no good ends. The core city, as stated, is no longer a place for a Jewish House of worship inasmuch as there is no longer the populace to support such an institution in such a location.

As stated above, because of the 'illegality' of the letter mailed out to the membership, no vote could be taken the discussion.

Board Minutes January 12, 1969

The New Building

Plans for the new building now proceeded rapidly. The shul needed an additional $100,000 for architectural and construction costs, so in April 1970 Allan Robinson sent out a successful fundraising letter.

Fundraising Letter by Allan Robinson (April 1970)

Look Homeward, Landsmann!

Once upon a time you lived in the West End. Once upon a time the finest people on earth, your parents, literally scraped up every penny they could either to send you to 'Cheder', or to engage a 'Rebbi', so that you could acquire the first principles of the forms and practice of traditional Jewish Communal Worship and at least a rudimentary concept of those moralities which have enabled the Jews to survive through the millennia and have so enriched the temporal and spiritual values, statutes and canons of all the world.

Do you remember 'Shabbas'? Your 'Bar-Mitzvah?' The 'Yom Tovim,' The Solemn High Holidays? Especially the High Holidays? When these irreplaceable people, Mama and Papa, and their wonderful counterparts, 'Alayhem Hasholem', in awe and indescribable prayerfulness gathered their respective clean-scrubbed progeny by the hand and propelled them to the Beth Hamidrash to thank 'Him' for life and ask for its continuation. Remember, if you were a 'Litvak', you went to 'Shull'. If you were a 'Rooshasha', you went to 'Shill'! What the heck difference did it make? G-d was and is everywhere. In the West End the chances were you went to THE BIG ONE, the beloved North Russell St. Orthodox Synagogue, more formally called the 'Beth Hamidrash Hagodol Beth Jacob'. Hagodol, 'THE CHIEF', That's us.

Thus, I come to business. The Boston Redevelopment Authority, in its wisdom also once upon a time, took our beloved 'Shull-Shill'. The 'Joy Street' people took us in and gave us a roof over our head. They've been grand. But somehow it wasn't 'Home'. Boston Redevelopment Authority gave us a lot of money which has been carefully and scrupulously conserved. We plan to build a new synagogue with it. We promised to build, and build we shall! We owe it to you, ourselves, and the Boston Redevelopment Authority. Our word is our bond! We learned that from our early teachings, remember? We have enough to build. NO

MORTGAGES! However, we need a little more. About $100,000 for fixtures and maintenance. Will you join us? Interested? Nostalgic? I hope and pray so...

I'm here, Dear Landsmann with my little Pushky. Not so little, that it can't take rubles, as well as kopeckes.

Please, do let's hear, and thanks no end. Mama and Papa would approve, I'm sure. You could donate in their name. I'm sure you will 'KLEIB A BISSEL NACHAS' too.

A new synagogue was erected at the current 55 Martha Road location, with initial dedication at Purim 1971 and High Holiday services beginning in September 1971. The building of the new shul was the subject of a June 29, 1970 *Boston Globe* article.

Gone but not forgotten synagogue to rise like Phoenix in West End

By Leo Shapiro
Globe Staff

Once, it now seems like a long time ago, there was a big Jewish community in what was known as the West End. But it was bulldozed out of existence and its inhabitants were scattered into many adjoining communities.

But the nostalgia remained. When the building of the old North Russell Street Synagogue whose official name is Congregation Beth Hamidrash Hagodol Beth Jacob, was demolished, arrangements were made to reserve a tract of land on which to rebuild when the time was right.

That time has come and at this moment work is proceeding on the new structure. The foundations are in and construction of the superstructure has started.

Instead of being surrounded by tenement buildings crowding on one another, it will be in the middle of the plush, highrise Charles River Park complex.

And when it is completed, sometime in October, it is expected to bring back to the site of the old haunts many who lived in the West End as children as well as some of the older folks who retain fond memories of the area and a bygone era of close neighborhood association.

The three-year-old Boston architectural firm of Childs Bertman Tseckares Associates Inc. has designed the synagogue not only as a meeting and worshipping center for members of the Jewish faith who live, work and visit in the downtown area, but also as a memorial to the original West End Jewish community that was uprooted by the West End Urban Redevelopment project back in the late 1950s.

The building, whose cost is estimated at $350,000, will be on a gentle sloping site fronting on Amy Court. It has been conceived as "a piece of sculpture consisting of interlocking garden walls "of fluted tinted concrete block. Some of the walls will enclose landscaped areas.

"This concept," explain the architects, "is intended to relate the building to the parklike setting of the West End and also to provide the people living high in the surrounding buildings with a pleasing view of the roof of the synagogue in harmony with the landscape."

They further point out that a sequence of spaces of open sky, with a courtyard and "intimate entry" has been worked out to help put the worshiper into the proper mood.

The sanctuary itself will be topped by a slanted roof made of translucent plastic. This will be the first use of such material for this purpose in a public building in Boston, they said.

Hyman B. Slate is president of the congregation. Maurice H. Seval is chairman of the building committee and Allan Robinson is chairman of the building fund committee.

The new shul was called the Charles River Park Synagogue with a new logo, reflecting the shul's location in Charles River Park.[110]

---

[110] Interestingly, the transliteration of the old shul name had changed from Amedrish Agudal to Hamedrash Hagodol.

> *Charles River Park Synagogue*
> New Home Of
> Congregation Beth Hamidrash Hagodol Beth Jacob
> (North Russell Street Synagogue)
> Amy Court - Charles River Park - Boston, Mass. 02114

Once North Russell moved from 8 Smith Court, Anshei Libavitz, which depended on North Russell's support for survival, sold its building to the African-American community (who intended to restore it to its original design as the African Meeting House).

Meanwhile, attendance at the Vilna Shul declined substantially. It ceased operating as a 52-week shul by the early 70s, with Mendel Miller being the only member for some time before the building closed in 1985:

> Until the mid-1970s the [Vilna] Congregation held religious services each day, on festivals and on the high holidays (the New Year and the Day of Atonement). Attendance then began to decline, causing reductions in daily and festival services. Rabbis and cantors served part-time.... Membership in the Congregation, at least since 1964, never exceeded twelve men. Because of attrition by death or resignation... the number of members dwindled in the early 1970s to not more than three or four, including Mr. Miller and his brother Nathan. Soon they were left as the only members, and when his brother died in 1985, Mr. Miller became the sole member. At no time was there recruitment or enrollment of new members.
>
> Alan J. Dimond *Master's Draft Report*, The Vilner Congregation vs. Attorney General of the Commonwealth, April 28. 1987

By 1971, the Charles River Park Synagogue was the only functioning shul in the West End, North End and Beacon Hill; perhaps the only major US city with such a small Jewish downtown presence.

Chapter 11

The Maurice Saval Era 1971-1989

The history of the Charles River Park/Boston Synagogue at the 55 Martha Road location spans three eras:

- The **Maurice Saval/Charles River Park era** (starting with the inauguration of the new building in 1971, and continuing through Saval's death in February 1989).
- The **Post-Saval era** (1989-1999), when a succession of shul presidents struggled to keep The Boston Synagogue alive without the financial support that Saval provided when he was alive.
- The **Recent era** (1999 to the present), when The Boston Synagogue took fundamental moves to adapt to the increasingly diverse needs of the Jews in downtown, and restored the shul to financial stability.

This chapter covers the Maurice Saval era. Chapter 12 covers the post-Saval era, while Chapter 13 discusses the recent era.

Maurice Saval: Background

Maurice Saval Memorial Plaque At The Boston Synagogue

Maurice H. Saval was an eighth-grade dropout who established six insurance companies and became wealthy. He lived in the Back Bay and was a member of the North Russell Street Shul when the BRA seized the property by eminent domain. He led the negotiations with the BRA that resulted in the construction of a new shul.

Aside from his North Russell Street/Charles River Park Synagogue activities, Saval was president of Maimonides School, where he developed a close relationship with Rabbi Joseph Soloveitchik (a.k.a.

"The Rav"), the founder of Maimonides and *rosh yeshiva*[111] at Yeshiva University. Saval became one of the Rav's major funders. A building at Maimonides is named "the Saval Campus"[112] and "in 1983, through an endowment by Maurice H. Saval, RIETS' [rabbinical ordination] Program [at Yeshiva University] was renamed the Rabbi Joseph B. Soloveitchik Center of Rabbinic Studies."[113]

As a result of these ties, Charles River Park Synagogue was informally affiliated with a national Jewish movement for the first time in its history – the Rav's form of Modern Orthodoxy. This would include such things as:

- Enlisting the Rav's son's help in obtaining an 'authentic' set of tablets of the Ten Commandments for the shul's ark.
- Hiring ritual directors/rabbis based on recommendations from the Rav (or his son-in-law, Isidore Twersky at Harvard)
- Resisting attempts by congregants to move from 'Orthodox' to 'Conservative'

Dedication of a Sefer Torah at Maimonides, 1979: Maurice Saval with Rav Joseph Soloveitchik.[114] *The Rav: The World of Rabbi Joseph B. Soloveitchik*, Volume 2, by Aaron Rakeffet-Rothkoff, Joseph Epstein

---

[111] Head of yeshiva; dean of rabbinical school.

[112] The gymnasium at the Saval Campus is named for Saval's friend Judge John Fox, a retired judge of the Norfolk Probate Court and before that, a Boston Municipal Court judge. Fox succeeded Saval as The Boston Synagogue's Chairman.

[113] Source: http://yu.edu/riets/about/ mission-history/rav/

[114] One of The Boston Synagogue's Torahs was donated by Israel Bonds in honor of Maurice Saval. The finials say "To Maurice H. Saval… from Maimonides School 1979."

Modernist Synagogue Design

Saval spent considerable time considering what the new synagogue should look like. In The Boston Synagogue's archives, there is a file with floor layouts for historical European shuls such as Regensburg and Worms as well as American synagogues. The end design clearly was neither casual nor directed solely by the architect.

Despite being in his late 60s, Saval presided over a modern design from a three-year-old architectural firm, breaking away from a natural tendency to recreate the old North Russell Street building. The design ended up winning a prestigious US Housing and Urban Development architectural award.

Charles River Park Synagogue, original architect's drawing

As noted in the following Charles River Park Synagogue descriptive document, the architect took care to create a building that was in harmony with the Charles River Park environment and created an appropriate space for meditation/prayer:

Harmonizing With Environment

The architects conceived of the building as a piece of sculpture consisting of interlocking garden walls positioned and shaped according to the movement of pedestrians. Some of these fluted concrete block walls enclose landscaped areas. This concept is intended to relate the building to the park-like setting of the West End and also to provide the people living high in the surrounding buildings with a pleasing view of the roof of the Synagogue in harmony with the landscape.

Scaling Down the Environment

Doors and windows are treated as abstract slots between the walls so as to prevent a correlation with surrounding high-rise buildings. As the architects explained, if the scale-giving elements such as doors and windows were the same sizes or shapes as those of the huge apartments, the tiny mass of the Synagogue would seem toy-like in comparison.

The designers further explained how a sequence of spaces was deliberately planned including the open sky, middle size courtyard, and intimate entry, to help the participant change his pace from that of noisy city routing to one of inner thought and worship. This "scaling down" is accomplished also through a series of transitional events – changes in level, screens of trees, changes in direction, changes in light quality, etc. The climax of this movement occurs in the sanctuary, which is bathed in diffuse natural light provided by a translucent plastic roof.

Undated Charles River Park Synagogue document

The result was a break with traditional shul architecture.[115] As Allan Robinson said (apologetically) in his April 1970 fund-raising letter,

> Please take a good look at the sketch of our projected edifice. They say it'll take the prize for design. **You'll see we've gone a bit 'Mod'. Do you mind?** [Emphasis added] It'll be a great place for a Library, Historical Society, Youth Activities, Engagement and other parties, Weddings, Banquets, Bnai Mitzvah, and all sorts of Communal life. Modern catering and entertainment facilities, of course!

Reactions to the new design were mixed. While the essay author in *Jews of Boston* appeared to be less than complimentary regarding The Boston Synagogue's 'inward facing' design, Charles Campbell, who won a Pulitzer Prize for his 35th anniversary critique of Charles River

---

[115] In The Boston Synagogue files is a memo from Saval dated Aug. 31, 1970 saying that an inactive shul in Chelsea had offered to donate a "beautifully hand carved and decorated" ark – presumably of the Sam Katz era. Obviously, the offer was never accepted.

Park, loved it:

> The Boston Synagogue of 1974, the designated heir to the West End synagogues destroyed by urban renewal, is the very picture of 'safe space.' [It is a] walled, windowless shelter… lit within by skylights. The synagogue was no longer aspiring to be a 'light unto the nations,' but rather, a place of interior illumination and spiritual sanctuary for Jews.
>
> David Kaufman, "Temples in the American Athens: A History of the Synagogues of Boston," in *Jews of Boston* p. 211.

* * *

> Only two things relieve the general disorder [of Charles River Park], and they're both interiors. One is a synagogue, designed by architects Childs, Bertman, Tseckares and built in 1970, an architectural gem where a mysterious golden light falls into the interior as if coming directly from God…
>
> Charles Campbell, "Charles River Park at 35;" in *Boston Globe* May 26, 1995; 1996 Pulitzer Prize-Winning Essay for Criticism

The Boston Synagogue today: Interior

Tablets of the Law

To decorate the new building, Saval spent considerable time thinking about the design for the tablets of the Ten Commandments, which are mounted above the minimalist ark design.

Tablets of the Law, seen as part of the overall ark and close-up

Designing and procuring the tablets took considerable time. As a result, the ark's top went undecorated for almost two-and-a-half years before the tablets were installed in August 1973.

The tablets were commissioned in Israel with the help of Rabbi Dr. Haim Soloveitchik, the son of Rav Joseph Soloveitchik.[116] At the time Haim was working in Israel as a professor at Hebrew University;

---

[116] The close relationship between Saval and Haim's father, Rav Joseph Soloveitchik, is seen in this interchange in the letters going back and forth on the tablet:

12/15/72 From Saval: "P.S. Your Father sat next to me at the head table at the Maimonides Donors Dinner last Sunday. He is in good form – in fact a number of people came over to me afterwards and pleasantly commented on the fact that your Father seemed to be enjoying himself immensely. We had an Israeli pop singer supported by an accordionist-saxophonist and a drummer, who were excellent. Your Father was keeping time with his hand on the table – it was really cute."

1/18/73 from Saval: " I saw your Father last Saturday night at the Shiur. He was in fine form, as I had a few words with him afterwards and he was almost gay. I also saw Atarah [Haim's sister, who married Isidore Twersky] the earlier part of the week as part of a committee at a meeting and she too seemed well."

2/22/73 from Haim: "Thanks for the report on my father – he writes so little its good to hear how he is."

Saval used his status as a major Maimonides donor to solicit Haim's help.

There was an involved process for deciding on the design. Saval wanted to use 'authentic' stone from Sinai, which Israel controlled in 1972. Haim responded, "Sinai is out. The stone is too hard to be quarried by ordinary drilling equipment. People have tried and broken drills. So other stone will have to be used." In the end, Galilee stone was used.[117]

Haim Soloveitchik

There also was learned discussion by Haim on color and shape, showing how important both Haim and Saval considered the tablets:

> **Color –** Midrash has it that the tablets looked like white fire on black fire, i.e. white letters on black background. Black stone is found in Sinai and its equivalent is in Jerusalem. But other colors could be used – .
>
> **Shape –**
> is out. First appears in Christian illustration in 13th century France. Jewish tradition is rectangular, but nothing in Jewish tradition that the two tablets linked, i.e., could equally be separate. As matter of fact in Sid[d]ur illustration of 14th century they appear as two separate blocks.
>
> Decision up to you or leave to discretion [of] the team here.

---

[117] The use of Israeli stone may have been influenced by Maimonides' commissioning a foundation stone from Israel for the dedication of its new Brookline building in 1962.

> **Script** – no one can say with certainty shape of letters in Moses time. I opt for oldest known Hebrew inscription from the first commonwealth times to 750 B.C.

Saval responded in favor of white letters on black detached rectangular stones:

> I opt for black, simply because I think that the contrast of the black against the reddish walnut wood would be more effective than the reddish stone against the wood.
>
> Two separate rectangular tablets I would think would be appropriate especially as you comment that the total of the two would weigh about 150 lbs.

There was also discussion of the impracticality of carving the entire text of the Ten Commandments. Saval agreed to include the first few characters only.

In the archives, there is a description of the final tablets by Haim Soloveitchik, prior to shipping them to Boston:

> The tablets were inscribed on three sides in accordance with the Palestinian Talmud, Tractate Megillah, which reports that the original tablets were inscribed on all four sides. I opted to forego the back as no one would see them.
>
> The stone is from Galilee, the cutting or inscribing done in Jerusalem.
>
> The shape is square by Talmudic tradition and the script patterned after the Shiloah inscription 8th century B.C.E.

To ship the tablets to Boston, Saval arranged for passage on the *Queen Elizabeth II* under the care of Sholom Cohen, the ritual director of the shul, who served as *machgiah* (Kosher certifier) on the cruise:

> The Queen Elizabeth II is making a trip to Israel and will be at Ashdad, April 21-23 – Haifa, April 24-May 3rd, and Sholom Cohen (you may remember him – he is a Maimonides graduate) who works for us in the Boston office, is going along as the Masgiach so I have pressed him into service. If the tablets were delivered to him on board the ship – presumably at Haifa during the period April 24 to May 2nd, just to be safe, he would guide them back to Boston. Several advantages of course. First: the shipping

charge is eliminated; second: time in transit would be minimized; third: presumably possibility of damage also reduced.

This also works in wonderfully well because I think the schedule is for the Elizabeth II to be back here about the 20th May, and with decent luck and co-ordination of services by the contractor we could have the tablets installed for Shavuot, Wednesday the 6th June. This of course would be a most appropriate day.

Saval to Haim January 18, 1973

The tablets arrived in Boston from New York in June 1973, on the first day of Shavuot in the middle of services. Saval considered this particularly appropriate since Shavuot commemorates the giving of the Torah to the Jewish people. Previously, the goal was for the stones to be delivered in time for Passover:

> [The tablets] came and arrived on the first day of Shavuot! I was not at our Synagogue that day – I was out of the country – but I am told it was pretty dramatic. It was just as they finished reading the Torah when the express man came in with the announcement that he had a package to deliver and needed some help for it was too heavy for him to handle.

Saval to Haim, 6/21/73

Each stone unexpectedly was 4 inches thick and 150 pounds, as the stonecutters were concerned about breakage with anything thinner. Saval decided to saw them in half to reduce the weight (this was done successfully). As he told Haim:

> Had you seen [the stones] before they left Israel? On the assumption that you did not let me tell you – each stone is about 16" square by approximately 4" wide and each one weighs about 150 lbs. The weight and the width made it impractical for us to position them above the Oren. I had the "brilliant" inspiration of sawing them in half, width-wise, thus making it feasible for us to mount two of the tablets that had been inscribed, in our Synagogue. We will have the

Ten Commandments cut into the face of the remaining tablets which I shall present to another Synagogue.

Saval to Haim, 6/21/73

The tablets cost $1,500, donated by Saval. Unlike the practice of typical shul donors who insist on acknowledgement plaques for everything, there was no plaque mounted by the tablets saying that they were donated by Saval.

Proposed New Cornerstone

Saval also enlisted Soloveitchik family help in crafting appropriate text for the new building's planned cornerstone. Apparently Saval sent to Rabbi Dr. Isidore Twersky[118] the following two initial drafts:

> This stone preserved from the Old North Russell Street Synagogue is a symbol of the everlasting continuity of Judaism.
>
> * * *
>
> This stone preserved from the Old North Russell Street Synagogue symbolizes the heritage of Torah from generation to generation.

Twersky responded with a note on Harvard University stationery, in which he suggested the following improved alternatives:

> Dear Mr. Saval,
>
> I tried to preserve your initial formulation, which was very precise and expressive. The Hebrew inscription means: "This building shall be witness and this monument shall be witness that God's Torah shall not depart from the children of Israel forever"
>
> As an alternate, it occurs to me, you might consider the following verse: Isaiah 59:21. ["And this shall be My covenant with them, said the Lord; My spirit which is upon you, and the words which I have placed in your mouth, shall not be absent from your mouth, nor from the mouth of your

---

[118] Twersky was Rav Joseph Soloveitchik's son-in-law. He was Professor of Jewish Literature and Philosophy at Harvard.

children, nor from the mouth of your children's children, said the Lord, from now on, for all time" (source: *JPS Tanakh*).]

If I can be of help, please call.

Warmest regards, Yitzhak Twersky

For unknown reasons, the new cornerstone was never commissioned, and the shul simply re-installed the 1940 North Russell cornerstone (shown previously).

Saval's Shul Management 1971-1989

Saval ran the Charles River Park Synagogue as a benevolent dictatorship,[119] paying for many of the shul's expenses over the nineteen-year period between 1971 and his death in February 1989. Membership dues were minimal and it has been said that his insurance company secretary handled shul administrative operations. In a memo from an unnamed shul Treasurer to his successor:

> The ability to authorize expenses has not been explicitly stated. However, the following can be a guide.
>
> There are a group of expenses that are paid because we all tacitly agree that we have to have the goods. Utilities, electricity, steam, and telephone, are such. We don't have a figure that we budget for, though usually last year's figures are the standard that we use. You should find our what these figures are. If current expenses are too big then you should raise questions I will refer to this level for authorization as level one.
>
> Level two authorization is when Mr. Saval himself <u>has</u> told you that he has authorized a payment. Areas where he will do so include fees to the Rabbi and religious direction.
>
> Level three authorization is an expense that an officer needs to fulfill his or her office.
>
> Level four authorization is for others who administer a program or project. Mr. Saval will tell you who they are.

---

[119] Saval was Chairman of the Board; the presidents included Michael Rosenberg, Frank Shapiro, Arthur Cohen and Allan Green.

This meant that Saval made most of the important decisions on how the synagogue would function, along a number of dimensions.

Ritual

While not Shomer Shabbat, Saval felt a strong affiliation with Orthodox ritual. As a result, the Charles River Park Synagogue maintained Orthodox Jewish ritual practice (e.g., all prayers in Hebrew, only males included in minyans and as prayer leaders).

Despite this, in an accommodation to the non-Orthodox demographics of the local community, Saval devised an "ecumenical" seating arrangement, in which: (a) the front sanctuary area would be reserved for men, with a separate side alcove for women; but (b) the rear of the building ("the social hall"), which had a separate flat roof, would be used for mixed-sex seating.[120] In practice, most congregants would sit in the mixed seating area.

> At the time of the building of the synagogue, Mr. Maurice H. Saval started to enunciate the concept of an ecumenical Jewish synagogue, one in which all Jews could be comfortable. Within this idea, our synagogue has a traditional core with the traditional service and separate seating for men and women. Separate from that core is the mixed section where people who don't want to separate or be in the separate seating can choose to sit. English translations are woven into the service depending on the need. And the siddurim have translations. This format created a warm and unthreatening environment and allowed our synagogue to grow.
>
> Harris Altman, Charles River Park Synagogue History Fact Sheet, undated

---

[120] 'Urban legend' says that Saval persuaded Rav Joseph Soloveitchik to approve this seating arrangement on the basis that the rear mixed seating area was a separate building with a separate roof. One wonders if this is true (perhaps Soloveitchik was persuaded to talk in generalities about the boundaries of a building being defined based on the contiguity of a single roof, without explicitly blessing Saval's mixed-seating compromise), but it appears to have been believed by synagogue members. For example, in a 1989 memo to the Boston Landmarks Commission, Jules Levine (Board Member) says "the structure is unique in that it is two separate buildings which are joined – one has separate seating for men and women, the other has optional mixed seating."

This arrangement, and what it suggested about the shul's affiliation, was controversial. As stated in the March 14, 1971 Board minutes (around the time that the new building was dedicated), "there was a great deal of discussion as to whether the congregation will remain Orthodox or not. Mr. Saval and Mr. Mindick pointed out that the charter calls for an Orthodox Synagogue. There was no resolution to this problem."

Interior of The Boston Synagogue showing the Sanctuary cathedral ceiling (top left) for men-only seating. Flat white roof in rear designates 'social hall' mixed seating.

Interior of The Boston Synagogue showing women's section in rear of photograph behind vaulted arches. Note lack of a high 'Kosher' mechitza.

The dispute did not go away. In late 1971, Ralph Gordon, of the Board's By-Laws Committee, drafted revised bylaws stating that "the purpose of this Congregation shall be the maintenance of a place of worship according to the (a) Orthodox (b) Conservative Hebrew rite, and for Jewish education and for such other kindred and incidental matters as my be fitting to said worship and purpose." In response, Allan Robinson crossed out the word "Conservative" and initialed the page. Saval then sent a letter to Gordon saying that the shul's incorporation papers explicitly referred to the shul's purpose being "the maintenance of a place of worship according to the Orthodox Hebrew Rite..," so that this change "is not permitted." To accommodate Gordon, Saval was willing to consider "Orthodox Hebrew Rite as currently (or modernly) interpreted and practiced." This change was never implemented.

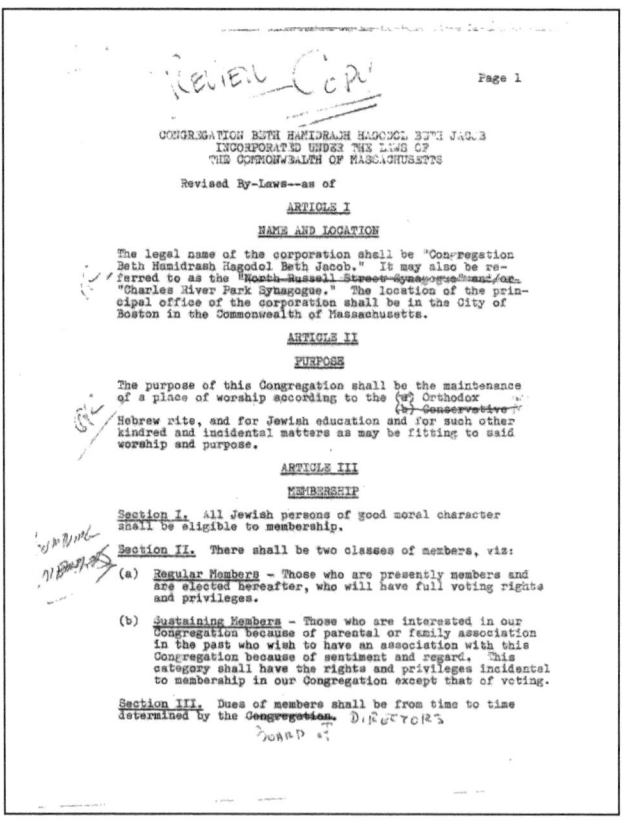

Draft Revised Bylaws with 'Conservative' Crossed Out, 1971

A similar pro-Orthodox view was expressed in a February 14, 1972 letter from board member Harris Altman to Maurice Saval:

> It takes little imagination to realize that since the turn of the century many generations of dedicated, devoted Orthodox Jew entered this sanctuary to pray to their God. How many names, unknown to us now, must be inscribed in the Heavenly Scroll of Honor for their sacrifice, their loyalty, their constant concern not only to their religious duties but to the upkeep and maintenance of the North Russell Street Synagogue. How many people of modest means still gave of their material substance, we shall never know. But that they gave, we do know. And beyond this, and even more importantly, they gave of themselves. The fact that in 1958 the North Russell Street Synagogue stood free of mortgage and of debt was silent but eloquent testimony of the enormous faith and work of these people.
>
> Now, in Charles River Park stands a new beautiful House of Worship - an outward manifestation of the inner faith and allegiance of countless Orthodox Jews of the North Russell Street Synagogue.
>
> If there is any we need - it is to try to regain the faith of these Loyal Pioneers to whom we owe so much.
>
> Altman to Saval, February 14, 1972

Two days later, at the February 20, 1972 membership meeting, there was a more complete discussion of the issue, with President Shapiro beginning the meeting and Saval making it clear that there would be no change:

> President Shapiro asked for a frank expression of views on the mater of changing over from an Orthodox congregation to a Conservative congregation. He said that was a topic of considerable interest and was the subject of discussion amongst some of our members during the past few months particularly. He made it clear that the purpose of this discussion was not to take any positive action at this time but to get the feeling of the membership.
>
> Dr. Joel Cooper expressed the view that he was strongly

for maintaining the Synagogue in its present form; that the congregation had made it possible for all members of the Jewish faith to be accommodated as we were using the Birnbaum Prayer Book;[121] we had arranged for separate seating in a portion of the Synagogue for those who were observers of Orthodox practices; and have mixed seating in another portion of the Synagogue so that those who were of the Conservative or Reform group could do so; and in every way we had made it possible for members of the three principal groups within Judaism to be at ease. He expressed the very strong convictions that there was an obligation on our part to carry on in the traditional manner, that there was no good purpose or need to change over from our present type of Jewish religious organization.

Messrs. Mike Rosenbaum, Arnie Cohen, Harry Kaminsky, Ed Kaminsky and Judge Fox spoke, each one affirming different facets of Dr. Cooper's theme.

Messrs. Harry Perlmuter, Sumner Edelstein and Ir[a] Lucas expressed the view that unless we converted to Conservatism we would not progress. They said essentially that the fact we were labeled "Orthodox" deterred prospective members from joining. Mr. Lucas particularly noted that five members had joined because they thought the congregation was going to convert and that they would probably withdraw if this did not happen. Comment was also made that some of the new members may feel that they had been misled because future affiliation was misrepresented to them. Some of the criticism was that we were not modern enough, not enough English was spoken in the services and that the services were too long.

Mr. Saval spoke in favor of maintaining our present form. He said that everything had been done to make all members

---

[121] The Birnbaum prayer book, first published in 1949 and used in Orthodox as well as Conservative shuls, was known for its use of a uniform Hebrew type face and more modern English translations. Here, Dr. Cooper is asserting that the availability of a good English translation but an Orthodox service would suffice for non-Orthodox Jews.

of the Jewish faith "comfortable" and "at home" and that we had met every reasonable suggestion that had been advanced by members. He said that in his opinion it appeared that the real problem was one of semantics; that the word "Orthodox" conjured up visions of old-fashioned narrow minded attitudes from which our Synagogue certainly did not suffer, as has already been proven, and that it was a matter simply of getting people to come in and see how we functioned to convince them that we were a new concept – a "Synagogue for all Jews" – best labeled "Liberal Traditional." He suggested that we use this term in response to any question as to what kind of a Synagogue we were

He further made the statement that in his opinion, just as we had faithfully performed the trust obligation to preserve the assets of the congregation, we also had a more sacred obligation to preserve the spiritual trust of maintaining our Synagogue in accordance with the traditions of our forebears.

Membership Meeting Minutes, February 20, 1972

Indeed, some members wanted to become *more* Orthodox. A draft letter from board member Richard Wimberley to Saval (unclear if it was sent) suggested a mechitza that would separate the mixed seating from the men's area. He also proposed increasing the women's mechitza height:

> On the matter of the mahitza, I don't think that it is entirely correct to say that changing the mahitza is impossible. Raised or stepped floor mahitzas exist only at our shul, Young Israel of Brookline, and the Old Vilna Schul. The mahitza is at the same floor level as the men's davening area at the Boston Rebbe's the Talner's Kedima Moshe Torah, Chabad House, Hai Odam, BU Hillel Orthodox minyan, and many other shuls I have been to. Separators, constructed of wood and fabric, are set up, permanently or temporarily at an appropriate place. There are several configurations that could be set up at our schul. We could expand the present one out into the men's section (where I usually sit). Or the present mixed section could

have a waist high wall going along the separation line of the sanctuary and the social hall.

Draft memo by Richard D. Wimberley to Maurice Saval, undated

This tension would continue in the post-Saval period, with attempts to put plants or a railing in front of the women's section to act as a more 'kosher' mechitza.

Increasingly, however, opinion would shift in favor of egalitarian services. The shul would face a classic problem, in which a number of the regular shul goers wanted things to stay as they were, while the people who wanted change came to the shul rarely or not at all. Making a radical change would threaten the short term, while not making changes would threaten the long term.

A visual illustration of the conflict facing the congregation is a 1974 photo of a shaharit service. There are only nine men pictured (ten are needed for a minyan), so that attendance was at the margin needed for conducting an official service. The number of seats reserved for men-only seating is small, suggesting that not many men wanted to sit there. With the exception of the person in front, all of the men are older. Finally, many of the men are not wearing tefillin and/or are wearing short shawl tallits rather than large 'Orthodox' tallits.

Charles River Park Shaharit Service, 1974. *Pictorial Living Coloroto Magazine*, August 4, 1974

The overall impression from this photo is of a small group of aging men who were not completely Orthodox themselves but who insisted that the old ways be continued. This would raise as key issues (a) how the shul could recruit younger observant Jews to replace the aging core membership, and (b) what the shul would do if it failed to recruit these younger Jews.

Rabbinical Support

During the initial period after the dedication of the Charles River Park shul in 1971, the shul employed a ritual director rather than a rabbi, with rabbinical support for the High Holidays. From an undated document *(Charles River Park Synagogue History Fact Sheet)*, "In the Fall and Winter of 1974... Shalom N. Cohen[122] was the religious director and Earl Lefkowitz was the cantor, and gave classes on the weekly Torah portion."[123]

From: Charles River Park Press Release 1972

Youth Carries On With Orthodox Traditions

Religious Director Shalom Cohen graduated from Maimonides School, Brookline in 1964 and received the Arthur Ellison Prize for excellence in Chumash (Bible). Following a year's attendance at Yeshiva University and Rabbi Isaac Elchonon Theological Seminary in New York, he returned to Boston, continuing his studies at Boston University's College of Business Administration. He received a Bachelor of Science Degree in Business Administration in 1968. In addition to religious teaching in the Dorchester-Mattapan Districts. Cohen has served on the staff of the Associated Synagogues' Kashruth Commission. In December 1971 he was appointed Religious Director of the Charles River Park Synagogue.

Cantor Earl Lefkovitz ... comes from a family of

---

[122] Shalom Cohen was a Maimonides 1964 graduate. Source: January 18, 1973 letter from Saval to Haim Soloveitchik and Internet search.

[123] David Fishman remembers Sholom driving up to shul in a motorcycle and leather jacket for weekday and Sunday shaharit services, showing a distinctively different look from the largely older men who were there.

distinguished Cantorial artists from whom he acquired personal instruction. A native of Cleveland, Ohio, he is currently a Press Officer with the Combined Jewish Philanthropies of Greater Boston, and has authored and edited numerous articles in Jewish Publications

Surprisingly for a shul with a mixed seating section, Rabbi Ira Korff (the future Grand Rabbi of Zvhill-Mezhbizh) conducted High Holiday services in the 1970s, and perhaps other services as well:[124]

A. [Alpert] We had Rabbi Korff in the '70s.

Q. As I understand it, Rabbi Korff came on high holidays. Apart from his coming occasionally on high holidays, have you ever had what you would call a year-round rabbi..?

Mr. Saval: Rabbi Korff

Mr. Baker: Rabbi Korff was your year-round - -

Mr. Saval: Yes, I think.

Q. What period of time do you think Rabbi Korff was there?

A. Early '70s.

Q. For how long? Two or three years?

Mr. Saval: No. A couple of years, at the most.

* * *

From: Charles River Park Press Release 1972

Charles River Park Synagogue (the North Russell Street Shul) at Leverett Circle, next to Whittier Place, Boston, one of the oldest active Orthodox Synagogues in Metropolitan Boston announces that High Holiday Services ushering in the year 5733 will be conducted by a group of young traditionalists, led by Rabbi Doctor Ira A. Korff, Cantor Earl Lefkowitz and Religious Director Shalom N. Cohen. Rabbi Dr. Korff graduated from the Hebrew College of Boston with a B.J.E. and received his B.A. from Columbia University, he furthered his studies at the Berlin Rabbinical

---

[124] Source: 1987 deposition of Israel Alpert and Maurice Saval on the Vilna Shul receivership matter:

Academy and the Kretz Israel Rabbinical Academy, where he received Smicha (Ordination). The degree Juris Doctor was conferred on him at Brooklyn Law School.

Starting in 1980, Saval hired Rabbi Allan Nadler as part-time rabbi for three years, through 1983. The apparent reason was that after nine years of ritual directors and cantors, the shul was not gaining sufficient traction and Saval decided that an investment in a rabbi might make the shul self-sustainable (see retrospective discussion on the next page).

At the time, Nadler was 25 years old and studying for a Ph.D. with Isadore Twersky at Harvard. One presumes that Nadler's hiring was due to the Soloveitchik and Twersky relationship. In short, Saval recruited someone young but with high upside.

Allan Nadler circa 1980

In September 1982, Nadler left on what was meant to be a one-year sabbatical to be the rabbi of Shaar Hashomayim in Montreal (Nadler was born in Montreal and had received rabbinical ordination there).

As a substitute, Nadler recommended David Fishman, a Harvard Ph.D. classmate also studying with Twersky. Although not a rabbi, David had an undergraduate degree from Yeshiva University and was Orthodox, and so was an acceptable substitute.

After the year was up, and it became clear that Nadler was not coming back (except for some High Holidays), Saval extended Fishman's employment without a specific title but effectively as part-time ritual director. This continued through 1988,[125] at which point David left Boston to join the faculty at Jewish Theological Seminary in New York City, where he is now Professor of Modern Jewish History.

---

[125] Fishman received his Ph.D. in Jewish Studies in 1985, and then worked as an assistant professor of Jewish History at Brandeis.

When asked why Saval did not replace Nadler with another rabbi, Fishman commented that the set of acceptable Orthodox candidates was small, since: (a) the job was part-time, (b) Saval appeared to want a smart young person, and (c) Saval had a preference for people studying with Twersky. In addition, the congregants at Charles River Park became comfortable with Fishman after his first year, so there was no impetus for change.

On the other hand, a 1987 Charles River Park document (written while Saval was still alive) suggested a financial consideration. Saval and his board believed that having a rabbi added substantial value for new prospective members (which is why he hired Nadler earlier in the decade). However the shul could not afford it, and Saval apparently was unwilling to contribute the necessary funds:

> Should the Charles River Park Synagogue receive substantial new monies, the board of directors has indicated that the first priority to ensure the longevity and viability of the congregation is to hire a full-time, permanent rabbi.
>
> Earlier this decade, the synagogue managed to hire a young rabbi [Nadler] on a full-time basis due to the generosity of a congregant [Saval], who agreed to underwrite the experiment. For a two-year period, the congregation saw a sharp increase in activity, with new and younger congregants attracted by the energy and creativity of the young man, who was also completing his doctoral studies at Harvard's School for Judaic Studies. The rabbi introduced a vigorous program of recruitment of members, adult education courses, social activities, and all the attendant amenities expected of an involved and concerned rabbi. He made shiva calls, visited the ill, wrote a newsletter -- and generally conveyed a sense of community and spiritual leadership.
>
> There was a discernible impact on the synagogue's finances because of the rabbi's presence: membership began to increase; and contributions became larger and more frequent. This was a gradual process that became more apparent towards the end of the rabbi's second year of tenure…

The two-year experience taught the synagogue's elders that a rabbi is essential to build membership and broaden participation. The city-dwelling Jew of today needs the sophistication and skill of a trained rabbi to spark and sustain his interest in synagogue membership. The board has determined to retain a permanent rabbi as soon as fiscally possible.

The cost of adding a rabbi's salary to the budget, together with a small "rabbi's discretionary fund," and other expenses relevant to retaining him, is estimated at $55,000 a year.

To replace Fishman, Saval in September 1988 took a low-budget route and hired Noah Feldman, a Maimonides graduate who had just started college at Harvard to read Torah and conduct shaharit (morning) services at the shul on Mondays and Thursdays. Rabbi Soloveitchik presumably recommended him. Feldman ended up graduating first in his class at Harvard, became a Rhodes Scholar, and is now a Professor at Harvard Law School, where he is a leading international law expert.

Noah Feldman

During this period, the shul also enjoyed the expert Torah reading of longstanding member Mark Schonfeld, an intellectual property litigator who lived in Back Bay and worked downtown.

In sum, Saval knew that a growing shul needed rabbinical presence, but he backed away from funding it.

Services

Due to declining attendance, the Shul no longer had minchah and maariv services except on holidays. It only held shaharit services on Sunday, Monday and Thursday mornings, as well as on Shabbat and holidays.

David Fishman recounted this amusing anecdote about one morning when they needed a tenth man for a minyan. To get to ten, one old timer (Izzy Alpert) went outside and said "a minyan, a minyan." He actually was able to get someone, but it quickly seemed that the new person did not know anything about the service. So they asked him if he was Jewish. He said, "No, I'm Armenian. I thought you were asking for an Armenian." Apparently in Alpert's thick Boston/Yiddish accent there practically was no difference between the pronunciation for 'a minyan' and 'ah-meenian.'

Hebrew School

Saval, although childless, felt strongly about the need for Jewish education, hence his support of Maimonides and Solomon Schechter. However he believed that Jewish children should go to Jewish day schools. As a result, the Charles River Park Synagogue had no Hebrew School and the building design made no provision for classrooms. In turn, families with young children who were not going to day schools perceived the Synagogue as unwelcoming and unaccommodating.

Programming

Programming was an area of focus during the Saval years. Here is a recollection by Harris Altman on shul activities in the early 1970s:

> In 1973, I came in contact with the synagogue through a chicken supper and later a Sisterhood sponsored dance. Eddy Ship made sure that I had plenty of chicken to eat.
>
> Harris Altman, Charles River Park Synagogue History Fact Sheet

During the Nadler years, there was emphasis on generating interesting lecture programs and activities like volleyball:

> The Program Committee chairman Bob Fox reported that the Committee was planning activities on a regular basis. The first program for Sunday May 27 7:30 PM would be on the subject of the Falasha Jews of Ethiopia. Mr. Moshe Nipress will personally sponsor this event. A barbeque is planned for the last Sunday in June the 24th. A September program on the history of the West End Jewry is planned. Publicity will include the *Jewish Advocate*, *Hagigah* and the *Boston Globe*. June's program may include volleyball. The purpose of the program committee is to attract many different types of Jews, and it looks like its programs will do that.
>
> Board minutes, May 6, 1984

There also were Friday night dinners and "a continuous Shabos presence of hospitality" for visitors.[126]

Shul Size

From a deposition statement by Israel Alpert, the claimed membership in 1987 was 120 and that the shul attracted up to 297 people (building capacity) on Yom Kippur.[127] Other references speak to membership being stable at 100.

In an undated *Jewish Advocate* article circa 1970, it was stated that membership prior to the completion of the new building was "approximately 100 families, 25 of which reside on Beacon Hill and in the Back Bay, the rest in Brighton, Brookline, Newton and other sections of Metropolitan Boston."[128]

In a reversal of the historical exodus from downtown to neighborhoods like Dorchester, some of the new members at Charles River Park (CRP) joined when their shuls in Dorchester closed. This included Arthur Cohen, who eventually became president of CRP in 1987-88; his good friend Irving Krutter, a regular attendee at services for many years who recently died at age 90;[129] Muriel Kantor and her son David -- all of whom joined CRP after Mishkan Israel in Dorchester shut down in 1977.

Despite the upbeat membership numbers, a contact list for a March 10, 1986 meeting regarding the asset disposition of the Vilna Shul only included 82 families or individuals. Husbands and wives were listed separately rather than as member units, and the list may have included non-members. Thus the actual number of member units was probably in the 60-80 range,[130] which was substantially smaller than the shul size for North Russell Street circa 1940 as

---

[126] Source: *History of the Synagogue*, undated.

[127] Source: *Israel Alpert Vilna Shul deposition* March 1987.

[128] Joseph G. Weisberg, "Rebirth of a Shul," in the *Jewish Advocate* approximately 1970.

[129] Krutter used to say that his participation consisted of getting together with his friends to tell jokes, interrupted by occasional aliyahs.

[130] The difference may be due to the Shul's practice of giving old West Enders 'lifetime memberships,' even if they never in fact were active members.

indicated by the number of names on the mortgage redemption plaque.

[Author's Note: when asked about membership size in the 80s, Fishman commented that membership was not a concept that was taken seriously or even relevant, since everyone knew that Saval was paying the bills whenever cash was short.]

Perhaps to boost membership numbers, dues were low compared to those for large suburban synagogues. For 1971-72, dues were $100 per year with no apparent difference for families versus singles; $25 per High Holiday seats for members/$35 for non-members. As there were minimal membership fees for 'grandfathered' old West End residents, this did not come close to covering expenses.

For Shabbat, Israel Alpert said that the shul would get 20 to 25 attendees.[131] Fishman says it was more like 15 to 25, with close calls for weekday morning minyans.

Thus the shul could tout reasonable membership numbers, but the reality of these totals was questionable, and the low dues meant that these members could not sustain a shul without Saval's help.

Situation at the end of the Saval Era 1989

During this period, the demographics of an aging population steadily eroded the shul population base, without being replaced by younger Jews, whether observant[132] or non-Orthodox.

As a result, the only thing keeping the shul viable was the willingness of one wealthy person to pay the bills. Even that willingness had limits, since Saval was unwilling to self-fund the cost of a full-time rabbi.

---

[131] Source: Israel Alpert deposition March 1987

[132] While there was a substantial and growing Orthodox population in Greater Boston, most of these people (outside of college students) lived in Brookline, Newton and Sharon. There were almost no young Orthodox Jews in downtown.

Postscript

One amusing yet poignant reflection of the 'old-timer' nature and experiences of some of the congregants in this era is a July 1974 letter from Ryfuel Abosch, a Holocaust survivor, to Shalom Cohen, the shul's ritual director, regarding Abosch's commissioning of four plaques for the shul's memorial board. As the last person left alive in his family, he asked in broken English/Yiddish[133] that the shul make a plaque in his memory once he died:[134]

> I Autorize You to make 4 Plates in The Memory of Main Father Mother and Sister... The nechst Payment 33%... Ist possible near plates to put a small electro Bulb and to Lighten wen the Yourzeit is... For Main Mother Kraincia Bodnar Bas Ruben Born 1877 Day I do not Remember Diet All Kidush HAshem From the Natzis Inwasion Armies on The First Day Cholomoid Sukkot October 6 1941. [Sister] Rebeka Abosch... Diet on the same Day First Day Cholomoid Sukkot October 6 from The Wild Hord of the Natzis Inwasion Armys.... Raphael of Ryfuel Abosch ben Aron... Open Line when i Will pas Away to the Officers from The Synagogue. Then I have Nobody Left and no Children the Synagouge must this Due.

Ryfuel Abosch letter to The Boston Synagogue

Abosch Family Yahrzeit Plaques at The Boston Synagogue Memorial Board

---

[133] Misspellings, miscapitalizations and grammatical errors have been left unchanged.

[134] The Synagogue's Memorial Wall has plaques for Abosch's father, mother and sister and for Ralph (Ryfuel) Abosch. Ryfuel's plaque does not have a date, although research indicates that he died on November 1, 1987.

Chapter 12

The Post-Saval Era 1989-1999

The unsustainability of the Saval era became apparent when Maurice Saval died in February 1989 at the age of 88, following injuries sustained in a car accident and a subsequent stroke.

One month before he died, the board met to discuss the potentially dire financial implications:

> Mr. Alpert raised for discussion the financial situation of the synagogue. Although the final figures for 1988 were not yet tabulated, it appears that the shortfall in the operating budget of the synagogue will be approximately $30,000, and this is likely to represent an annual figure. Mr. Nipress raised for discussion the possibility of obtaining support from the Combined Jewish Philanthropies, either for programmatic events or for general support. Mr. Cohen raised the possibility of mailing an additional appeal letter. Dr. Stearns suggested contacting potential benefactors directly rather than by a mass mailing. Mr. Saltzman raised for discussion an increase in dues to improve the financial base of the synagogue. Mr. Alpert raised the possibility of contacting potential new members from the local voting lists. Mr. Nipress felt that the hiring of a full-time rabbi would help rejuvenate the synagogue. If initial salary support were provided by benefactors, the presence of a rabbi might result in an increase in new members that would cover his salary on a long-term basis. Professor Levine noted that it is hard to hire a rabbi in the face of an uncertain financial base and a shortfall in operating expenses.
>
> Mr. Alpert announced he will convene a meeting with Judge Fox and Allan Green to consider strategies for raising funds and discussing long-term needs regarding a rabbi.

January 2, 1989 board minutes

While Saval left substantial bequests to other charities (including a $5 million trust fund established for Maimonides – invested with Bernie Madoff), The Boston Synagogue only received a $250,000 legacy – which was not enough to permit hiring a rabbi. Per the September 18, 1989 board meeting minutes:

> Mr. Alpert distributed a statement of CRP's income and expenses of January through August 1989. There followed a discussion of the financial feasibility of having a full-time rabbi, even with Mr. Saval's endowment of $250,000, of which 10% maximum is allotted each year to CRPS for expenses.
>
> Board Minutes, September 18, 1989

The result was that the Synagogue was left in difficult financial circumstances. Under the leadership of Judge Fox as Chairman and a variety of lay leaders as presidents including Allan Green, Jules Levine, Robert Stern and Larry Baras, the Synagogue tried to figure out how to survive.

One early move was changing the shul's name. Thinking that the name 'Charles River Park' might have been hurting its ability to attract people from other neighborhoods, the shul board adopted the name 'The Boston Synagogue' -- reflecting its desire to attract members from a wider downtown geography. The change was made at Purim 1990.

The Boston Synagogue
at Charles River Park
55 Martha Road, Boston, MA 02114

A year later, despite limited available funds, the shul decided to invest part of its Saval/Fox endowment by hiring a new rabbi, Marc Gopin, on a part-time basis starting on October 1, 1991. The apparent hope was that a dynamic rabbi would enable the shul to gain sufficient traction with new members to cover the shul's annual operating cost in future years.

Gopin came from the same promising young rabbi mode as Nadler and was a 1975 graduate of Maimonides. Just as in a previous era, Rabbi Friederman was proud of receiving ordination from Rabbi Yitzchak Elchanan Spektor, Marc Gopin states in his Wikipedia biography that in 1983, he "was ordained as a rabbi at Yeshiva University, where he was a student of Rabbi Joseph Soloveitchik." He was also studying for a Ph.D. in religious ethics from Brandeis.[135]

Unfortunately, due to a combination of dwindling funds and conflicts with congregants regarding the Israeli-Palestinian issue, Gopin left after a year. After this the Synagogue gave up on the rabbi experiment and relied on a lay chazzan (Norman Rosenfield) and Torah reader (Chuck Hartholz) at a lower monthly operating cost. While this was more affordable, the lack of rabbinical talent deterred new people from joining the shul, since there was no 'rabbi' available for life cycle events.

Although the shul board saw the need to make changes in rabbinical support, it took an opposite position on ritual, choosing to make no changes in this area. In large part, this was because the post-Saval leadership came from the same core observant group that ran the shul during the Saval period and was happy with the status quo. Reinforcing this was their belief that Orthodox ritual was required by the bylaws as well as the Saval bequest terms.

As a result, the same issues that had begun surfacing in the Saval era continued unabated – as it became increasingly difficult to offset the loss of the shul's aging core with new members. In several instances, parents with daughters left the shul because they could not have a bat mitzvah.

The effect of ritual stasis was also seen in declining attendance at services. As core observant members died and were not replaced, the Shul could no longer sustain shaharit services on Sunday, Monday and Thursday mornings. It therefore retrenched to Friday night and Saturday mornings only, with Friday night attendance also becoming

---

[135] Given that Joseph Soloveitchik lived until 1993, one suspects that he continued to have a relationship with the shul via Judge Robert Fox and that Gopin's hiring as a Maimonides/Yeshiva University graduate was not coincidental In addition, Marc's father, David Gopin, is pictured in Farber's *An American Orthodox Dreamer* at the Maimonides construction site in 1960 -- showing that he was a *macher* at Maimonides whose son presumably was worthy of Joseph Soloveitchik's job placement assistance.

marginal. From a Norman Rosenfield report to the board, dated January 17, 1996:

> Friday night in particular is of major concern because this is when most prospective members, newcomers and travelers come to shul. People don't generally choose when they have to say kaddish, and aren't necessarily sure what moves them to attend one Friday over another. But we can't pretend to service the downtown Jewish community when our Friday night welcome mat consists of maybe three or four people on average
>
> Norman Rosenfield, report to the board. January 17, 1996

Larry Baras (President) and Jonathan Slate (Vice Chairman) worked hard to offset the loss of core observant people via better programming, including Christmas Day fairs and auctions of sports memorabilia. One particularly well-attended event was when Dana Rosenblatt, a leading Jewish boxer, came to the shul. Some of these programs were successful in generating good single-event attendance, but they did not attract a regular group of congregants. Similarly, the shul attracted large turnouts for community Seders, but most of the attendees did not return for other services.

In another attempt to gain traction with potential new members, Larry Baras decided that the shul needed a Hebrew school and hired Janice Rosenfield, Norman's wife, to run it. This was modestly successful; within a few years, the Hebrew school had 5-7 children as well as some new members with children. However there was an unresolved issue about what to do with Hebrew school girls wanting bat mitzvahs.

In addition to declining membership, a second major problem was the need to deal with maintaining a now-aging building. By the 1990s, the building was over twenty years old – which meant that things like the roof, which had a twenty-year life, needed replacement. Unfortunately, there was no money to pay for this.

Susan Weingarten, who joined the synagogue Board in the 1990s, recalls a contentious meeting regarding the roof, in which one member said that repairing the roof properly would require $250,000, while another said that he could fix the problem temporarily with duct tape and more permanently for $1,500-$2,000. After a long period of unproductive and increasingly heated argument, Judge John Fox slammed down his gavel, and told the board attendees to 'shut up and behave yourselves.'

For the short term, the shul adopted the duct tape solution. Longer term, when Susan became president in the late 90s, she would opt for a staged professional solution.

The Vilna Shul Conflict

During this period, the Synagogue also engaged in a protracted conflict over the disposition of the Vilna Shul property, lasting from 1989 to 2000.

The Vilna Shul (Anshe Vilna) was formed in 1903 by Lithuanian immigrants. In 1919-1920, it moved to a new building at 18 Phillips Street on the flat of Beacon Hill. It then suffered from the same declining Jewish population as The Boston Synagogue predecessor shuls. In 1958, Tifereth Israel – the Chambers Street Shul – joined Vilna when it lost its building as a result of the West End urban redevelopment effort. As previously noted, this merger did not bring in sufficient revenues or membership to make a meaningful difference for Vilna.

By 1985, Mendel Miller, the sole surviving member of the congregation, shut the facility. Three years later in 1988, he sought permission from the Massachusetts Superior Court to liquidate the property and send the proceeds to selected Israeli charities. The Court responded by putting Vilna into receivership and appointing a special master to consider what should be done.

At this point, there was a multi-party fight over the property:

- Miller argued that the proceeds from the property should go to his designated charities. He opposed giving the proceeds to the Charles River Park Synagogue, arguing that it was not an Orthodox synagogue, due to its mixed seating.
- Rabbi Abraham Halbfinger of Kadimah-Toras Moshe (KTM) in Brighton argued that a Torah from the Vilna Shul in KTM's possession belonged to KTM.
- The Charles River Park Synagogue argued that as the closest synagogue to Vilna, it should be the recipient of the funds; and

that the funds were needed by CRP to maintain the financial viability of the last remaining shul in downtown Boston.
- A group of preservationists felt that, as the last immigrant-era shul in downtown, the Vilna property should receive historical landmark status and be preserved as a Jewish museum/cultural center.

Ultimately, the Special Master recommended that The Boston Synagogue should be the recipient of any assets, on the basis of the doctrine of *cy pres* (the phrase comes from Norman French and means 'near enough,' i.e., that CRP was 'near enough' in practice to Vilna and so should receive the funds).

On December 18, 2000, Justice Abrams of the Massachusetts Supreme Court ruled that the Vilna property should be sold to the Jewish cultural center group, with the proceeds going to The Boston Synagogue. In addition, Kadimah-Toras Moshe, which had taken possession of the Vilna Shul Torah, was directed to pay the value of this Torah to The Boston Synagogue.

> 4. The claim of the Congregation Kadimah Toras Moshe to ownership of the "Ladies Auxiliary" Torah is denied as a claim against the estate of the Vilner Congregation.
>
> 5. The Court hereby decrees that The Boston Synagogue shall be the charitable beneficiary of the estate of the Vilner Congregation under Massachusetts General Laws c. 180, §11A, and the principles of *cy pres,* and the Receiver shall pay and transfer to The Boston Synagogue all of the net assets of the estate, after the payments set forth hereinabove. The Receiver is authorized to execute such assignment or other document as necessary to transfer to The Boston Synagogue the Vilner Congregation's receivable associated with the "Ladies Auxiliary" Torah, as set forth in the Report and Recommendation.
>
> Massachusetts Supreme Court, Order On Report And Recommendation Of The Temporary Receiver Of The Vilner Congregation, December 18, 2000

In total, this legal effort took eleven years. After paying for legal costs, The Boston Synagogue only received around $100,000 from the sale for a building that was assessed by the City of Boston in 1985 at $963,000. The synagogue also never received, despite the Court ruling, payment for the Kadimah Toras Moshe Torah. It later was donated by KTM to Vilna Shul, with no proceeds to The Boston Synagogue.

In retrospect, the Vilna conflict can perhaps be viewed as a 'pyrrhic victory' for The Boston Synagogue. It consumed substantial Board-level attention that might better have been placed in growing The Boston Synagogue, and in the end did not generate a transforming level of endowment for the shul.

Situation at the end of the Post-Saval Era 1999

The greatest accomplishment of the post-Saval leadership was that the shul survived the death of Saval and began to be weaned away from what had become an unhealthy dependency.[136]

On the other hand, The Boston Synagogue operated with continual deficits that were exacerbated by declining membership. As a result, it survived only by tapping into the Saval principal each year (allowed under the terms of the bequest). The shul's poor financial condition was highlighted by Michael Weingarten when he became treasurer in 2001 and determined that the $250,000 bequeathed by the Saval estate had been largely spent to cover continuing operating losses. While much of this had been replaced by other bequests and/or the Vilna proceeds, there was no assurance that this would continue. Without new bequests, the shul would be insolvent within a decade.

During this period, Susan Weingarten recalls board meetings in the 1990s in which the board was talking about shutting down and giving the keys to Chabad,[137] or tearing down the shul and building an income-generating 'Synagogue Towers.'

This situation was unsustainable.

---

[136] Ruth Fein, when she moved from the suburbs to downtown and joined The Boston Synagogue in 1980, was told by a CJP communal leader shortly after her move that 'The Boston Synagogue would be dead within five years.'

[137] Given that Chabad Rabbi David Rabinovitz was the first recorded rabbi of North Russell Street, this would have been ironic.

Chapter 13

The Recent Era 1999-2013

Susan Schreiner Weingarten was elected president of The Boston Synagogue in 1999 and served in this capacity until 2002. She then became Vice Chairman and since 2008 has been Chairman of the Board.

Also serving as presidents during this period were Michael Rubin, Michael Weingarten (Susan's husband) and Bette Siegel.

Susan Schreiner Weingarten

*   *   *

During this period, the shul implemented a number of important changes, based on leadership's assessment of local Jewish population demographics and needs.

First, the board perceived that there was an important shift in the desirability of downtown Boston as a place for Jews to live. As seen in the Chapter 9 BRA population chart, Boston's population bottomed out in 1980 and was recovering by the late 90s. More importantly, the shul's key downtown neighborhoods were experiencing gentrification.

From The Boston Synagogue's perspective, this was good news. The prior history of Boston's Jewish population was that as the community prospered, Jews moved from poorer to richer neighborhoods. Given downtown Boston's increasing attractiveness, it made sense that the local Jewish population would rebound. Therefore if The Boston Synagogue managed itself properly, it could have a viable future.

[These hypotheses were later confirmed by the *2005 CJP Boston Community Survey*, which found that the Jewish population in Boston, Cambridge and contiguous towns increased by 83 percent from 1995-2005, while Brighton/Brookline/Newton only grew by 10 percent and Sharon declined.]

Jewish Population Estimates By Area

	1995	2005	Percent Change
Brighton, Brookline, Newton and Contiguous Areas	56,000	62,500	11.6%
Central Boston, Cambridge, and Contiguous Towns	24,000	44,000	83.3%
Greater Framingham	17,000	19,000	11.8%
Northwestern Suburbs	19,000	25,000	31.6%
Greater Sharon	22,000	21,500	-2.3%
Other Towns	42,000	42,000	0.0%
Total	181,995	216,005	18.7%

2005 *CJP Boston Community Survey* and The Boston Synagogue Analysis

On the other hand, there was no indication that downtown was becoming an attractive neighborhood for Orthodox Jews, who continued to live in the suburbs.

A second important leadership conclusion that what Jews were looking for in a synagogue was changing. Over the previous hundred years, bigger typically was better than smaller. As a result, synagogues like Ohabei Shalom and Temple Israel repeatedly swapped their old buildings for ones that were larger and more elaborate, and they prospered.

The problem with this was that many of the most committed Jews, and in particular day school graduates, were becoming increasingly attracted to small (and often lay-led) services inspired by the havurah movement of the 1980s and reminiscent of the old immigrant *shtibls*. As noted in Sarna's *American Judaism*:

> The havurah movement... focused on intimacy and worship in family-like settings, as opposed to large impersonal "sanctuaries," helping to break down the formality that had for so long characterized the American synagogue. Whereas an earlier generation concerned itself with decorum and solemnity, postwar children, influenced by new cultural surroundings, sought cozier religious settings where they could come to worship far less formally attired and feel right at home. The American synagogue, as a result, became less performance-oriented in the late twentieth century. Where once congregants expected to sit back passively to watch a service choreographed by the rabbi and

the cantor.., now more of them expected to participate in the service actively: praying aloud, singing, and even dancing in the aisles. Formal sermons in many synagogues became less frequent, replaced by interactive discussions and "words of Torah" prepared by lay members.

Sarna, *American Judaism*, p. 324

A related element was the Chabad movement, where uncommitted Jews were finding comfort in joining the local Chabad Rabbi and Rebbetzin for a warm Friday night dinner and drinks.

This suggested that after years of being 'subscale,' The Boston Synagogue was in a position to take advantage of its smallness, by redefining 'smallness' as 'intimacy.'

A third leadership realization was that The Boston Synagogue supports a transient population in downtown with diverse needs. Indeed, the backgrounds of the shul's members suggested that many of the Jews in downtown did not grow up in Massachusetts, and moved here for college or job opportunities.

On one hand, this was bad news, as each year the shul needed to recruit new members to replace people who moved out. However it suggested that if The Boston Synagogue became more attractive to new prospects, it would have more opportunities to make a good first impression – something easier to do than convincing someone turned off by a bad experience that happened years before.

It also was becoming clear that the shul needed to focus on young people, families with interfaith issues and gay/lesbian (GLBT) Jews. If The Boston Synagogue could do a better job of dealing with their needs, it could attract a new member base.

* * *

Based on these insights, a number of key changes were made during this era. These included:

Recruiting rabbinical talent

For the shul to survive, it needed high quality rabbinical talent. Since The Boston Synagogue could not afford a full-time rabbi, this meant that it had to find good part-time people (like the West End shuls of the 1880s/1890s).

While shopping one Friday morning in 1999 at the Butcherie in Brookline, Susan Weingarten ran into Rabbi Daniel Lehmann (the then headmaster at the New Jewish High School). When Susan described the shul's need for part-time support and asked Lehmann whom he could recommend, he suggested that he might find it of interest.

This became the start of a relationship in which Rabbi Lehmann and his family would spend one Shabbat a month at The Boston Synagogue. When Lehmann had to cancel a Shabbat commitment, due to the death of his father, he arranged for Ebn Leader to serve as substitute (Ebn at the time was head of Judaics at the New Jewish High School; he is now a rabbi and faculty member at the Hebrew College Rabbinical School). Leader soon became part of The Boston Synagogue 'family' as well.

Rabbi Daniel Lehmann   Rabbi Ebn Leader

One unanticipated benefit from the Lehmann/Leader relationship was the emergence of Noah Weingarten as unofficial ritual director of the shul in the 2002-2008 period. Noah, who was a student at Solomon Schechter School in Newton (and then Gann Academy), was tutored by Ebn Leader for his bar mitzvah in 2002. Ebn taught him so well that the week after his bar mitzvah, he read the entire Torah and Haftarah portion of the week, as well as serving as chazzan. This continued on most weeks for five years, until Noah left for college.

Noah Weingarten (circa 2003)

Once Lehmann and Leader moved to Hebrew College (as President and head of the Rabbinical School Bet Midrash, respectively), the shul established a close relationship with the Rabbinical School by hosting a rabbinic student intern each year starting in 2006 (seven in all through 2013). In some ways, these talented people (all of whom were Ebn's protégés) were Noah's linear successors. They collectively made a tremendous contribution to the quality and energy of the shul's services and programming.

Supplementing this, the shul engaged Rabbi Ben Lanckton, the Jewish chaplain at Massachusetts General Hospital; and more recently, Rabbi Daniel Klein of Hebrew College Rabbinical School, to be part-time 'rabbi-in-residence.'

For High Holidays and Passover, the shul has enjoyed the support of Dr. David Fishman, Professor of Modern Jewish History at the Jewish Theological Seminary, whose relationship with The Boston Synagogue dates to the 1980s.

The synagogue also has developed a close relationship with Rabbi Al Axelrad, the head of Hillel at Brandeis for thirty years and more recently Chair of Student Spiritual Life at Emerson as well as Jewish Chaplain at Massachusetts Eye and Ear Hospital.

As a result, even without a full-time rabbi, The Boston Synagogue has benefited from access to world-class rabbinical talent.

Hebrew College Rabbinical School Interns

Top (Left to Right): Rabbi Judi Ehrlich (2005-6); Rabbi Alyson Solomon (2006-7); Rabbi David Cohen-Henriquez (2007-9).

Middle (Left to Right): Rabbi Tamar Grimm (2009-10); Rabbi Eric Cohen (2010-11).

Bottom (Left to Right): Getzel Davis (2011-12); David Finkelstein (2012-2013).

Top: (Left to Right): Rabbi Ben Lanckton; Rabbi Daniel Klein (with wife and son).
Bottom (Left to Right): Rabbi Al Axelrad, Dr. David Fishman.

Egalitarian services

It became clear to shul leaders that for The Boston Synagogue to survive in the absence of Orthodox members, it needed to become egalitarian. To foster this and to deal with opposition from shul 'regulars,' The Boston Synagogue sponsored a series of classes led by Ebn Leader on the subject of egalitarianism, based on Talmudic sources.

Anecdotally, when the class participants learned that the Talmud says that 'even a woman or child may read from the Torah,' and that the traditional prohibition on women's participation was based on offending 'the dignity of the congregation,' a general (albeit facetious) reaction was that the shul did not have all that much dignity that could be offended.

> Everyone can be counted towards the seven [who are called to the Torah on *Shabbat*], even a child and even a woman, but the Sages said, a woman should not read in the Torah because of the dignity of the congregation (*kevod ha-tsibbur*).
>
> Baraita, Megillah 23a

Based on this, the shul began trial egalitarian services, and voted to make the move permanent in 2002.

This was a painful episode for the congregation. The leader of those in opposition to the change was Jonathan Slate (Hyman Slate's grandson and part of the Slate family with longstanding ties to the shul). While not personally Orthodox, Slate felt that it would be a betrayal of his ancestors for the shul to become egalitarian. He also argued that he wanted to make it possible for Orthodox Jews visiting Boston to feel comfortable at the shul, and that the Saval bequest as well as the shul's bylaws required it to remain Orthodox.

The key counter arguments were the following:

- The Saval bequest had been spent in the past ten years of deficits
- The bylaws could be changed by membership vote
- Orthodox Jews were already uncomfortable visiting The Boston Synagogue due to its mixed seating and 'non-Kosher' women's mechitza
- Without change, the shul would die
- Maurice Saval was a practical businessman who would understand this – he was, after all, the one who came up with the mixed seating solution in the first place.

In December 2001, Slate and other dissidents attempted to adjudicate the matter before the Boston Orthodox Beth Din. A month later, the head of the Beth Din, Rabbi Abraham Halbfinger, sent Michael Rubin, The Boston Synagogue's president, a letter summoning him to a proceeding:

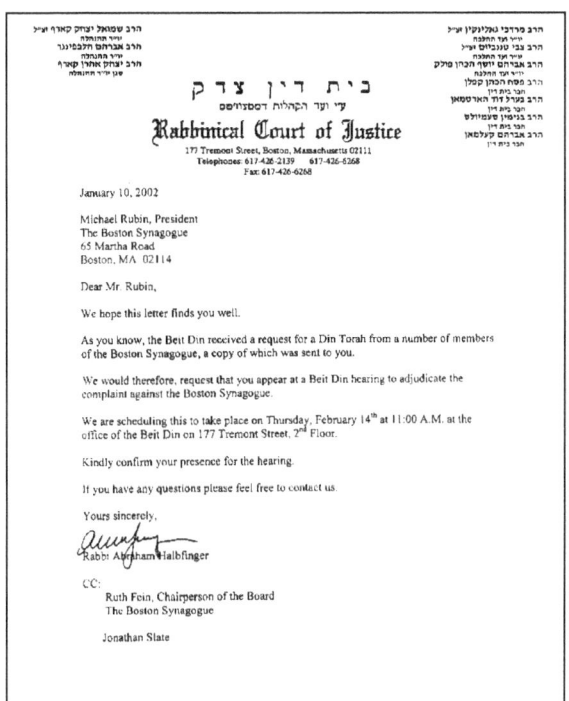

Beth Din Summons Letter, 2002

The Board had three reactions to the letter: (a) if it agreed to the proceeding, a negative outcome was certain; (b) it was upset that the letter appeared to be an involuntary summons, despite the fact that Bet Din adjudication requires the consent of both sides; and (c) it felt that Rabbi Halbfinger, the head of the Beth Din, had a conflict of interest with respect to The Boston Synagogue dating back to the Vilna Shul receivership proceedings.

After considering the matter at a Board meeting, Ruth Fein, Chair, and Michael Rubin, President, responded to Halbfinger that the Board was the appropriate party for ruling on these issues, and it declined to participate in the Bet Din process.

> **The Boston Synagogue**
> *"Your downtown neighborhood synagogue"*
>
> located at Charles River Park
> 55 Martha Road
> Boston, MA 02114
> Tel: (617) 523-0453
> Fax (617) 723-2863
> www.bostonsynagogue.org
>
> February 4, 2002
>
> Rabbi Abraham Halbfinger
> Rabbinical Court of Justice
> 177 Tremont Street
> Boston, MA. 02111
>
> Dear Rabbi Halbfinger:
>
> Thank you for your letter of January 10, 2002, which invited Officers of the Boston Synagogue to attend a hearing before the Beit Din for a Din Torah on February 14, 2002.
>
> This matter was discussed at a special meeting of the Synagogue Board of Directors. The Board thanks you for your invitation, but has voted unanimously that we respectfully must decline to participate.
>
> The Board notes that the By-Laws of the Synagogue provide for a grievance procedure which has not been implemented by Mr. Slate and the three other co-signers of the letter to the Beit Din. The Board has authorized the President to remind the signers of this procedure and encourage them to exercise this right.
>
> Sincerely,
>
> Ruth Fein
> Chairperson of the Board,
> The Boston Synagogue
>
> Michael Rubin
> President,
> The Boston Synagogue

The Boston Synagogue Response to Bet Din Summons

The shul officers also considered the possibility that opponents would file litigation in Massachusetts Superior Court. In preparation, a legal review was performed -- which suggested that Massachusetts courts consistently had declined to rule on religious ritual issues (based on First Amendment considerations). As the Vilna Shul Special Master stated over a decade earlier on the subject of Boston's Synagogue's religious status (due to its mixed seating):

> ... judicial inquiry into Charles River Park's orthodoxy is forbidden. Mixed seating is a matter of pure religious doctrine, an area into which judicial intrusion is barred by both the common law and the First Amendment to the United States Constitution. <u>Solomon</u> v. <u>Congregation Tiffereth Israel of Revere</u>,[138] 344 Mass. 755, 756 (1962); <u>United Kosher Butchers Association</u> v. <u>Associated</u>

---

[138] In *Solomon*, members of an Orthodox Jewish congregation sued to prevent a move to mixed seating, claiming it violated their property rights as members. The court dismissed the case on First Amendment grounds.

Synagogues of Greater Boston,[139] 349 Mass. 595, 598 (1965); Wheeler v. Roman Catholic Archdiocese of Boston, 378 Mass. 58, 63 (1979); Antioch Temple, Inc. v. Parekh, 383 Mass. 854, 859-860 (1981).

Alan J. Dimond, Master; *Master's Draft Report* April 28, 1987, The Vilner Congregation vs. Attorney General of the Commonwealth, Massachusetts Supreme Judicial Court for Suffolk County No. 85-290

Fortunately no lawsuit was filed. The Boston Synagogue proceeded with the change, with the membership amending the shul's mission statement in the bylaws from:

OLD[140]

The purpose of this congregation shall be the maintenance of a place of worship according to Orthodox Hebrew Rites and for other related matters such as educational, cultural and social activities.

to:

NEW

The purpose of this congregation shall be the maintenance of a place of worship and for other related matters such as educational, cultural and social activities, all of which are designed to serve the diverse and ever changing needs of the community of Jews in Downtown Boston while maintaining Jewish traditions, practices and customs.

The Boston Synagogue bylaws

---

[139] *United Kosher Butchers* involved an association of Kosher butchers that employed a Orthodox rabbi for Kosher supervision. The rabbi formerly was associated with the 'official' V'aad Harabbonim (a division of the defendant), but had a falling out with the V'aad and resigned. In response, the V'aad, which provided the supervision for most Kosher caterers, told the caterers that they could no longer buy food from these butchers, since the butchers were now using a non-V'aad affiliated rabbi. The butchers sued the V'aad for restraint of trade; the Court dismissed the case on First Amendment religious grounds.

[140] The use of the word 'old' is relative. As previously noted, the original incorporation papers for Beth Jacob and Amedrish Agudal Anshi Sfard only referred to Jewish worship and said nothing about Orthodox rites. The latter only was added in the 1940 incorporation papers at the time of the North Russell/Beth Jacob merger. In this context, the 'new' bylaws, which are not limited to a particular Jewish denomination, are more consistent with the verbiage of the 1888 and 1902 charters.

In conjunction with this change, the shul's articles of incorporation now state:

> The purpose of the corporation is to engage in the following activities: To conduct worship services and to engage in other religious, social and cultural activities; and to engage in and carry on any other activities permitted to a corporation organized under Chapter 180 of the Massachusetts General Laws, but only to the extent that such activities shall not preclude the classification of the corporation as an organization exempt under Section 501(c)(3) of the Internal Revenue Code.

The egalitarian conflict was a painful episode and it resulted in a small number of people leaving the shul. As a result, however, others who would have found the previous ritual unacceptable began to perceive the synagogue as more welcoming and attractive. As a result, membership grew – something that was vital for restoring the synagogue to financial sustainability. In particular, the shul became an acceptable place for parents with daughters who wanted bat mitzvahs – as well as for young professional women.

In conjunction with the ritual change, the shul needed to decide how it would characterize itself in response to inevitable affiliation questions. After considering different choices, the shul adopted the term 'transdenominational' to reflect the new mission statement. Not coincidentally, this was the term used by the Hebrew College Rabbinical School, with whom The Boston Synagogue had developed a close relationship.

One poignant story regarding the egalitarian move comes from Susan Weingarten, who commented that shortly after the change, Michael Rubin was contacted by an elderly lady from Brookline. The woman told him that many years earlier she had been an officer of the North Russell Street Ladies' Auxiliary, and that they still had a bank account with an approximately $1,000 balance. She and her friend, also part of the Auxiliary, appreciated the changes at the shul and decided that they should now close out the account and donate the money to the shul – thereby terminating their organization.

Investing in the Building

One result of the increasing membership (and with it, increased operating funds) was that the shul could deal with building maintenance, which had been neglected in the 1990s. The synagogue stopped using duct tape to repair the roof, which the roofers advised only made matters worse. After consulting with competent contractors, the roof was replaced in stages over a period of years, while also shoring up the roof – in danger of collapse -- with steel girders.[141]

When the shul's air conditioning system failed in 2008 (requiring a complete HVAC replacement) the board decided to invest in an innovative, high-efficiency ductless heat pump system, which in addition to being socially responsible (there was a 70% BTU reduction), led to a 57% reduction in energy costs with a five-year payback.

In 2012, the shul decided that it needed to convert underutilized coat closets and spare office space into multipurpose rooms to accommodate Hebrew School classes and small meetings/functions. This corrected a serious design oversight from the Saval days.

Current Situation

As a result of these efforts, the shul has been operating with an operating surplus for some years and membership is growing. Unlike 10 to 15 years ago, when people were asking how long the shul could survive, the issue going forward is how it can do better. There is an increasing sense of optimism about the future.

---

[141] Despite a previously mentioned board member's fears, the total cost was less than $100,000 including roof reinforcement, not $250,000.

Chapter 14

Looking Back: The Past 125 Years

Looking at the narrative of The Boston Synagogue and its predecessor shuls over the past 125 years, one can observe several broad themes:

A. Demographics rule

The history of The Boston Synagogue needs to be considered as part of broader demographic trends and not in isolation:

- When immigrant Jews came to America and moved into the West End, the shuls thrived.
- When increasingly prosperous Jews left the immigrant strongholds of the North and West Ends and moved to 'better' neighborhoods in Dorchester, Mattapan and Roxbury, the shuls came under severe distress and were forced to merge to survive.
- As the remaining Jewish population in downtown became less observant, the continuation of an 'Orthodox' shul, even one with mixed seating, became problematic.
- More recently, as downtown Boston began to gentrify (either through normal gentrification processes or via Charles River Park-style urban renewal), an increasing population of Jews has made it increasingly possible to sustain a shul in the area.

Fortunately, recent Boston Development Authority data published in the *Boston Globe* (March 3, 2013) suggests that demographic trends are in the shul's favor:

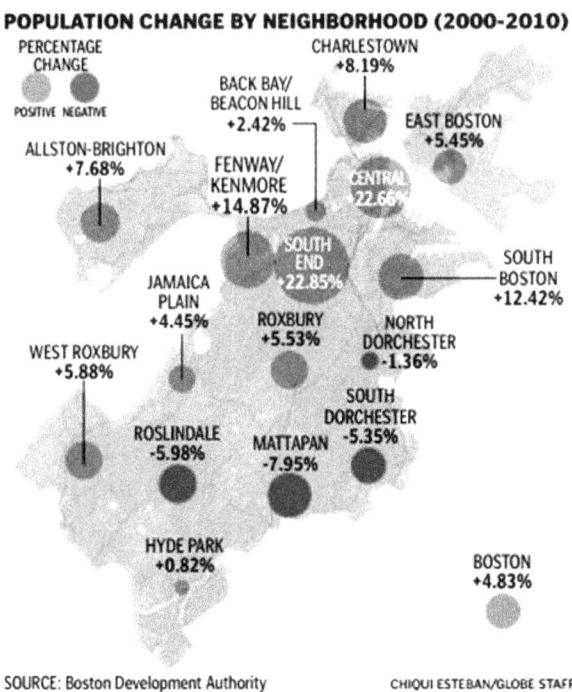

B. Not the rich people's shul

The Boston Synagogue's history largely has been the story of relatively poor Jews (with the noteworthy exception of Maurice Saval) who decided that having a shul as a focus for a warm Jewish communal life was important to them. Compared to places like Temple Israel, the predecessor shuls never were places for the rich and powerful.[142]

C. Association with prominent rabbis and ritual leaders

One of the greatest surprises coming out of this history was the extent to which some eminent rabbis and ritual leaders have been associated with the shul, starting with the Ramaz and Rabbi

---

[142] Although for a time, North Russell Street was the establishment shul in the West End.

Friederman at the turn of the 20th century. This extends to the Soloveitchiks in the Saval years; the smart young talent recruited by Saval and Fox (Nadler, Fishman, Feldman and Gopin); more recently, Rabbis Lehmann/Leader and the others at Hebrew College; as well as Rabbi Axelrad, Rabbi Lanckton and Dr. David Fishman.

To a great extent, these relationships are the result of being located in Boston, one of the great centers of Jewish population and learning in America. However it also reflects favorably on lay leadership's ability to find and recruit high quality rabbinic talent.

D. No movement affiliation

Most synagogues in America today are defined by their movement affiliation; e.g., Reform, Conservative, Orthodox, Chabad, or Reconstructionist. In contrast, The Boston Synagogue and its predecessors never have been a part of a movement.

In the early days, the nature of the synagogue was determined by 'rebbe/grand rabbi' type rabbis such as Margolies, Friederman, Margolis and Yudlevich. If Margolies and Friederman were founders of Agudath Harabbonim, then the predecessor shuls were Agudath-leaning as well.

Increasingly, as lay leadership asserted greater control, the predecessor shul rabbis became rabbis rather than rebbes. However the previous rebbe-affiliation was never replaced by shul-affiliation, for the following reasons:

- Being in Boston, it was easy to hire new rabbis in a manner that would not be possible in places like the rural Midwest. As a result, there was never a need to affiliate to gain access to movement rabbis.
- Given the increasing financial stress on the predecessor shuls as the population declined, the annual dues would have been burdensome.

Particularly in recent years, the lack of affiliation facilitated flexibility. As one illustration: even when the Charles River Park Synagogue under Saval was informally aligned with Soloveitchik and modern Orthodoxy, it had mixed seating (which presumably made Rav Soloveitchik less than happy; and it is unclear that he ever visited the building).

E. At the epicenter of some major trends in American Judaism

By being associated with prominent rabbis in Boston yet never being part of a movement, the predecessor shuls have been part of some major trends in American Judaism:

- Starting with the Agudath Harabbonim resistance to Reform Judaism in the Margolies/Friederman period
- Moving to more mainstream Orthodoxy in the 20s (Sharfman and Lifland dealing with the pain of real life issues for secularizing Jews)
- Embracing a form of modern Orthodoxy with Soloveitchik in the Saval days (yet having mixed seating)
- More recently, embracing the egalitarian/transdenominational approach taken by the rabbis at Gann Academy and Hebrew College; and borrowing from the intimacy of the havurah and Chabad approaches to Judaism.

F. Need to stay nimble

One thing that has become clear is that over 125 years, one cannot rely on static business models. In 1888, President Robensohn of CBJ could count on a rising tide of Jews that would lift all shuls in the West End. On that basis, building a large modern shul commissioned by a well-known local architect (Norcross) made sense.

And in general, bigger was better, as seen by the success of Ohabei Shalom, Temple Israel et al. By way of a reminder, note that "Beth Hamedrash Hagodol" (the formal name for the North Russell Street Shul) means **Big** House of Study.

Fast-forward 50 years, and demographic change made the business model of Beth Hamedrash Hagadol untenable. There were not enough Jews in downtown to fill a place that large, and those that were still in the neighborhood generally were not Orthodox and rarely attended services. Even without urban renewal, it is unclear that North Russell Street would have survived without radical changes.

Fast-forward 100 years, and The Boston Synagogue's leadership changed its business model to reflect its belief that for many Jews, being small and intimate increasingly trumped large and formal. As a result, the shul is now doing relatively well.

This is not to say that things can stay as they are. The clear lesson of the past 125 years is that one needs to be nimble to survive, and evolve as needed.

G. A few laypeople have made a big difference

The Boston Synagogue exists today because of the dedication of lay leaders who decided that having a shul in the West End was important and whose families devoted significant time to the shul. This began with Elias Kamberg in the 1890s along with other members of his family through the 1941 merger. It continued with the Slate family, beginning with Hyman Slate at the time of urban renewal and including Jonathan Slate as Vice Chairman in the 1990s during a period of desperate survival. Then there was Maurice Saval, who refused to accept the destruction of the North Russell Street Shul without seeing to its replacement; and, once the shul was built, ran it for twenty years. After Saval died, without the support of Judge John Fox and leaders like Bob Stern and Larry Baras, the shul would not have survived the 1990s. More recently, Susan Weingarten and her family, along with Mike Rubin and Bette Siegel, have played a vital role in making The Boston Synagogue a viable and vibrant community.

In addition, numerous other people who were not shul presidents have provided important week-in week-out support, such as:

- *Muriel Kantor* Z"L, a Radcliffe graduate and chemistry teacher. On a regular basis, Muriel would volunteer to clean up after Shabbat morning Kiddush as her contribution to the shul, and then would sit reading books from the shul library afterwards.
- *Alan Gelb*, who has been at virtually every service for years; and *Gerry Kleinstein*, who in addition has been a regular chazzan and Torah reader. Those who attend also serve, and those who serve make a real contribution.

- *Rachel Semigran*, who post-Bat Mitzvah has been helping to prepare Kiddush on Shabbat mornings on a regular basis.
- *Florrie and Henry Einhorn*, who volunteered for years to clean the laundry in the rabbi's apartment.
- *Shlomo Pinkas*, who has been acting as the shul's gabbai for years.
- *Kelly Burnett,* The Boston Synagogue's administrator, who helped propel the shul into the world of social media. Without good administrators, very little happens.

Running a shul takes work by a lot of people. The Boston Synagogue honors those who have served over the past 125 years, in whatever capacity.

Chapter 15

Looking to the Future

While we respect the people who preceded us (and in honor of whom we created this 125th anniversary retrospective), we believe that the mission of the shul is to look forward and to find new ways to meet the diverse and evolving needs of Jews in downtown Boston. We are not a museum commemorating a dead past, we are a living organic community. As Maurice Saval once wrote:

> It's important to understand that we did not rebuild this historic house of worship merely out of filial devotion to the dead or to erect a monument to what was, but we hoped to inspire and challenge a new generation of urban residing Jews to restore a communal religious spirit.
>
> Maurice Saval, unattributed quote from The Boston Synagogue archives

If we accomplish our objectives successfully, our hope is that other Jews will be in a position to do a retrospective on us in 2038 or 2088 (our 150th and 200th anniversaries, respectively). Hopefully, they will have nice things to say about us; but more importantly, we hope that they will be able to point to a vibrant shul and Jewish community in downtown Boston.

Appendices

Appendix 1

A Geography Lesson

Given that the only predecessor shul building that exists today is Anshei Libavitz at 8 Smith Court, two obvious questions are: where were the other buildings located and what are on the sites today? The following chart from *The Last Tenement* superimposes the locations of the pre-urban renewal streets on a modern map.

On this map, we also show where each of our predecessor shul streets was located, along with the current location of The Boston Synagogue. These shuls include:

- **Congregation Beth Jacob:** Originally at 11 *Minot Street*, then moved to 24 *Wall Street* (also had a building at 30 Wall)
- **Beth Hamedrash Hagadol (Anshe Sfard)/Beth Hamedrash Hagadol Beth Jacob:** 28/30 *North Russell Street*
- **Ein Jacob (Anshe Vilna):** 16 *Poplar Street*
- **Mishkan Shlomo/Anshai Birsh:** 71 *Poplar Street*
- **Anshei Libavitz:** 8 *Smith Court*
- **Charles River Park Synagogue/ The Boston Synagogue:** 55 *Martha Road*; at the bottom of the Amy Court *cul de sac*

Map Superimposing The Pre-Urban Renewal Map With The Current Map

Source: *The Last Tenement* and The Boston Synagogue analysis

The next step in the process is to determine the modern location for each predecessor shul. Looking first at Congregation Beth Jacob, Minot and Wall Streets were a short block to the north of Leverett. This suggests that these shuls were located near what is now Martha Road/Lomasney Way.

Given that Wall Street was located parallel to North Station, the location of 24 Wall is close to the rear of where the Basketball City/Propark garage is located, on the side nearest to West End Place. [In the way of continual change, the garage owner is seeking to replace this with a new mixed use high-rise, so future readers may need to see what is built at 15/21 Lomasney Way.]

**Propark Garage Today
(West End Place to the Left)**

Looking next at North Russell Street Shul, a detailed 1917 map from the Boston Public Library's Norman Leventhal Map Center shows the synagogue in the center of the block bounded by: North Russell (to the east); Cambridge (to the south); Blossom (to the west); and Parkman (to the north). In addition, by 1923, the shul also owned 24-26-30 North Russell, to the right of the 28 North Russell parcel.

1917 Map of North Russell Street Shul and Environs

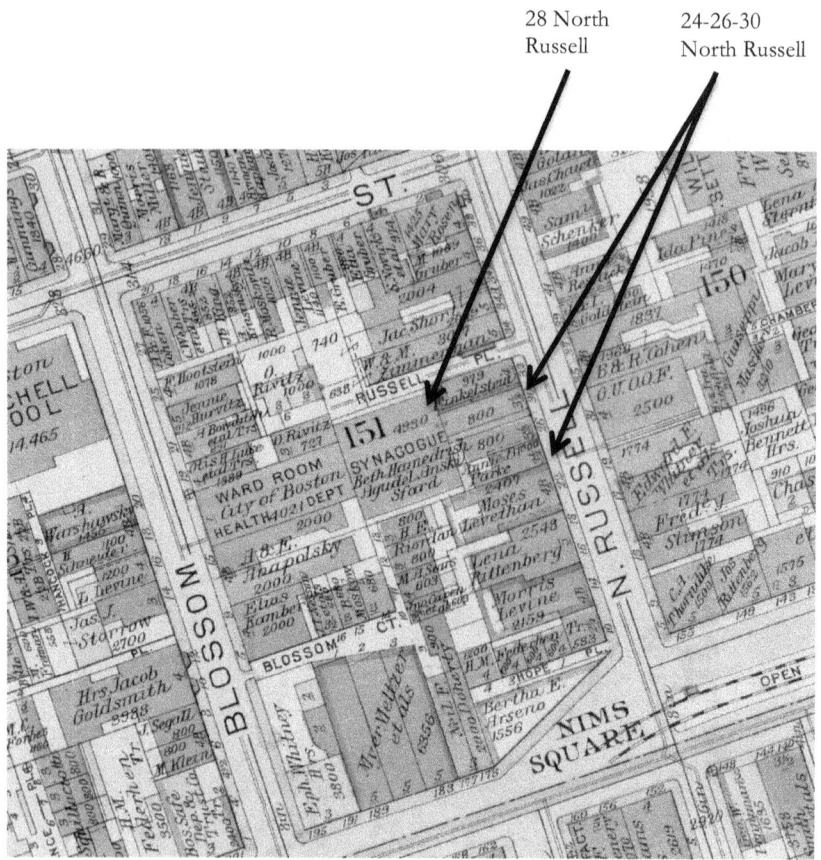

Courtesy of Boston Public Library's Norman Leventhal Map Center

Given that three of the four streets of this block still exist (and the location for the fourth, North Russell Street, can be determined by extending a line north from South Russell Street), it is clear the North Russell Street Shul site is now part of parking lot of the Charles River Plaza garage.

Approximate Location of North Russell Street Shul Superimposed on Modern Map

(lighter shade is entire block; darker shade is shul footprint)

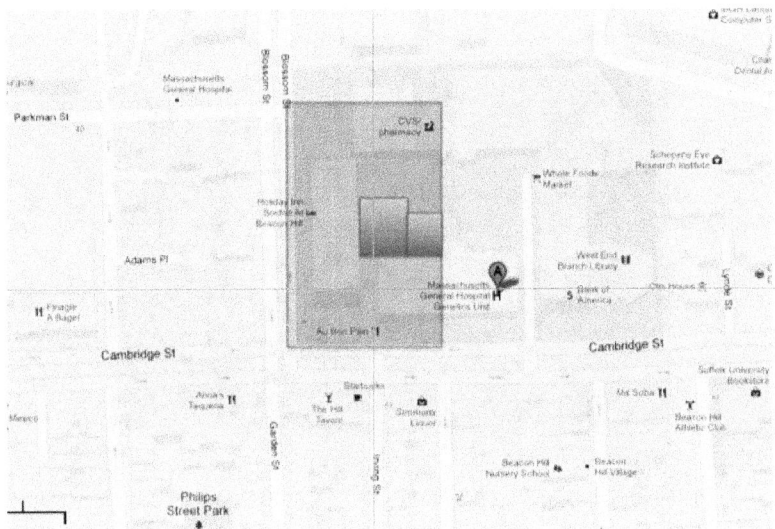

View of Charles River Plaza from Irving Street Side:
Synagogue site is directly north of Irving
(past Cambridge Street, which runs left to right) in CRP parking lot

A pre-urban renewal shot taken from approximately the same Irving Street vantage point shows the rear of the North Russell Street Shul in the background center left.

**Man and a Produce Cart at the Corner
of Irving and Cambridge Streets, 1957**

Source: The Bostonian Society

With respect to the Poplar Street shuls: Poplar was located one block north of Massachusetts General Hospital (bounded by Allen Street running East/West, which terminated at Blossom running North/South).

Based on a review of detailed 1917 maps, Miskhan Shlomo was located on the grassy knoll to the left of the Blossom Court cul de sac, while Ein Jacob was near the two Hawthorne buildings.

**Approximate Location of Poplar Street Shuls
In Shaded Circles**

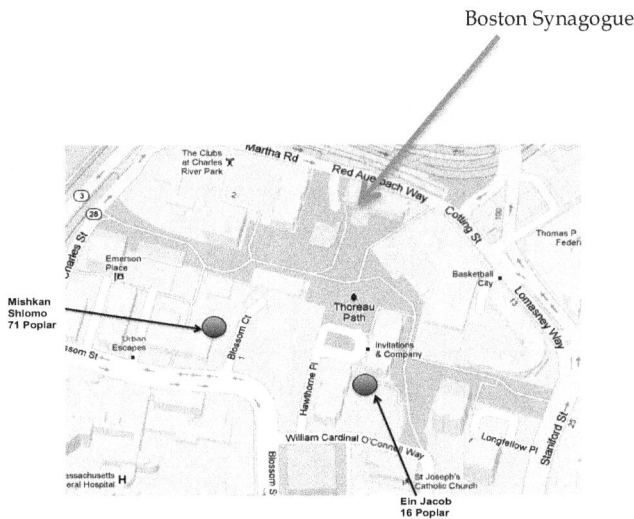

Finally, the location of Anshei Libavitz on Beacon Hill is easy to locate, since the building still exists at 8 Smith Court. In 1972, it was sold back to the African-American community, who owned the building in the 19th century. The community's goal has been to restore the building to its original appearance as the African Meeting House.

Appendix 2

Listing of Predecessor Shul Rabbis and Ritual Directors

The following is a listing, to the best of The Boston Synagogue's current knowledge, of all rabbis/cantors/shammases/ritual directors who worked at the predecessor shuls of The Boston Synagogue as well as the current facility. An 'x' indicates that the shul was in existence, but that there is no available information on rabbis/ritual directors; grey shading indicates that the shul was not in existence in that particular year.

To the extent that anyone can add to the shul's knowledge base, please contact the synagogue office at office@bostonsynagogue.org.

1888-1940

	Cong Beth Jacob	Ein Jacob (Anshe Vilna)	Mishkan Shlomo/ Anshai Birch	Anshei Libavitz	Adath Jesura Nusach Ari	Beth Hamedrash Hagadol (Anshe Sfard)
1888	no listing					
1889	no listing					
1890	no listing			no listing		
1891	no listing			no listing		
1892	no listing			no listing		
1893	no listing			no listing		
1894	M.S. Margolies, Lewis Kamper sexton			no listing		
1895	M.S. Margolies, I. Beresofsky sexton	no listing		no listing		
1896	M.S. Margolies, Jacob Oshray sexton	no listing		no listing		no listing
1897	M.S. Margolies, Jacob Oshray sexton	no listing		no listing		no listing
1898	M.S. Margolies, J Rachkorsky sexton	no listing	no listing	M.S. Margolis	no listing	no listing

	Cong Beth Jacob	Ein Jacob (Anshe Vilna)	Mishkan Shlomo/ Anshai Birch	Anshei Libavitz	Adath Jesura Nusach Ari	Beth Hamedrash Hagadol (Anshe Sfard)
1899	M.S. Margolies, J Rachkoosky sexton	no listing; Amer Jewish Yearbook lists Rabbi Friederman	no listing	M.S. Margolis	no listing	no listing
1900	M.S. Margolies, J Rachkoosky sexton	no listing	no listing	M.S. Margolis	M.S Margolies	no listing
1901	M.S. Margolies, J Rachkoosky sexton	no listing	no listing	M.S. Margolis	M.S Margolies	no listing
1902	M.S. Margolies, J Rachkoosky sexton	no listing	no listing	no listing	M.S Margolies; David Pearlson sexton	no listing
1903	M.S. Margolies, J Rachkoosky sexton	S.J. Friederman in AJY	no rabbi	M.S. Margolis in AJY	M.S Margolies David Pearlson sexton	no listing
1904	M.S. Margolies, J Rachkoosky sexton	no listing	Isaac Baritz Rabbi, Abram Illman sexton	no listing	M.S Margolies; David Pearlson sexton	D.M. Rubinovitz
1905	M.S. Margolies, J Rachkoosky sexton	no listing	Isaac Baritz Rabbi, Abram Illman sexton	no listing	M.S Margolies; David Pearlson sexton	D.M. Rubinovitz
1906	J Rachkoosky sexton	no listing	Isaac Baritz Rabbi, Abram Illman sexton	M. Kopelowitz (Globe wedding artifle)	David Pearlson sexton	D.M. Rubinovitz
1907	H. Epstein, J Rachkoosky sexton	S.J. Friederman and Isaac Baritz rabbis; I. Rabinovitz sexton	Isaac Baritz Rabbi, Abram Hillman sexton	no listing	no rabbi	no rabbi
1908	H. Epstein, J Rachkoosky sexton	S.J. Friederman and Isaac Baritz rabbis; I. Rabinovitz sexton	Isaac Baritz Rabbi, Abram Hillman sexton	no listing	Wolf Margolis; Abraham Pantanowich sexton	Marcus Hillman rabbi
1909	H. Epstein, J Rachkoosky sexton	Isaac Baritz; L Rabinovitz sexton	Isaac Baritz Rabbi, Abram Hillman sexton	no listing	Wolf Margolis; Abraham Pantanowich sexton;	Marcus Hillman; Harris Lerner sexton
1910	H. Epstein, J Rachkoosky sexton	Isaac Baritz; L Rabinovitz sexton	Isaac Baritz Rabbi, Abram Illman sexton		Wolf Margolis	Marcus Hillman and Hyman Sharfman, rabbis; Harris Lerner sexton
1911	H. Epstein, J Rachkoosky sexton	Isaac Baritz and I Rabinovitz rabbis	Isaac Baritz Rabbi, Abram Illman sexton		Wolf Margolis; Abraham Pantanowich sexton;	Marcus Hillman and Hyman Sharfman, rabbis; Harris Lerner sexton
1912	Harry Epstein and Samuel Goldstein, Rabbis; S. Robinson, sexton	no listing	Isaac Baritz Rabbi, Abram Illman sexton		Wolf Margolis; Abraham Pantanowich sexton	Marcus Hillman and Hyman Sharfman, rabbis; Harris Lerner sexton
1913	no rabbi; S Robinson Sexton	Isaac Baritz and I Rabinovitz sexton	Isaac Baritz Rabbi, Abram Illman sexton		A.A. Yudlevitz; Abraham Pantanowich sexton	Hyman Sharfman, rabbi; Harris Lerner sexton
1914	Simon Price rabbi; S Robinson Sexton	Isaac Baritz and I Rabinovitz Sexton	Isaac Baritz Rabbi		A.A. Yudlevitz; Simon Cohen sexton	Hyman Sharfman, rabbi; Harris Lerner sexton

	Cong Beth Jacob	Ein Jacob (Anshe Vilna)	Mishkan Shlomo/ Anshai Birch	Anshei Libavitz	Adath Jesura Nusach Ari	Beth Hamedrash Hagadol (Anshe Sfard)
1915	Simon Price rabbi; S Robinson Sexton	Isaac Baritz	Isaac Baritz Rabbi		A.A. Yudlevitz; Simon Cohen sexton	Hyman Sharfman, rabbi
1916	Simon Price rabbi; S Robinson Sexton	Isaac Baritz	Isaac Baritz Rabbi		A.A. Yudlevitz	Hyman Sharfman, rabbi
1917	Simon Price	Isaac Baritz	no listing		no rabbi listed	Hyman Sharfman, rabbi
1918	Simon Price	Isaac Baritz	no listing	Joseph Lifland	A.A. Yudlevitz	Hyman Sharfman, rabbi
1919	Aaron Mancovitz; Morris Levin rabbis	Isaac Baritz	Isaac Volk	Joseph Lifland	no rabbi listed	Hyman Sharfman, rabbi
1920	Aaron Mancovitz; Morris Levin rabbis	Isaac Baritz	Isaac Volk	Joseph Lifland	Samuel Lefland	Hyman Sharfman
1921	Aaron Mancovitz; Morris Levin rabbis	Isaac Baritz	Isaac Volk	Joseph Lifland	Samuel Lefland	Hyman Sharfman
1922	Aaron Mancovitz; Morris Levin rabbis	Isaac Baritz	no rabbi listed	no name	no name	Hyman Sharfman
1923	Aaron Mancovitz; Morris Levin rabbis	Isaac Baritz		Joseph Lifland	Samuel Lefland	Hyman Sharfman
1924	Aaron Mancovitz; Morris Levin rabbis			x	x	x
1925	Aaron Mancovitz; Morris Levin rabbis			x	x	x
1926	Aaron Mancovitz; Morris Levin rabbis			x	x	x
1927	Aaron Mancovitz; Morris Levin rabbis			x	x	Jacob Shohet
1928	Morris Levin			x	x	Jacob Shohet
1929	Morris Levin			x	x	no name
1930	Morris Levin			no name	no name	no name
1931	x			x		x
1932	x			x		x
1933	x			x		x
1934	x			x		x
1935	x			x		x
1936	x			x		x

	Cong Beth Jacob	Ein Jacob (Anshe Vilna)	Mishkan Shlomo/ Anshai Birch	Anshei Libavitz	Adath Jesura Nusach Ari	Beth Hamedrash Hagadol (Anshe Sfard)
1937	x			x		x
1938	x			x		x
1939	x			x		x
1940	x			x		x

1941-2013

	Anshei Libavitz	Beth Hamedrash Hagadol Beth Jacob	Boston Synagogue
1941	x	x	
1942	x	x	
1943	x	x	
1944	x	x	
1945	x	x	
1946	x	x	
1947	x	x	
1948	x	x	
1949	x	x	
1950	x	x	
1951	x	x	
1952	x	x	
1953	x	x	
1954	x	x	
1955	x	x	
1956	x	x	
1957	x	x	
1958	x	x	
1959	x	x	
1960		x	
1961		x	
1962		x	
1963		x	
1964		x	
1965		x	
1966		x	
1967		x	
1968		x	
1969		x	
1970		x	
1971			Shalom Cohen, Ritual Director

	Anshei Libavitz	Beth Hamedrash Hagadol Beth Jacob	Boston Synagogue
1972			Shalom Cohen, Ritual Director
1973			Shalom Cohen, Ritual Director
1974			Shalom Cohen, Ritual Director
1975			Shalom Cohen, Ritual Director
1976			Shalom Cohen, Ritual Director
1977			Shalom Cohen, Ritual Director
1978			Shalom Cohen, Ritual Director
1979			Shalom Cohen, Ritual Director
1980			Rabbi Nadler
1981			Rabbi Nadler
1982			Rabbi Nadler
1983			David Fishman, ritual director
1984			David Fishman, ritual director
1985			David Fishman, ritual director
1986			David Fishman, ritual director
1987			David Fishman, ritual director
1988			David Fishman, ritual director
1989			x
1990			x
1991			Rabbi Gopin
1992			Rabbi Gopin
1993			Norman Rosenfield ritual director
1994			Norman Rosenfield ritual director
1995			Norman Rosenfield ritual director
1996			Norman Rosenfield ritual director
1997			Norman Rosenfield ritual director
1998			Norman Rosenfield ritual director
1999			Rabbi Daniel Lehman/Ebn Leader Periodic Shabbats
2000			Rabbi Daniel Lehman/Ebn Leader Periodic Shabbats
2001			Ebn Leader periodic Shabbats; Mike Rubin ritual director
2002			Ebn Leader periodic Shabbats; Mike Rubin ritual director
2003			Noah Weingarten, ritual director
2004			Noah Weingarten, ritual director
2005			Noah Weingarten, ritual director
2006			Judi Ehrlich intern; Noah Weingarten ritual director
2007			Allison Solomon intern; Noah Weingarten ritual director
2008			David Cohen Henriquez intern
2009			David Cohen Henriquez intern

	Anshei Libavitz	Beth Hamedrash Hagadol Beth Jacob	Boston Synagogue
2010			Rabbi Ben Lanckton Rabbi in Residence; Tamar Grimm intern
2011			Rabbi Ben Lanckton, Rabbi in Residence; Eric Cohen Intern
2012			Rabbi Ben Lanckton, Rabbi in Residence; Getzel Davis Intern
2013			Rabbi Daniel Klein Rabbi in Residence; David Finkelstein intern

Appendix 3

Bylaws: North Russell Street Mishnah Study Group

The Regulation of The Mishnayos Study Group of Beth HaMedrash Hagadol Anshi Sfard Boston
[Translation from the Hebrew]

First Regulation
Each and every one of the above Study Group is obligated to learn 26 chapters of Mishnayos every month if he is a scholar.

Second Regulation
One member of the Study Group is required to study his share of Mishnayos between Mincha and Maariv, so people who are interested to study in a group could join him.

Third Regulation
In addition, one of the members of the Study Group is required to study in each and every Shabbat, Hilchos Shabbat [Shabbat rules and regulations] in order to join the people who are not required to study the 26 Mishnayos on their own since they do not have the time to come to the Synagogue to study a chapter of Mishnayos with the group between Mincha and Maariv. Consequently one is obligated to come on Saturday to study Shabbas rules and regulations.

Fourth Regulation
The Sium of the Mishnayos [completion of the 26 chapters of Mishnayos] must take place exactly at the end of the respective month.

Fifth Regulation
If it will transpire that one of the group did not complete his required share of Mishnayos, he must inform the Gabbai of the above Study Group prior to the Sium how many

chapters he did not study and during the Sium he should set a fine for himself. If, God forbid, he will do that again, he should also set a fine for himself; however, if after two times he again would not study the share he took upon himself the Gabbai may impose a fine on him according to his own judgment up to three times and then if still he did not fulfill what he undertook, the Gabbai together with two other members of the Study Group can dismiss him from the above Study Group.

Sixth Regulation
If any member of the above Study Group passes the one hundred and twenty years mark [i.e., dies], the members of the Study Group must study chapters of Mishnayos in the name of the deceased for the holy soul and to assemble a Minyan at the home of the deceased in the morning and in the evening for 7 days, and to divide saying the Kaddish up to 11 months. Also on the Shlosheem the above Study Group should get together and study Mishnayos in the name of the deceased and should mention his soul for the good, because the memory of a Zadik is a blessing.

That should be the case when there will be about twenty people who are able to study Mishnayos. But, when God will bless them and the number of those who are able to study Mishnayos will grow to forty or more then they should divide the complete Six Divisions of the Mishna into thirty, which is in accordance with the opinion of our Holy Fathers; and also, they should distribute Chapters of Mishnayos, in the name of the deceased, on his Yahrzeit every year.

Seventh Regulation
If somebody comes to join the Study Group, and be a part of it, then the Gabbai would decide how much he has to pay. The Gabbai will make his decision according to the place, the time, and the man.

Eighth Regulation
The person who is elected from the above Study Group to be a Gabbai, should not deter from reminding the members

at every opportunity and any time, if they are diligent in the Mishnayos to study every day, and he should be concerned with every detail which contributes to the well being of this Study Group.

Ninth Regulation

It is an obligation of every member of the Study Group to make sure that the Gabbai fulfills what is stated in the Eighth Regulation. And if it transpires that he does not, another person should be very quickly appointed irrespective of offending the Gabbai, since the tardiness of the Study Group is a consequence of the laziness of the Gabbai.

Tenth Regulation

The money that belongs to the Mishnayos Study Group should be deposited in a bank acceptable to the Study Group and the Bank's books should be maintained by two people selected by the Study Group.

Eleventh Regulation

It is customary for the Study Group to buy books and mend books and also to have a dinner when appropriate. In these cases the Gabbai has the power and permission to do whatever he finds appropriate.

Twelfth Regulation

Each and every member of this Study Group must pay 18 cents to the Study Group on any occasion that he has a Yahrzeit and the Gabbai can do with this money whatever he pleases.

Thirteenth Regulation

On every Holiday the Mishnayos Study Group must study the appropriate Masechta for that Holiday and also study on the day when Yizkor takes place.

Fourteenth Regulation

The money that is held at the Mishnayos Study Group belongs to the Mishnayos Study Group Beth Hamedrash Hagadol Anshi Sfard at North Russell Street; however the Beth Hamedrash has no claim whatsoever on this money.

Fifteenth Regulation

Every year, in the week of Parsha Noach, the Study Group should have a general meeting where seven arbitrators would be selected by a lottery, who would be responsible to select two Gabbais, a First Gabbai and a Second Gabbai.

Sixteenth Regulation

The seven arbitrators will select the Gabbais during the Hanukah holiday every year and the Gabbais should be from the members who are studying 26 Mishnayos per month.

Seventeenth Regulation

If somebody is interested to join the Study Group the Gabbai should first read to him all of these regulations and then ask him if he accepts of all these regulations. The Gabbai then will consult with the seven arbitrators regarding this person and together they decide his case.

Eighteenth Regulation

If a person comes and he is interested to join the Study Group based on the Second and Third Regulations by saying that he too can come every evening to study a chapter of Mishna with the group, and he says in addition that he would come every Shabbat to learn Hilchos Shabbat with the group, then his name would not be included in the books until a period of a half a year in order to verify that indeed he can carry out his claim.

Translation: Gerald Kleinstein

Appendix 4

Rabbi Moses Margolies Boston Shul Affiliations

	Beth Jacob	Anshi Libawich	Adath Jesura Nusach Ari	Beth Israel	Chawre Thilim	Shaari Jerusalem	Shaari Zion	Count
1893				x				1
1894	x			x				2
1895	x			x		x		3
1896	x			x		x		3
1897	x	x		x	x	x		5
1898	x	x		x	x	x		5
1899	x	x		x	x	x		5
1900	x	x	x	x	x	x		6
1901	x	x	x	x	x	x		6
1902	x		x	x	x		x	5
1903	x		x	x	x		x	5
1904	x		x	x			x	4
1905	x		x	x			x	4

Source: Boston City Directories

Appendix 5

Rabbi Solomon Friederman Boston Shul Affiliations

	Ein Jacob	Sfardis Cong	Anshe Stonier	Anshe Wilkomeer	Anshe Zhitomer	Shaari jerusalem	An Tagi Jacob	Count
1896		x						1
1897		x						1
1898								0
1899			x	x				2
1900				x	x			2
1901				x	x			2
1902					x	x		2
1903	listed in AJY				x	x		3
1904						x	x	2
1905						x	x	2
1906						x	x	2
1907	x					x		2
1908	x					x		2
1909						x		1
1910						x		1
1911						x		1
1912						x		1
1913						x		1
1914						x		1
1915						x		1
1916						x		1
1917						x		1
1918						x		1
1919						x		1
1920						x		1
1921						no rabbi listed		1
1922						no rabbi listed		1

	Ein Jacob	Sfardis Cong	Anshe Stonier	Anshe Wilkomeer	Anshe Zhitomer	Shaari jerusalem	An Tagi Jacob	Count
1923						no rabbi listed		1
1924						no rabbi listed		1
1925						no rabbi listed		1
1926						no rabbi listed		1
1927						x		1
1928						x		1
1929						x		1
1930						x		1

Source: Boston City Directories and American Jewish Yearbook

Appendix 6

Rabbi Isaac Baritz Boston Shul Affiliations

	Ein Jacob	Miskan Shlomo	Adas Israel	Ahavach Archin	Anshei Vilna	Chawre Slivick	Chawre Thilim	Sharai Tefila	Sharai Zedek	Beth Abraham (Blue Hills Ave)	Count
1901			x						x		2
1902			x						x		2
1903			x			x			x		3
1904		x	x			x	x		x		5
1905		x	x						x		3
1906		x	x						x		3
1907	x	x	x	x	x				x		6
1908	x	x	x	x					x		5
1909	x	x	x						x		4
1910	x	x	x						x		4
1911	x	x	x					x	x		5
1912	x	x	x					x			4
1913	x	x	x						x		4
1914	x	x	x						x		5
1915	x	x	x						x		4
1916	x	x	x						x		4
1917	x		x						x		3
1918	x		x								2
1919	x		x							x	3
1920	x		x							x	3
1921	x										1
1922	x										1
1923	x										1

Source: Boston City Directories

Appendix 7

Charles River Park/Boston Synagogue Officers

	Chair	Vice Chairman	President	Treasurer	Secretary
1970-71	Maurice Saval	NA	Hyman Slate	Harry Kaminsky	
1971-72	Maurice Saval	NA			
1972-73	Maurice Saval	NA	Frank Shapiro	Ralph Gordon	Seth Goldschlager
1973-74	Maurice Saval	NA	Michael Rosenbaum	Ralph Gordon	Frances Talcove Feldman and Diane G. Davis
1974-75	Maurice Saval	NA			
1975-76	Maurice Saval	NA			
1976-77	Maurice Saval	NA		Shalom Cohen	
1977-78	Maurice Saval	NA			
1978-79	Maurice Saval	NA			
1979-80	Maurice Saval	NA			
1980-81	Maurice Saval	NA			
1981-82	Maurice Saval	NA			
1982-83	Maurice Saval	NA			
1983-84	Maurice Saval	NA			
1984-85	Maurice Saval	NA			
1985-86	Maurice Saval	NA			
1986-87	Maurice Saval	NA			
1987-88	Maurice Saval	NA	Arthur Cohen	Israel Alpert	Myles Lopatin and Robert Fox
1988-89	Maurice Saval (d 3/89)	NA			
1989-90	John Fox				
1990-91	John Fox		Allan Green		
1991-92	John Fox				
1992-93	John Fox		Bob Stern		

	Chair	Vice Chairman	President	Treasurer	Secretary
1993-94	John Fox				
1994-95	John Fox				
1995-96	John Fox	Jonathan Slate	Larry Baras		
1996-97	John Fox	Jonathan Slate	Larry Baras		
1997-98	John Fox	Jonathan Slate	Larry Baras		
1998-99	Mark Schonfeld	Jonathan Slate	Susan Schreiner Weingarten	David Crane	Muriel Kantor
1999-00	Ruth Fein	Jonathan Slate	Susan Schreiner Weingarten	David Zimbalist	
2000-01	Ruth Fein	Jonathan Slate	Susan Schreiner Weingarten	Ruth Aaron	
2001-02	Ruth Fein	Susan Schreiner Weingarten	Mike Rubin	Michael Weingarten	Howard Speicher
2002-03	Ruth Fein	Susan Schreiner Weingarten	Mike Rubin	David Zimbalist	Howard Speicher
2003-04	Ruth Fein	Susan Schreiner Weingarten	Mike Rubin/Jacob Hadar	David Zimbalist	Howard Speicher
2004-05	Ruth Fein	Susan Schreiner Weingarten	Mike Rubin/Michael Weingarten	Marshall Schribman	Howard Speicher
2005-06	Ruth Fein	Susan Schreiner Weingarten	Michael Weingarten	Jeffrey Steinfeld	Howard Speicher
2006-07	Ruth Fein	Susan Schreiner Weingarten	Michael Weingarten	Jeffrey Steinfeld	Howard Speicher
2007-08	Ruth Fein	Susan Schreiner Weingarten	Bette Siegel	Mark Paul	Howard Speicher
2008-09	Susan Schreiner Weingarten	NA	Bette Siegel	Michael Weingarten	Jeffrey Steinfeld
2009-10	Susan Schreiner Weingarten	NA	Bette Siegel	Michael Weingarten	Jeffrey Steinfeld
2010-11	Susan Schreiner Weingarten	NA	Bette Siegel VP	Michael Weingarten	Jeffrey Steinfeld
2011-12	Susan Schreiner Weingarten	NA	Bette Siegel VP	Michael Weingarten	Jeffrey Steinfeld
2012-13	Susan Schreiner Weingarten	NA	Bette Siegel VP	Michael Weingarten	Jeffrey Steinfeld

Bibliography-For Further Reading

Books, Journals, Unpublished Materials, and Web Sites, Including Blogs:

Aarons, Jules. *Street portraits, 1946-1976: the photographs of Jules Aarons.* Lincoln, Mass.: DeCordoba Museum and Sculpture Park, c2002. ISBN 189102471X

Altman, Harris. *Charles River Park Synagogue history fact sheet.* Undated.

American Jewish Year Book. Philadelphia (etc.): American Jewish Committee, 1899/1900-

Angoff, Charles. "Memories of Boston" in *The Menorah Journal* (New York: Menorah Association), volume 49, autumn-winter 1962, numbers 1-2, the Henry Hurwitz memorial issue – valedictory issue; pp. 136-147.

_____. *Something about my father, and other people.* New York: T. Yoseloff, [1956].

_____. *When I was a boy in Boston.* New York: Beechhurst Press, [1947].

Antin, Mary. *The Promised land.* Boston: Houghton Mifflin, 1912.

Axelrod, Morris. *A community survey for long range planning: a study of the Jewish population of greater Boston* by Morris Axelrod, Floyd J. Fowler, and Arnold Gurin. Boston: Combined Jewish Philanthropies of Greater Boston, 1967.

Behrman, S[amuel] N[athaniel]. "Daughter of the Ramaz," *The New Yorker*, November 21, 1953; pp. 45-82.

The Boston directory...: including all localities within the city limits... Boston: Sampson & Murdock company, various years.

The Boston Synagogue archives.

Buch, Yehoshua. *The Libin family: from the Chernigov Country in the 19th and 20th centuries.* 2011 Internet edition edited by Joshua B. Hurwitz. http://www.zevindescendants.org/Libin.pdf Accessed: February 2013.

Catholics in the American century: recasting narratives of U.S. history. Edited by R. Scott Appleby and Kathleen Sprows Cummings. Ithaca, N.Y.: Cornell University Press, 2012. ISBN 9780801451409

A Chassidic journey: the Polish chassidic dynastics of Lublin, Lelov, Nikolsburg and Boston. New York: Feldheim, 2002. ISBN 1583305688

City-Data.com Accessed: February 2013.

Clingan, Carol. *Massachusetts Synagogues and Their Records, Past and Present* (the "Clingan Spreadsheet"). Compiled for the Jewish Genealogical Society, 2010. http://jgsgb.org/pdfs/MassSynagogues.pdf Accessed: February 2013.

Combined Jewish Philanthropies of Boston. *The 2005 Boston community survey: preliminary findings: a report by the Steinhardt Social Research Institute, Brandeis University.* November 2006. http://www.cjp.org/local_includes/downloads/16072.pdf Accessed: February 2013.

Congregation Anshei Libovitz archival collection. 1907-1965, 1982. Four manuscript boxes and one oversized box. Held at the American Jewish Historical Society, Boston.

Congregation Beth Hamedrash Hagadol Anshe Sfard archival collection. Ledger, 1909-1910. One manuscript box. Held at the American Jewish Historical Society, Boston.

Dimond, Alan J. (Master). "Master's draft report, April 28, 1987, The Vilner Congregation vs. Attorney General of the Commonwealth, Massachusetts Supreme Judicial Court for Suffolk County, No. 85-290."

Ein Yaakov: the ethical and inspirational teachings of the Talmud. Compiled in the sixteenth century by Yaakov ibn Chaviv; a translation with commentary by Avraham Yaakov Finkel. Northvale, N.J.: Jason Aronson, [c1999]. ISBN 0765760827

The Encyclopedia of Cleveland history. Edited by David D. Van Tassel and John J. Grabowski. Bloomington: Indiana University Press, 1987. ISBN 0253313031

Farber, Seth. *An American Orthodox dreamer: Rabbi Joseph B. Soloveitchik and Boston's Maimonides School.* Hanover, New Hampshire: University Press of New England, c2004. ISSBN 1584653388

Fein, Isaac M. *Boston – where it all began: an historical perspective of the Boston Jewish community.* Boston: Boston Jewish Bicentennial Committee, 1976.

First generation: in the words of twentieth-century American immigrants. Compiled by June Namias. Urbana: University of Illinois Press, 1992. ISBN 0252061705

FitzPatrick, Maura E. *From template tenements to beaux arts boulevards: the architecture of Fred A. Norcross.* Unpublished M.A. Thesis, Boston University, 1993.

Gamm, Gerald H. *Urban exodus: why the Jews left Boston and the Catholics stayed.* Cambridge, Mass.: Harvard University Press, 1999. ISBN 0674930703

Gans, Herbert J. *The urban villagers, a study of the second generation Italians in the West End of Boston.* Philadelphia, Pa.: University of Pennsylvania, Institute for Urban Studies, 1959.

Greenberg, Steven M. "Just beneath the surface," *Vilna Scribe,* v. 15, no. 2 (Fall 2009/Tishrei 5770), p. 2 http://www.vilnashul.org.images/uploads/VilnaSCRIBE-Fall2009.pdf Accessed March 2013

Guide to Jewish cemeteries. Newton Centre: Jewish Cemetery Association of Massachusetts, 1985- 2010 edition has the distinctive title: "Bridging past, present, and future: history and guide: Massachusetts Jewish cemeteries" http://cemetery2010_Guidebook.pdf Accessed: February 2013

Gurock, Jeffrey S. *A modern heretic and a traditional community: Mordecai M. Kaplan, Orthodoxy, and American Judaism* by Jeffrey S. Gurock and Jacob J. Schacter. New York: Columbia University Press, c1997. ISBN 0231106262

History of the Jews of Boston and New England: their financial, professional, and commercial enterprises, from the earliest settlement of the Hebrews in Boston to the present time...together with biographies of noted men, and other matters of interest. Boston: The Jewish Chronicle Publishing Co., 1892.

Hoffman, Joshua. "The Changing attitude of Rabbi Gavriel Zev Margolis towards RIETS," *The Commentator*, updated as of August 12, 2009. http://admin2collegepublisher.com/preview/2.2469/2.2843/1.299300#.URbODWfvXfo Accessed: February 2013

Jewish women in America: an historical encyclopedia. Edited by Paula E. Hyman and Deborah Dash Moore. New York: Routledge, 1997. ISBN 0415919363

The Jews of Boston. Revised and updated edition edited by Jonathan D. Sarna, Ellen Smith, Scott-Martin Kosofsky. New Haven, Conn.: Yale University Press, 2005. ISBN 0300107870

Kaplan, Mordecai Menahem. *Communings of the spirit*, edited by Mel Scult. Detroit: Wayne State University Press; [Wyncote, Pa.]: The Reconstructionist Press, c2001. ISBN 0814325750

Kleinstein, Lisa C. *Echoes of the Old West End Boston, 1900-1914.* Unpublished typescript, May 1989.

The Last tenement: confronting community and urban renewal in Boston's West End. Edited by Sean M. Fisher, Carolyn Hughes. Boston: Bostonian Society, 1992. ISBN 0934865000

Levine, Julius B. *A Plea to the Boston Landmarks Commission and a tiny Beacon Hill Group: do not obstruct the progress of the Charles River Park Synagogue.* Unpublished typescript, 1989.

Lifland, Yosef. *Converts and conversion to Judaism.* Jerusalem: Gefen, c2001. ISBN 9652292354

Lisitzky, Ephraim E. *In the grip of cross-currents.* Translated from the Hebrew by Moshe Kohn and Jacob Sloan and rev. by the author. New York: Bloch Pub. Co., [1959].

Lyman, Thomas K. "Vilna Shul: a remnant of Beacon Hill's Jewish History," 3-page insert in the fall 1996 issue of *Guides' Gazette: newsletter of the activities of the tour guides of the State House...,* Boston, Mass.: Massachusetts State House.

Multilingual America: transnationalism, ethnicity, and the languages of American literature. Edited by Werner Sollors. New York: New York University Press, c1998. ISBN 081478092X

Nimoy, Leonard. *I am not Spock.* Milbrae, Calif.: Celestial Arts, c1975. ISBN 0890871175

_____. *I am Spock.* New York: Hyperion, c1995. ISBN 0786861827

Rakeffet-Rothkoff, Aaron. *The Rav: the world of Rabbi Joseph B. Soloveitchik.* Edited by Joseph Epstein. Hoboken, NJ: KTAV Pub. House, 1999. ISBN 0881256145 (v. 1); 0881256153 (v. 2)

Rappaport, Ellen R. *The community history forgot: the Jews of Boston's North End, 1890-1915.* Unpublished senior honors thesis, Brandeis University, Department of American Studies and Department of History, 1992.

Robinson, Ira. *Translating a tradition: studies in American Jewish history.* Boston: Academic Studies Press, 2008. ISBN 9781934843062

Rosen, Benjamin. "The trend of Jewish population in Boston: a study to determine the location of a Jewish communal building," *Monographs of Federated Jewish charities of Boston,* vol. 1, January 1921, no. 1.

Ross, Michael Alan. *BostonWalks' the Jewish friendship trail guidebook: Jewish Boston history sites.* 2[Nd] ed. Belmont, Mass.: BostonWalks, 2003. ISBN 0970082517

_____. *BostonWalks* web site. http://www.angelfire.com/biz/LikeJACKnMARIONS/shulsWE.html Accessed: February 2013

Sammarco, Anthony Mitchell. *Boston's West End.* Charleston, South Carolina: Arcadia, 1998. ISBN 0752412574

Sarna, Jonathan D. *American Judaism: a history.* New Haven: Yale University Press, c2004. ISBN 030010197X

Sherman, Moshe D. *Orthodox Judaism in America: a biographical dictionary and sourcebook.* Westport, Conn.: Greenwood Press, 1996. ISBN 0313243166

Stein-Milford, Amy. "Eldridge Street's Rabbi Yudelovitch – Between admiration and controversy," posted December 6, 2011. Museum at Eldridge Street blog. http://www.eldridgestreet.org/blog/2011/12/eldridge-streets-rabbi-yudelovitch-between-admiration-and-controversy Accessed: February 2013

Temple Israel web site. http://www.tisrael.org/TIHistory.asp Accessed: February 2013

Thomas F. McSweeney Associates (Hingham, Mass.). "Consulting study for Congregation Beth Amedrich Agudal Beth Jacob, 28 North Russell Street, Boston, MA, No. 3283," Valuation analysis dated March 9, 1959.

Van Hise, James. *The man between the ears: Star trek's Leonard Nimoy.* Las Vegas, Nevada: Pioneer Books, c1992. ISBN 9781556983115

Weinstein, Lewis Hyman. *Masa: odyssey of an American Jew.* Boston: Quinlan Press, c1989. ISBN 1557701296

_____. *My life at the bar: lawyer, soldier, teacher, and pro bono activist.* Hanover, Mass.: Christopher Pub. House, c1993. ISBN 0815804768

_____. "Urban renewal in Massachusetts," *Massachusetts Law Quarterly*, March 1962, vol. 47:1, pp. 5-27.

Wieder, Arnold A. *The early Jewish community of Boston's North End: a sociologically oriented study of an Eastern European Jewish immigrant community in an American big-city neighborhood between 1870 and 1900.* Waltham, Mass.: Brandeis University, 1962.

Yood, Barry. "Zayde's shul revisited" Congregation Or Zarua (New York City) Newsletter, volume 21:2, p. 8
http://www.orzarua.org/Newsletters/Newsletter_2008_NovDec.pdf
Accessed: February 2013

Newspaper articles:

Boston Advocate
-----June 15, 1906: table showing real estate ownership on Hale Street

Beacon Hill Paper
-----August 4, 1998: "Boston Synagogue: a David-and-Goliath story" (Ingrid Thaler)

Beacon Hill Times
-----September 7, 1999: "The Boston Synagogue welcomes Rabbi Lehmann" (Abbe Colodny); and "The Boston Synagogue makes news with its changes" (Susan Schreiner Weingarten)

Boston Evening Transcript
-----November 13, 1903: "New educational centre: Jewish meeting held in North Russell Street synagogue"

Boston Globe
-----March 30, 1903: Mittel-Rubin wedding announcement
-----September 5, 1903: "Congregation Beth Jacob to replace its present house of worship"
-----June 20, 1906: Yaffe-Glaser wedding announcement
-----January 5, 1913: "Synagogue service in Boston ghetto: Impressions of a Gentile visitor there"
-----August 1, 1931: "Thirteen-year-old Shloimele youngest cantor in Boston"
-----March 24, 1960: "N. Russell St. shul notes interim move"
-----June 29, 1970: "Gone but not forgotten synagogue to rise like phoenix in West End" (Leo Shapiro)
-----March 12, 1973: "'Old West End' residents recalled in book to be kept by new synagogue" (Leo Shapiro) (*Evening Globe* edition)
-----May 26, 1995: "Charles River Park at 35" (Charles Campbell)

Jewish Advocate
-----April 5, 1940: "Hecht Neighborhood House celebrates its jubilee"
-----"Rebirth of a shul" (Joseph G. Weisberg)
-----March 22, 1990: "New name for Charles River Park Shul" (letter

to the editor from J. John Fox, Allan Green, and Israel Alpert)

Los Angeles Times
-----October 19, 1995: "A higher authority: overseeing the kosher boom" (Joseph Hanania)

New York Times
-----January 15, 1922: "Denial by Rabbi Margolis"
-----August 26, 1936: "Rabbi Margolies dies of pneumonia"; "Tributes by leading Jews"

Newsweek
-----March 13, 1972: "The Exodus"

Newton Times
-----July 31, 1912: front page coverage of Adams Street synagogue dedication

About the Author

Michael Weingarten is Treasurer of the Boston Synagogue and served on the on the Archival/Historical Committee that performed the research for this book. He has lived in Boston's Back Bay since the late 70s/early 80s with his wife Susan – where they raised two sons. His relationship with the Boston Synagogue community goes back to the early 1990s.

Professionally, he is a Managing Director at Signal Lake, a high-tech venture fund located in Boston and Westport, Connecticut. In a previous lifetime, he received a B.A. and M.A. in European History from Columbia University before deciding to pursue a career in business (receiving an M.B.A. from Harvard Business School).

Writing this book is therefore a return to his aspirations as a young adult.

Celebrating
THE **BOSTON SYNAGOGUE**
1888 **125** 2013
YEARS

1888 Congregation Beth Jacob • 1890 Anshei Libovitz • 1895 Ein Jacob (Anshe Vilna)
1896 Beit Hamedrash Hagadol (Anshe Sfard) • 1898 Mishkan Shlomo/Anshai Birsh
1898 Adath Jesura Nusach Ari • 1923 United Congregation Beth Jacob
1941 Beth Hamedrash Hagadol/Beth Jacob • 1971 Charles River Park Synagogue
1990 The Boston Synagogue

www.ingramcontent.com/pod-product-compliance
Lightning Source LLC
Chambersburg PA
CBHW071821300426
44116CB00009B/1388